THE BREAD OF AFFLICTION: THE FOOD SUPPLY IN THE USSR DURING WORLD WAR II

SOVIET AND EAST EUROPEAN STUDIES: 76

Soviet and East European Studies

Series list continues on page 252

THE BREAD OF AFFLICTION

The Food Supply in the USSR During World War II

WILLIAM MOSKOFF
Lake Forest College

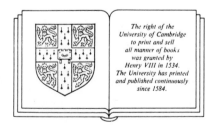

The right of the
University of Cambridge
to print and sell
all manner of books
was granted by
Henry VIII in 1534.
The University has printed
and published continuously
since 1584.

CAMBRIDGE UNIVERSITY PRESS
Cambridge
New York   Port Chester   Melbourne   Sydney

Published by the Press Syndicate of the University of Cambridge
The Pitt Building, Trumpington Street, Cambridge CB2 1RP
40 West 20th Street, New York, NY 10011, USA
10 Stamford Road, Oakleigh, Melbourne 3166, Australia

© Cambridge University Press 1990

First published 1990

Printed in the United States of America

Library of Congress Cataloging-in-Publication Data
Moskoff, William.
The bread of affliction : the food supply in the USSR during World
War II / by William Moskoff.
  p.   cm.
Includes bibliographical references.
ISBN 0-521-37499-5
1. Food supply – Soviet Union – History – 20th cen-
tury. 2. World War, 1939–1945 – Food supply – Soviet
Union. I. Title.
HD9015.S652M67   1990
363.8'0947'09044 – dc20   90–1365
                                                      CIP

British Library Cataloguing in Publication Data
Moskoff, William
The bread of affliction : the food supply in the USSR during
World War II.
1. Soviet Union. Food supply, history
I. Title
338.1947

ISBN 0-521-37499-5 hardback

For Carol Gayle
Wife, Historian, Best Friend

Contents

Foreword

June 22, 1941, was a momentous date for both the Soviet Union and the United States. The Nazis turned their armies eastward to begin their triumphal progress across the steppes, which was to be reversed only with the successful defense at Stalingrad. Winston Churchill and Franklin D. Roosevelt made a quick decision in 1941 to help Stalin's armies defeat Hitler, a decision that reversed long years of hostility between the West and the East. Stalin was invited to submit a list of military supplies that he thought were necessary to hold the line, and Harry Hopkins and Averell Harriman were sent to Moscow to discuss further needs. Out of the negotiations, which were clouded by Stalin's secretiveness as to his resources and his plans, came a protocol listing the supplies Stalin needed from the West. On November 7, 1941, the USSR was placed under the Lend-Lease Act by Roosevelt.

At the time, the emphasis was upon materiel: tanks, trucks, aircraft, military telephone equipment. A Lend-Lease Administration was established in Washington to coordinate the effort being made by the United States Army, Army Air Force, and Navy, and the civilian agencies supplying textiles, chemicals, and food. Not only the military forces but the population generally were recognized as indispensable to ultimate victory. Roosevelt told his Lend-Lease staff that without Soviet participation in the struggle against the Nazis the war could not be won. The United States with its British ally and the forces of DeGaulle's Free French were thought inadequate to meet the Nazi drive. We of the Lend-Lease staff were given one basic directive: Keep the Soviets in the war. They must not be driven to the point of despair, lest they make a separate peace with Hitler, leaving the Western forces to struggle on alone. To those who did not live through those frightening days, it may seem incredible that the United States' leadership worried about endless years of warfare, if not defeat, without the Soviets, but it must be remembered that German submarines were sinking U.S. freighters faster than U.S. shipbuilders could replace them. Also the Japanese advance across Burma toward India and the Nazis' advance across the Soviet Union toward Stalingrad looked ominous. The Lend-Lease staff was told that the Japanese and the Nazis might join forces in Iran and close the noose around the Soviet armies, cutting off any possibility of supply.

William Moskoff has pieced together the dreadful picture of starvation that threatened both the troops and the population of the USSR in those fateful years. It presents such a compelling need for food that it is hard from this distance in time to imagine how Washington bureaucrats could have doubted its need. Yet there were doubts. Some were exacerbated by the doubt, which Dr. Moskoff describes, that the Stalinist forces could hold the line, suggesting that the program was a waste of U.S. taxpayers' money; some were relics of the years during which the Bolshevik menace had loomed large to many Americans, leading to a somewhat suppressed feeling that it could help the United States in the long run if Stalin were defeated; some sprang from the fact that information was scant on food conditions in the USSR. Perhaps because Stalin feared that his Western allies might stop supplying goods if they knew how limited his stocks were, he never permitted his supply officers in Washington to provide much to justify his requests for aid. Routine verification of Soviet needs, as required by Lend-Lease procedures, had to be based on reports from U.S. officials in the USSR, on estimates of specialists in the United States Department of Agriculture who had followed for years Soviet crop reports and consumption needs, and on general common sense that as the Red Army retreated from the grain fields of the Ukraine, they lost the major source of food.

Stalin's interpreter, who has survived to the present day, has reported on Soviet television while reminiscing about World War II that Lend-Lease was "too little and too late." Dr. Moskoff's statistics confirm that quantitatively Lend-Lease supplies of food seem pitifully small: less than a month's supply of grain and flour for the Red Army out of a total Lend-Lease shipment in all categories reaching nearly $11 billion in 1940 prices. Dr. Moskoff adds, however, that in meats and oils the U.S. supplies were important. He has heard from those he has interviewed that *tushonka* was a lifesaver. From the U.S. point of view it had seemed inedible, being a can of solid animal fat that when tried out on the members of the Lend-Lease staff had turned stomachs. Yet it had been prepared in accordance with specifications submitted by the Red Army and was said to provide stomach heat to the troops sitting in snowbanks on the front lines.

Even at the time U.S. supply officers realized that some needs were pressing, although not supported by justification of need. Great quantities of vitamin C were requested and sent. Now Dr. Moskoff shows how important it was to suppress scurvy and gum disease.

Transporting food and other supplies presented a great problem. Three routes were available: north around Norway's North Cape to Murmansk in the Soviet North, south around South Africa's Cape of Good Hope to the Persian Gulf to be shipped by a hastily built railroad across Iran to Azerbaidzhan in the USSR, and via Seattle by ship across the Pacific Ocean through the Kurile Islands to Magadan in the Soviet Far East. The North Cape route was the most dangerous, as Nazi submarines lay in wait for convoys to dash through the British Navy escorts and sank considerable numbers of Lend-Lease freighters. The Iranian route was difficult because of the great heat. A photograph sent home to Lend-Lease officers showed barrel staves strewn around a field as barrels fell apart when the edible margarine they held was melted away. The Pacific route proved dangerous because of the Aleutian storms that on occasion split hastily built Victory ships in two before they could reach their ports.

Some routings of food were necessary to feed populations in Siberia for whom scarce railroad transport could not be provided from what grain fields remained in Soviet hands in European Russia and the Ukraine, as Dr. Moskoff indicates. Lend-Lease officials realized that Soviet requests for food in the Far East were as important as those for troops in Stalingrad, because workers in the factories moving ahead of advancing Nazi troops from the Ukraine to Siberia could not be expected to produce war materiel if they were exhausted from short rations.

Dr. Moskoff has rightly emphasized the importance of food production in the tiny household gardens of the peasants on the collective farms. Families could meet their own needs and even have a surplus to sell on the peasant markets. Factories turned their workers into fields made available by local authorities for subsidiary farming in off hours. Hand labor was critical, as fuel for farm machinery was scarce, and even farm machinery was often inadequate as it could not be brought from the Ukraine during evacuation. Draft animals were often milk cows, as they alone were available to pull the plows.

Some of this shortage was evident to Vice-President Henry Wallace when he crossed Siberia during the summer of 1944. As a world-renowned agricultural geneticist, he visited experimental farms to see what was being developed and to get a feel for local conditions. He had been shocked as a geneticist by the claims made by the academician Lysenko. Indeed he had concluded that stopping genetic work in plant development was a major blow to Soviet agricultural progress, just as Dr. Moskoff has concluded. To be sure, such work had not been entirely stopped in spite of Lysenko, because Wallace praised one scientist in Siberia for his experiments with alfalfa. Later he was told that the man had been awarded the Order of Lenin, the highest Soviet decoration, on the basis of this commendation.

Wallace also experienced some of the hospitality to foreigners that Dr. Moskoff reports as the food provided at Kremlin dinners. When Wallace reached the first Siberian airfield on his progress from Alaska across the Far East to China, he had been offered just such a meal as Dr. Moskoff describes. As he was a man of great simplicity, he asked that in the future he be given sandwiches, and, of course, his hosts complied with his request, but the banquets continued all the way to China. The food had been brought with the chefs and waitresses from Moscow because the Russians as a proud people wanted to show hospitality even if it hurt. Perhaps I bear some responsibility for the continuation of the feasts, as I told the vice-president that if the feasts were discontinued, the large company invited at each overnight stop to share an evening meal with Wallace would be deprived of the only good meal they had enjoyed throughout the war. Wallace agreed to let the hospitality continue, so long as he could have his modest sandwich.

The heartrending story of starvation in Leningrad during the Nazi siege was beyond Lend-Lease rectification. The city was cut off, except during winter when some food was delivered over the ice of Lake Ladoga to the east. But death from starvation and cold was everywhere, as visitors to Leningrad can verify by visiting the vast cemetery with mound after mound of mass graves.

Soviet citizens have not forgotten the privations of wartime, as tourists from the West can easily verify. In every city there are tombs of unknown soldiers with eternal flames flickering and lugubrious music emerging from concealed tapes. Rebuilding devastated villages and cities began immediately after the war, as I was able to verify in 1957 when I took a bus tour from Warsaw through Minsk and Smolensk to Moscow, passing through villages already restored after the devastation of scorched earth policies implemented by both the Red Army in retreat and the Nazi Army in its retreat after defeat at Stalingrad in February 1943.

The Russians, Ukrainians, and Belorussians proved themselves to be plucky people and they rebuilt rapidly, but those years of privation, as described by Dr. Moskoff, have left indelible memories. The public never wants to return to such privation. To be sure the leaders during the war concluded that almost any privation would be tolerated. I recall a conversation with the lieutenant general heading the USSR Supply Mission in Washington at the end of the war in Europe. I had asked the general how his leaders could expect the people to tolerate a continuation of the war in the Far East against Japan, as Stalin had committed them to do. His reply was simple: "Our people are a disciplined people!" Indeed they have been for decades, but perhaps the tide is turning. Mikhail Gorbachev's policy of open discussion of problems, hopes, and fears has seemingly released long-suppressed feelings. Food is again an issue, and this time belt tightening is not acceptable. There is no Nazi force at the gates to be resisted at whatever personal cost. Provision of food is a test of government to the contemporary generation, and the Soviet leadership gives evidence that it knows it must meet the test if it is to survive.

Dr. Moskoff's account of a period that may seem rather distant to contemporary U.S. readers is not only moving, but it can sharpen our minds to evaluate how the peoples of the Soviet Union tolerated the shortage of food.

John N. Hazard
Deputy Director of the Lend-Lease
    Supply Program to the USSR, 1941–45

Acknowledgments

There are many people and institutions whose generosity made this book possible. I hope that all will accept mention as reflecting my deep gratitude for their contribution.

A number of people worked for me as research assistants. I wish to thank Natasha Dragunsky, Veronika Shapovalov, Inna Shapovalov, and Mikhail Spektor for their able research assistance. I want to thank a number of students at Lake Forest College who did research for me: Will Cronenwett, Jill Glassman, Holly Grabelle, Kris Hill, and Helen Tachkov. But I mostly want to note the especially valuable contributions of Cristen Kogl and Mike Minerva, each of whom worked a full year for me; it is a joy to have students who have the gifts of intellect and independence.

The librarians at Lake Forest College, both past and present, handled my seemingly infinite requests for interlibrary loans and assorted other services with much grace and competence. I thank Martha Briggs, Pat Cardenas, Emily Miller, and Guynell Williams for all their help. I would also like to thank Harold Leich at the Library of Congress for his help during the summer of 1987. The archivists at the National Archives were also very helpful during two summer trips to Washington. Douglas Bowers at the U.S. Department of Agriculture helped me find the appropriate archives in the department's inner sanctum and I am grateful for his guidance.

As always, the manifold resources of the University of Illinois – Urbana-Champaign were critical to my work. Two summer grants to the university's Summer Research Laboratory for Soviet specialists were very beneficial. Both the library and the librarians are a state treasure.

I am indebted to Lake Forest College, which gave me a great deal of sustenance over the several years I worked on this project. Several summer grants, a research fund associated with my chair, and a sabbatical for the 1988 and 1989 academic year contributed immeasurably to the completion of this book. I am especially grateful to former Dean of Faculty, Bailey Donnally, for all his support. My colleagues in the Department of Economics read pieces of the book and I appreciate their comments.

Over a period of about two years I interviewed over thirty Soviet émigrés to the United States. I walked into their homes and their lives and asked them to dredge up memories that at times must have been painful. For some, the idea of answering questions about this period created apprehension about reprisals against relatives still in the Soviet Union. Therefore, although I would like to mention each by name, I will in fact identify no single individual. Their wartime experiences enriched my work, taught me a great deal about the human spirit, and at times moved me deeply. I will never forget them.

Mark Harrison read both an early prospectus for the book and the final version. I have greatly profited from his knowledge of the war period. James R. Millar read the entire penultimate version with great care and a number of his suggestions are incorporated in the final version. Susan Woodward's comments gave me early insights into the questions I was asking. Gordon White was generous with his time and took several pictures that appear in this book. I am also in the debt of George Bolotenko, of the National Archives of Canada, who went out of his way to help me.

I save my biggest thanks for last. My wife Carol Gayle, to whom this book is dedicated, spent many hours over a period of several years discussing my ideas in all manner of places: at school, at meals, in the car, and in her garden. And then she helped shape the final product with her astonishing editorial skills. She continually gave me loving support as well as the wisdom of an able historian's eye. I cannot thank her enough.

List of abbreviations

The following abbreviations are used in the footnotes:

CBS   Foreign broadcasts as monitored by the Columbia Broadcasting System, August 1939 to March 1945

CDR   *Records of the Department of State Relating to the Internal Affairs of the Soviet Union, 1940–1944. Decimal file, 861. Calamities, Disasters, Refugees.*

DOA   U.S. Department of Agriculture Archives, World War II files.

FBIS   *Daily Report of Foreign Radio Broadcasts.*

FRUS   U.S. Department of State, *Foreign Relations of the United States.*

Istoriia   *Istoriia Velikoi Otechestvennoi Voiny Sovetskogo Soiuza 1941–1945.*

NFAS   USSR: Crop Conditions and Production, 1942–1945. Records of the Foreign Agricultural Service. Record Group 166.

Opyt   *Opyt sovetskoi meditsiny v Velikoi Otechestvennoi Voine 1941–1945 gg.*

Reich   *Records of the Reich Ministry in the Occupied Territories*, T454.

SDDF   *U.S. State Department Decimal File, 1940–1944.*

I have given the full citation for each source when it first appears in each chapter.

Introduction

On June 22, 1941, nearly two years after World War II had begun in Europe, the war came to the Soviet Union. German invaders, some 175 divisions of them, motorized, with massive armor and air support, rolled swiftly and irresistibly forward like lava across Soviet territory. They struck northeast toward Leningrad, due east toward Moscow, and southeast toward Kiev. In their path were the lives of millions of people, already buffeted by the stormy events of Soviet history. Only twenty-four years earlier, revolution had overturned the nation's rulers; then civil war ruptured the country, setting brother against brother; and a decade later the peasantry was brutally torn apart by collectivization.

There is a common theme in all these struggles: Food. The abiding, underlying theme of Soviet political economy during its early years was the struggle to feed the population. At times that struggle had been lost. A Soviet citizen who was 55 years old or more in 1941 could remember the famine of 1891, one who was 25 or older could remember the famine of 1921 to 1922, and one who was only about 15 years old could remember the famine of 1932 to 1933.

Ensuring that famine would not occur was connected to the question that goes to the heart of Soviet political economy: Could a proletarian dictatorship rule in a peasant country and at the same time find ways to persuade or force the peasants to produce enough food to feed the population? The food issue is thus a major part of the fabric of Soviet history. War Communism, for example, was born of the need for the new Soviet regime to requisition food to survive the Civil War. The New Economic Policy (NEP) had a twofold purpose; it was designed, first, to provide peasants with incentives to produce more so that the towns would not starve and, second, to heal the breach between the party and peasantry caused by the forced requisitioning of food during the Civil War. The failure of NEP to solve

1

the food problem in the 1920s provided the justification for collectivization that emerged as a result of real or imagined fears that enough food would not be supplied to the urban population. To ensure that the industrialization drive would succeed, the Soviets used violence and even famine against the peasantry in the early 1930s.

World War II once again forced the regime to contend with the threat of extinction and the danger of food shortages. Major food-producing areas were lost to the Germans very early. Indeed, by the end of November 1941 the Germans held Soviet territory that had produced 84 percent of the nation's sugar, 38 percent of its grain, and 60 percent of its pigs.[1] There was also a loss of agricultural machinery in these territories and a decline in the male labor force because of the military draft. Almost overnight, the nation's capacity to feed itself fell with dramatic force.

In 1941 the Soviet people once again faced the ugly specter of starvation, less than a decade after the mass starvation of 1933 and barely two decades after the hungry years of the Civil War. Relief supplies were sought from food-rich countries, but the response was only grudging. And what food was received from the West was allocated by the Soviet government almost entirely to the armed forces, rather than being used to improve the civilian food supply.

Nevertheless, the Soviet Union won the war. This book is the story of how the Soviet Union, specifically how Soviet planning, dealt with feeding its people during World War II. Most often, the Soviet victory, achieved in the face of enormous human and economic losses, is seen as a sign of the effectiveness of the centralized institutions of the planned industrial economic system created by Stalin. In the words of James Millar: "Stalinist political and economic institutions proved their stability, flexibility, and durability in World War II."[2] But there are many reasons to think that these institutions worked quite imperfectly in respect to the food supply or, more accurately, that the institutions worked better to feed the army than they did to feed the civilian population. In fact, the war demonstrated the limitations of central planning, which works best because it channels resources to areas that have been given priority status. But once everything has priority, as happens during war – supplying hardware to the armed forces, feeding the military, feeding civilians, protecting precious natural resources – the weaknesses of central planning are demonstrated.

[1] Alec Nove, *An Economic History of the U.S.S.R.*, London: Penguin, 1969, p. 270.
[2] James R. Millar, *The ABCs of Soviet Socialism*, Urbana: University of Illinois Press, 1981, p. 43.

My fundamental argument in this book is that, in respect to feeding the civilian population, a decision was made early in the war to decentralize production and distribution and to require the population explicitly to rely on local resources for most of its food, a policy that created severe difficulties for the population. Understandably, feeding the army was given a higher priority than feeding civilians, a policy that further complicated the food situation in the rear. It was not until the tide of the war turned that the central authority resumed its primacy in feeding the population. Thus, while Soviet power was used to feed the armed forces, the solution to the problem of feeding the civilian population was not to use the strength of the centralized Soviet planning system, but to force the population to find the capacity to feed itself. The new emphasis on local initiative fostered the creation and expansion of institutions that relied on private economic activity. Not since the years of NEP had there been so much license given to the private sector. People displayed a rather remarkable degree of ingenuity, born largely out of a sense of desperation, in finding ways to produce and distribute food.

Notwithstanding the chronic food problems of the civilian population, those in the unoccupied areas fared better than those who lived under German occupation. With the exception of the nightmarish experience of Leningrad, the only mass starvation appears to have taken place in occupied areas, although starvation was not absent in the hinterlands.

A very special aspect of this study is a series of interviews with Soviet émigrés about their experiences during the war in regard to the food situation. The interviews were generally an hour or more in length and those interviewed fall into several important categories, soldiers as well as civilians. One of the major handicaps for scholars who are working on the war period is the inaccessibility of adequate archival material to balance the one-sided testimony of the official press and other self-serving accounts. The thirty-one interviews I completed provide an extraordinary window into a set of experiences we know of only at a superficial level. The stories I have heard add specific detail and texture to our knowledge of the food issue during the war. What I found is that the memories of those interviewed are extremely keen. They remember many events during this period as though they occurred yesterday. Some of them still recall the precise date they were evacuated from their home city. What has emerged from these interviews is an astonishing set of stories that in part confirm what was printed in the official press. However, often the content of the interviews seriously contradicts official Soviet claims as to what happened. Those who lived through the experience bear a special witness.

Thus unfolds the tale of how a nation fed itself after experiencing a massive invasion of its territory, including critical food-producing areas, carried out a frantic evacuation of people and factories to the depths of the country, and then swiftly gathered up its energies to fight and conquer Nazi Germany.

1   On the eve of the war

The unrelenting shortage of food that the Soviet people would face after the catastrophic German invasion of June 1941, was directly linked to the prewar situation. The blow inflicted by the Germans worsened a set of prewar circumstances that were already precarious at best. Although the past did not fully ordain the future, it did severely limit the options available to planners. A number of preexisting conditions contributed to the awful predicament in which the nation found itself after the Germans marched through major food-producing areas and forced the Soviets to place the economy on a war footing. The major problem was the impact of forced collectivization and the destruction of a predominant share of the food production base. Other problems included the insufficient transportation network, the absence of food reserves that could sustain the population for any protracted period of time, and the ways that practical agricultural policy were undermined by ideology.

There were three major strands that would create a knot around the country during the war and lead to the terrible food shortages that ensued. First, there were the near-term events of 1939 and 1940, in which the nation careened, albeit in fits and starts, toward war with Germany. Second, there was the set of reversals for the food supply marking the early years of Soviet history. These included the expropriations during the Civil War after the 1917 revolution, which ended with the famine of 1921, and the debacle of collectivization imposed upon the peasantry, whose crowning catastrophe was the great famine of 1932 and 1933. The third factor was the press of Russian history, which was tragically dotted with famine through the centuries.

The backdrop to the invasion

The Soviet Union was eager to keep the rising tide of militarism away from its door. After the appeasement at Munich in September 1938, when the British and French acquiesced to Hitler's demands, they looked for ways to avoid the coming war. They were suspicious of the West, and although they detested the Nazis, Soviet leaders still signed a mutual nonaggression pact with Hitler. Free now to face only the West, Germany invaded Poland on September 1, 1939. A secret protocol divided Poland between Germany and the USSR and eastern Poland was added to the Ukraine and Belorussia. The next step was the signing of defense treaties with the three Baltic republics, Estonia, Latvia, and Lithuania in late September and early October 1939, which gave the Soviets access to military bases. The Soviets made similar demands on Finland in November, including the movement of the Finnish boundary twenty more miles away from Leningrad. When these demands were rejected, the Russians invaded Finland on November 30, 1939, and after some early military setbacks, finally defeated the Finns in mid-March 1940. Following this victory, the Soviets occupied the Baltic countries in July 1940 and they were forced to merge with the Soviet Union as union republics. Nonetheless, time was running out for the Soviet Union. The efforts it was making in Europe to strengthen its position and its struggles at home to bridge the gap between German military and industrial might and its own position were too little, too late. The surprise attack came on June 22, 1941; the Soviet Union was at war with Germany.

Food and Soviet and Russian history

Russia had endured throughout its history. Whether created by God or man, hunger seemed like a time bomb that went off every so often, taking many lives with it when it exploded. There was the great famine during Boris Godunov's regime at the beginning of the seventeenth century. The crops failed in each of the three years from 1601 to 1603 and more than 100,000 are said to have died in Moscow alone.[1] There was a major famine in European Russia at the end of the nineteenth century in 1891 and 1892. It is estimated that more

---

[1] Nicholas V. Riasanvosky, *A History of Russia*, 2nd edition, New York: Oxford University Press, 1969, p. 178.

than 400,000 people died in the 16 provinces most seriously affected by the famine.[2] In the Soviet period two major famines gripped the nation. A drought in 1920 and 1921 led to a massive famine centered in the Volga region. The Soviets estimated that about 25,000,000 people were jeopardized by the famine.[3] Crop output was about half of the pre–World War I average.[4] Probably the worst famine to strike the nation was the manmade starvation concentrated in the Ukraine during 1932 and 1933.[5] There are substantially differing estimates of the number who died in this period. Wheatcroft contends that 3 to 4 million died, whereas Mace estimates that 7½ million died in the Ukraine.[6] Living on the margin was nothing new for the peoples of the Soviet Union.

The impact of collectivization

The forced collectivization drive at the beginning of the 1930s and the damage it inflicted on Soviet agriculture was probably the watershed event determining the amount of food available to the country on the eve of the war. The peasantry's violent reaction, which included the destruction of implements and animals, has been well documented.[7] What is crucial is how it diminished the food base of the country. Collectivization was an unmitigated disaster. Table 1.1 shows the livestock figures at the beginning of 1929, just before collectivization began; 1934, at a nadir in the aftermath of livestock destruction; and 1940, a year before the war started. The number of cattle and cows was about 20 percent less than it had been a decade earlier, the number of sheep and goats fell by about 30 percent, and the number of horses was virtually half of the 1929 level; only in the

[2] Richard D. Robbins, Jr., *Famine in Russia 1891–1892*, New York: Columbia University Press, 1975, p. 189.
[3] H. H. Fisher, *The Famine in Soviet Russia*, New York: Macmillan, 1927, p. 51.
[4] Lazar Volin, *A Century of Russian Agriculture*, Cambridge: Harvard University Press, 1971, p. 173.
[5] Probably the most complete exploration of this cataclysmic event is Robert Conquest's *The Harvest of Sorrow*, New York: Oxford University Press, 1986.
[6] Stephen G. Wheatcroft, "New Demographic Evidence on Excess Collectivization Deaths: Yet Another *Kliuvka* from Stephen Rosefielde?" *Slavic Review*, Fall 1985, p. 508; James E. Mace, "Famine and Nationalism in Soviet Ukraine," *Problems of Communism*, May–June 1984, p. 39.
[7] There are several good overviews of this period. See, for example, Alec Nove, *An Economic History of the U.S.S.R.*, London: Penguin, 1969, Chapter 7, or Zhores A. Medvedev, *Soviet Agriculture*, New York: Norton, 1987, Chapters 3 and 4.

Table 1.1. *Livestock in the Soviet Union as of January 1 (millions)*

	Horses	Cattle	Cows	Pigs	Sheep and goats
1929	32.6	58.2	29.2	19.4	107.1
1934	15.4	33.5	19.0	11.5	36.5
1940	17.7	47.8	22.8	22.5	76.7

Source: Narodnoe khoziaistvo SSSR za 70 let, p. 253.

Table 1.2. *Gross output of crops as of December 31 (in millions of tons)*

	Grain	Potatoes	Vegetables
1928	73.3	46.4	10.5
1939	73.2	40.7	9.7

Source: Narodnoe khoziaistvo SSSR za 70 let, p. 208.

case of pigs did the numbers recover.[8] Because horses were the essential tractive power in the fields, this huge decline adversely affected agricultural production. There were further ramifications for wartime production because the army confiscated many of the already diminished number of draft animals.[9]

The decline in the livestock herd had major implications for meat and milk production. At the end of 1928, the nation produced 4.9 million tons of meat; by the end of 1940, production was down to 4.7 million tons. Milk production was up only slightly for this same twelve-year period, from 29.8 million tons to 33.6 million tons.[10] Gross output of the three major field crops upon which the Soviet diet depended – grain, potatoes, and vegetables – was also down, as shown in Table 1.2. It is fair to say that the food base from which the nation could support itself had fallen severely. The situation was aggravated by the fact that the population had grown from 165.7 million in 1932 to 194.1 million in 1940.[11]

These data suggest that food shortages were probably independent

[8] Pigs recovered first probably because of their ability to bear young at an early age, their larger litter size, and their shorter gestation period.
[9] See Chapter 2 for an analysis of this policy.
[10] *Narodnoe khoziaistvo SSSR za 70 let*, p. 258 (*Narkhoz*). Here, as in Table 1.2, all prewar data correspond to Soviet boundaries for the corresponding year.
[11] Nove, p. 180; *Narkhoz 1987*, p. 373.

of the war and, in fact, 1940 was not a good year. There were shortages of potatoes, vegetables, and milk of sufficient magnitude that prices in government food stores around the country were raised 35 percent and Western sources reported popular discontent.[12] Even at the beginning of the year, conditions had become so bad that the Soviet government was censoring all press dispatches that mentioned food.[13]

One Soviet study of peasant diets maintained that per capita consumption worsened between 1923 and 1924, which was quite a poor year in agriculture, and 1937, which was an excellent harvest. Although annual per capita consumption of bread and bread products remained about the same, falling from 253 to 249 kilograms per capita, the consumption of milk and other dairy products fell by about half, from 242 kilograms to 127 kilograms a person, and meat and fat consumption, already at a low of 18 kilograms a person, fell to just below 16 kilograms. Only potato consumption rose, going from 172 kilograms to 199 kilograms.[14]

This difficult situation was probably aggravated when, in February 1940, as the Finnish war was winding down, the Soviets signed a commercial agreement with Germany. Among other obligations, the Soviets agreed to deliver 1 million tons of feed grains and cereals and 120 million Reichsmarks worth of legumes within the first twelve months of the signing.[15]

Not only was there an overall decline in food, but there was also a maldistribution of the existing provisions. There were substantial differences among the various social groups in their feelings about the supply of food. When people were asked if they thought the food supply was "adequate," 66 percent of the intelligentsia thought it was, as did 43 percent of the white-collar workers, 38 percent of the skilled workers, 28 percent of workers, and only 3 percent of the

---

[12] *The New York Times*, January 28, 1940, p. 1. The situation had gotten bad enough to provoke the Moscow raion and city party organizations to discuss the deficits.
[13] *The New York Times*, February 11, 1940, p. 5. In part this may have been triggered by such pieces as the January 25, 1940 *The New York Times* article that cited unnamed "experts" who predicted famine in the Soviet Union if the war with Finland continued. Even if this was a hyperbolic assessment, it confirms the sense of severe shortage experienced by others.
[14] M. A. Vyltsan, *Zavershaiushchii etap sozdaniia kolkhoznogo stroia*, Moscow, 1978, p. 208. The situation was even worse in 1932, a year coinciding with the depths of destruction in the countryside. In that year, per capita peasant consumption of potatoes was 136 kilograms, milk and dairy products was 132 kilograms, and meat and fat consumption was less than 12 kilograms. The 1932 bread figure was not given.
[15] Raymond James Sontag and James Stuart Beddie, eds., *Nazi-Soviet Relations, 1939–1941*, New York: Didier, 1948, pp. 108–9, 131–3.

peasantry.[16] The disaffection of the peasantry from the system seemed quite complete. The toll of collectivization, still fresh in the minds of the peasantry, as well as the severe delivery quotas imposed in the 1930s, left farmers with a bitter taste of injustice; they knew how much food they could have produced. The considerably lower level of discontent of urbanites was also possibly rooted in the fact that they ate better than collective farmers. In 1937, although Muscovites consumed 238 kilograms of bread, about the same as farmers, they ate 36 kilograms of meat and lard a person, considerably more than the peasantry.[17] Even greater were the complaints about the "extremely limited and monotonous nature of the diet and its high cost."[18]

The railroad system

A second major problem was the bottleneck in the distribution system caused by inadequate rail facilities. This showed up in the winter following the invasion of Poland in September 1939. Equipment that had previously been used to transport food was recruited for the war with Finland. This would be a foretaste of what would happen in the much more demanding war with Germany, when Soviet transportation would only be adequate to the task of moving military personnel and supplies. In an article written to stimulate discussion that appeared in *Pravda* at the end of January 1940, Trade Commissar Pavlov suggested that small, local enterprises begin to produce more food, such as fish, cheese, wild berries, and mushrooms, "to relieve a burden on the transportation system."[19] The inability of central authorities to accomplish multiple goals became even more apparent during the war. Pavlov's idea would reappear in about eighteen months when the invasion put astonishing pressure on all resources, including the railroad system. The wager on local food sources would become a cornerstone of Soviet wartime food policy.

A review of how the rail system evolved in the years before the war will help us understand its performance during the war. The

[16] Alex Inkeles and Raymond Bauer, *The Soviet Citizen*, New York: Atheneum, 1968, p. 121.
[17] Medvedev, p. 121.
[18] Inkeles and Bauer, p. 121.
[19] *Pravda*, January 28, 1940, p. 2.

focus must be on the railroad system because the nation increasingly depended on it to move freight. When the industrialization drive began in 1928, 80 percent of the freight went by rail; by 1940, this figure had reached 87 percent.[20] The development of the railroad system went through several phases in the period before the war. In the early 1930s, railroads were of secondary priority in the industrialization scheme. As a consequence, a severe bottleneck was created in the economy. When the Soviet leadership recognized the problem in 1934, more resources were trained on the rail system to solve the so-called transportation crisis. While investment in railroads had a checkered pattern in the 1930s, the overall impact of expenditures was to increase the freight car stock by 42 percent from 1932 to 1940. The growth in freight traffic during the same period, however, increased by 140 percent.[21] The demands on the system grew at a rate that clearly outpaced the development of facilities.[22] Therefore, the railroads were already inadequate to meet Soviet needs before the war. The war could only worsen this condition as the vast new demands of the military fell on the overstretched rail network. This view runs counter to the conventional wisdom about the performance of the Soviet rail system during the war, which has been to give it high marks. The key to the puzzle can be found in Holland Hunter's praise for the performance of the railroad system during the war: "The Nazi invasion eliminated from the demands placed on railroads more than it eliminated from their ability to meet those demands, and this provided a margin of capacity for dealing with military traffic."[23] The demands that were eliminated were the demands of the civilian economy, including the use of railroads to carry food. Therefore, during the war there was a new version of the transportation crisis, although it was never spoken of as such. The crisis was partly a result of the prewar inadequacies of the transport network. The central government's response to this crisis would be a devolution of responsibility for the civilian food supply to the local level.

[20] Ernest W. Williams, Jr., *Freight Transportation in the Soviet Union*, Princeton: Princeton University Press, 1962, p. 14.

[21] Holland Hunter, *Soviet Transportation Policy*, Cambridge: Harvard University Press, 1957, p. 77.

[22] Hunter (pp. 81–2) speculates on why the rate of improvement slowed down. His tentative hypotheses include the negative effect of the purges on the administration of the railroads and the reaching of technological as well as administrative limits in running the existing system.

[23] Hunter, p. 109. See Chapter 5 in his *Soviet Transportation Policy* for a more complete analysis of the railroad system during the war.

Food reserves

Food reserves are a government's hedge against disaster. The size of reserves relative to need can provide some indication of how great a government's fears of disaster are and also how much it intends to do should disaster strike. It now seems beyond dispute that Stalin did not want to believe that Hitler would invade Russia, at least not as early as 1941.[24] From Stalin's perspective, the signing of the nonaggression pact with Germany on August 23, 1939, was a way of buying time. In respect to the food situation, however, little had been accomplished by June 1941.

For instance, there were some shifts to the east of both industry and agriculture as a concession to the presumed eventuality of war with Germany. But the shift in grain production away from the traditional grain-growing areas since the Revolution was not very significant. The share of grain production coming from the Urals regions went from 8.4 percent in 1913 to 9.7 percent in 1940; the Siberian share rose from 7.0 percent to 11.7 percent; and Kazakhstan's share went from 2.8 percent to 3.4 percent.[25] These movements did not constitute the creation of a readiness for war. The same can be said about the level of reserves. Soviet historians say that there were 6,162,000 tons of grain, flour, and cereal reserves as of January 1, 1941.[26] At best, these reserves amounted to about a month's worth of grain.[27] In the U.S. intelligence community it was reported that at some unspecified time before the war, the Soviets were maintaining a substantially larger reserve of 10 million tons of grain,[28] but there

[24] See, for example, Harrison Salisbury's discussion in *The 900 Days: The Siege of Leningrad*, Avon: New York, 1979, pp. 74–103 and Vladimir Petrov, *June 22, 1941*, Columbia: University of South Carolina Press, 1968. The latter has A. M. Nekrich's stinging critique of Stalin for refusing to believe the evidence that Germany was preparing to invade the Soviet Union.

[25] Nikolai A. Voznesensky, *The Economy of the USSR During World War II*, Washington, D.C.: Public Affairs Press, 1948, p. 49.

[26] See, for example, *Istoriia Velikoi Otechestvennoi Voiny Sovetskogo Soiuza 1941–1945*, Vol. 1, Moscow, 1960, p. 412 and U. G. Cherniavskii, *Voina i prodovol'stve*, Moscow, 1964, p. 22.

[27] The average level of grain production for the fourteen-year period from 1925 to 1937, 1940 was about 75 million tons. The prewar reserves constituted one-twelfth of that figure. See Volin, *A Century of Russian Agriculture*, Cambridge: Harvard University Press, 1970, p. 232; Nove, pp. 239, 303. From another perspective, the Soviets believed they had four to six months of reserves for the military. See *Istoriia Vtoroi Mirovoi Voiny 1939–1945*, Vol. 3, Moscow, 1973, pp. 387–8.

[28] NFAS, American Embassy at Kuibyshev, Despatch No. 468, January 15, 1942, and *Foreign Relations of the United States*, 1942, Vol. 3, Washington, D.C., 1961, p. 423 (*FRUS*).

was never any confirmation of this number. Nor is it known whether some of the wheat held in reserve was used to meet Soviet obligations under the terms of the commercial agreement between the Soviet Union and Germany. The Germans never claimed that they found large caches of grain in occupied Soviet territory. There were reports prior to the invasion that food was being stockpiled in Ural regions.[29] The Soviets could have stored huge amounts of grain in the area behind the Urals, but that would have created a mismatch between the largely western location of the population and the rail system and eastern grain reserves.[30] There were so-called special granaries, but not all of them were in the hinterlands. When the Germans invaded, slightly more than 54,000 tons of grain were rescued and moved to safety.[31] It is possible that the Germans captured some of these reserves or that some reserves were destroyed when the Soviets implemented their scorched earth policy. There were also reports that the stringency in Moscow in 1940 was designed to conserve food that was put into emergency reserves.[32] Indeed, Stalin rigidly enforced the idea that grain reserves were not for civilians and only for soldiers when there was no other alternative. In part, this niggardly, albeit defensible, position contributed to the rigorous rationing system that was imposed early in the war.

There are other factors that worked against the buildup of reserves. The Soviet Union had sent substantial amounts of food to Germany in the eighteen months prior to the invasion. Deliveries (all measured in tons) included: grain – 1,604,000, oilseeds – 365, soya beans – 28,539, vegetable oil – 9,350, whale oil – 78,114, fish oil – 24,761, fats oil – 4,981.[33] Although grains and potatoes were by far the most important part of the traditional Soviet diet, the loss of these oils would cost dearly when the war started, when areas providing significant amounts of fats and oils to the population were lost. Finally, the adverse climatic conditions in three of the five years preceding the war must have made it more difficult to accumulate reserves.[34]

[29] *FRUS*, 1942, Vol. 3, pp. 423–4.
[30] Lazar Volin, "German Invasion and Russian Agriculture," *Russian Review*, Vol. 3–4, November 1943, pp. 79–80.
[31] Dmitri A. Pavlov, *Leningrad 1941: The Blockade*, Chicago: The University of Chicago Press, 1965, p. 44.
[32] *The New York Times*, October 29, 1940, p. 31.
[33] NFAS, American Embassy at London, Despatch No. 8015, March 5, 1943. This is based upon a secret British report given to the U.S. State Department.
[34] Lazar Volin, "The Russo-German War and Soviet Agriculture," *Foreign Agriculture*, October 1941, p. 405.

The rise of Lysenko and political agronomy

The pernicious effects of Lysenkoism seriously affected the Soviet Union's food supply during the war, and the wrongheaded theories he and his disciples championed during the 1930s had negative ramifications for all agriculture throughout the war and beyond. From the point of view of the war, there were two practical effects of Lysenkoism: the absence of the technology of hybrid corn production, which according to Zhores Medvedev cost the Soviets a minimum of 30 to 50 billion kilograms of corn in a twenty-year period[35] and the proliferation of a myriad of pseudoscientific ideas that not only never panned out, but also diverted resources from more sensible research projects.

In 1935 and 1936, Lysenko and a theoretician named I. I. Prezent rejected the universally accepted chromosome theory without offering any scientific basis for their conclusion. In its place they offered a theory that was more consistent with the ideas of social engineering that informed the economic, political, social, and ideological climate of the Soviet Union in the 1930s.[36] Lysenko had resurrected the long-dead Lamarckian theory that environmental changes in plants and animals cause structural changes that are inherited by future generations. Specifically, Lysenko claimed he could change winter wheat into spring wheat and then back again. This appealed to the Stalinist ideologues because it meant that nature was not immutable, and so the view that acquired characteristics were inherited came to rule Soviet biology from the mid–1930s well into the Khrushchev years.

Lysenkoism was opposed to the inbreeding of plants, which was necessary to develop hybrids. Hybridization was well known in the Soviet Union in the 1930s as was its success in the United States and other countries. Indeed, its adoption was proposed in 1938 and 1939 by N. I. Vavilov and others.[37] Lysenko and his adherents, however, fought mightily and successfully against its introduction into the Soviet Union, based on their opposition to the genetic theories that gave

[35] Zhores A. Medvedev, *The Rise and Fall of T. D. Lysenko*, New York: Columbia University Press, 1959, p. 181.

[36] I am summarizing Lysenkoism based upon a reading of Medvedev and David Joravsky's definitive work, *The Lysenko Affair*, Cambridge: Harvard University Press, 1970.

[37] Nikolai Ivanovich Vavilov was one of the world's giants in the field of plant genetics. He was head of the All-Union Institute of Plant Breeding and was elected president of the International Congress of Genetics. He was arrested in August 1940 and, after an initial death sentence was commuted to ten years, he wallowed in prison for about a year before his death in January 1943. His arrest was followed by those of a virtual who's who in Soviet and international plant genetics.

rise to hybrids.[38] A number of bizarre Lysenkoist ideas can be viewed as attempts at finding a quick fix for Soviet wartime food shortages, but instead led to a great waste of land and other agricultural resources during the war. The three ideas examined here by no means exhaust the list. One experiment involved trying to grow winter wheat in Siberia. Lysenko and Vil'yams, a self-anointed theoretician, claimed that frost-resistant strains could be developed within two to three years. Hundreds of thousands of hectares were given over to this enterprise, which failed quite badly.[39] The Soviets finally gave up on the idea just after the war ended. A second major failure attributable to Lysenko was the proposal to plant sugar beets in Central Asia during the summer. Without any prior testing, the project was implemented in 1943 and 1944 on thousands of hectares. The plants literally withered in the midst of the ferociously hot summers of Central Asia. It was a total loss. The third idea involved Lysenko's attempt to deal with the worldwide drop in potato output (which affected the Soviet Union) because of deadly viruses. Lysenko attributed the problem to the incorrect timing of planting. Potatoes, he argued, should be planted in the summer and be allowed to develop during this period. When the tubers formed in the cooler fall months, this would willy-nilly halt the decline. The idea had no scientific basis. Rather than devoting resources to research for fighting the viral disease affecting the potato crop, the nation followed the pied piper.[40]

---

[38] Medvedev, pp. 179 and 181. Hybrid corn was finally introduced into the USSR in the early 1950s. It is produced either by inbreeding or artificially produced self-induced fertilization in order to produce pure strains that are then crossbred to achieve specific traits. The virtues of hybrid corn rest in increased yield, hardiness against disease, and faster growth, among others. Former Vice-President Henry Wallace first marketed hybrid seed corn. See Edward L. Schapsmeier and Frederick H. Schapsmeier, *Encyclopedia of American Agricultural History*, Westport, Conn.: Greenwood Press, 1975, p. 76. One can get a good sense of what the absence of hybrids meant for Soviet agriculture by examining the results of U.S. production. It is estimated that the 1945 corn crop in the United States increased by 400 million bushels because of hybrid seed. That translated into enough output to feed twenty million pigs, or 25 percent more than were raised from 1938 to 1940. Looked at somewhat differently, in 1944 and 1945 it is estimated that without hybrid seed, total feed grain production would have been 10 percent lower than it was. See Walter W. Wilcox, *The Farmer in the Second World War*, Ames: Iowa State College Press, 1947, p. 290. In 1930, less than .1 percent of the corn acreage in the U.S. corn belt was planted to hybrid seed; by 1943, all of the corn acreage of Iowa was using hybrid seed. See *Encyclopedia Americana*, Vol. 7, Danbury, Conn.: Grolier, 1976, p. 802.
[39] The Soviets tried to pass off the Siberian experiment as a great success. *The Times* (London) of July 27, 1942, p. 4, asserted that: "Moscow has been looking ahead for years. Wheat fields have been developed in Siberia. Great reserves have been stocked."
[40] These experiments are described by Medvedev, pp. 161–2, 164–5. There is a certain perverse irony to Lysenko's domination during the war in the pages of *Sotsialisticheskoe*

The costs of Lysenkoism are literally incalculable. Although it would be excessive to argue that sound, scientific agriculture would have turned around the food situation in Russia, nevertheless Lysenko's theories had a negative effect on the wartime food supply. The politicization of science not only cost the lives and careers of many scientists, but probably the loss of a good deal of food.

Conclusion

The events of the Soviet Union's brief history had increasingly strained food resources that were already limited. The war against the peasantry during collectivization in particular severely diminished the capacity of the country to feed itself. In addition, Soviet granaries were not overflowing with reserves. The unwillingness of Stalin to tap what reserves there were may smack of brutality; but the truth is that there was little choice in the matter because there was probably little grain supporting the immediate stocks. The ideology and paranoia that helped make collectivization a reality also spawned Lysenko. The politicization of scientific inquiry in the Soviet Union simply added to the burden imposed by limited resources. Finally, although substantial investments in railroads had been made in the last half of the 1930s, the enhanced capacity could not be used to carry food.

There was darkness in the days following Germany's invasion, because on the eve of its most dreadful challenge, the nation was insufficiently prepared to feed its people. Already living close to the margin, it could not create the reserves that would ensure food for all. Planners were left with limited options. The rest of this book tells the story of how the nation survived after the German invasion.

sel'skoe khoziaistvo, the leading academic agricultural journal. For example, in the January–February 1943 issue, he had a twenty-three-page article, "O nasledstvennosti i ee izmenchivosti" ("On Heredity and its Changeability"). The next longest article was nine pages. Part two of the article occupied sixteen pages in the next issue of the journal.

2 The desperate months of 1941: invasion and evacuation

The German invasion of the Soviet Union on June 22, 1941, created immediate chaos. Stalin's lack of response to the growing evidence that Hitler would invade left the country vulnerable when the actual attack came and ill-equipped to fight a great war. One critical area left untouched because of the absence of planning for war was what to do about the food supply if the unthinkable should occur. It appears that only with the onset of war itself did the leadership actually develop policies about how to feed the nation. First of all, there were three decisions taken about food in the fields as the Germans' push eastward brought them into key agricultural areas: (1) gather in the harvest as soon as possible in order to salvage as much grain as possible; (2) evacuate as much agricultural machinery and livestock as possible; and (3) destroy anything that would be valuable to the Germans that could not be moved. Second, the decision to evacuate millions of people to areas of safety in the eastern regions, where they would become the backbone of a relocated industrial labor force, would have major repercussions on the food supply in areas receiving the refugees.

Although there were some real successes, such as removing certain key elements of the livestock herd, there were important ways in which the Soviets failed quite badly, such as in the actual relocation of people that had to be fed. The report card is mixed, but when one considers the lack of preparation for a possible invasion, the Soviet response to the invasion was extraordinary. And the immediate response became more important than might have been thought initially, because by the fall of 1942, the Germans controlled 40 percent of the prewar crop regions.[1]

[1] Lazar Volin, *A Survey of Soviet Russian Agriculture*, Washington, D.C.: U.S. Department of Agriculture, 1951, p. 184.

Collective farm family near the ruins of their house, which was burned down by the Germans. *Source:* National Archives.

The 1941 harvest

The 1941 harvest, especially in the grain-rich Ukraine, was expected to be a bumper crop, the best since the exceptional yield of 1937. After the invasion, the task of bringing in the crop before the Germans got to it was made much more difficult by the speed with which the Germans devoured Soviet territory and moved ever closer to the Ukrainian grain areas and by cool, rainy weather that slowed the ripening process.[2] The decision to act came only four days after the war started. On June 26, the Ukrainian Party Central Committee and the Ukraine *Sovnarkom* issued a directive regarding the organization of the harvest under these extraordinary conditions. It included

---

[2] It had rained excessively and temperatures were unusually low. *Ukrainskaia SSSR v Velikoi Otechestvennoi Voine Sovetskogo Soiuza 1941–1945gg.* (*Ukrainskaia*), Vol. 1, Kiev, 1975, p. 136.

Soviet village burned down by Germans. *Source:* National Archives.

orders to recruit the entire rural population and certain urban groups to work and to substitute animals for machinery.[3]

The flowing wheat fields of the Soviet Union became a second battlefield as men and women, children and old people struggled mightily to bring in the crop. Time was the enemy; the pace was unbelievable. One collective farm pledged to bring in the harvest in ten to twelve days, instead of the originally planned seventeen or eighteen days.[4] Some people worked twenty hours a day. Around-the-clock operations were organized using moonlight to see the crops. The prewar shortage of machinery worsened as the army commandeered a substantial part of the best draft power and related equipment. In the Ukraine 9,300 tractors and a large number of horses were immediately taken by the army.[5] Cows, unless pregnant, were used

[3] Ibid., p. 133.
[4] Ibid.
[5] Iu. V. Arutiunian, *Sovetskoe krest'ianstvo v gody Velikoi Otechestvennoi Voiny,* Moscow, 1963, p. 28.

Russian collective farmers driven out of their homes living in dugouts with several families in each. *Source:* National Archives.

in the fields.[6] Because they worked round the clock, the farmers simply changed animals during the course of the day and night, resting the ones that had worked and bringing in fresh animals.[7] Using animal draft power to compensate for the loss of tractors meant that collective farmers were forced to turn virtually all of their attention to the socialist sector and away from their private plots. What machinery there was operated at an intensive level, as in Georgia, where combines worked two or three shifts a day at the peak of the harvest.[8] During the first month of the war, 35,000 new tractor drivers were trained, although surely they were less productive at first than those

[6] In the Saratov oblast they used almost 100,000 cows to cart away grain and straw and in the Penza oblast almost 40,000 cows were used for the same purposes. M. I. Likhomanov, *Khoziaistvenno-organizatorskaia rabota partii v derevne v pervyi period Velikoi Otechestvennoi Voiny (1941–1942gg.)*, Leningrad, 1975, p. 52.
[7] *Ukrainskaia*, p. 135.
[8] *Pravda*, July 18, 1941, p. 3.

they replaced.[9] Urbanites were brought in to help with the harvest, including hundreds of teachers and more than 84,000 senior-level high school students in the Sumy district and 70,000 and 50,000 students and schoolchildren in the Zaporozhe and Voroshilov oblasts.[10] For them and the farmers who worked with them, it must have been a nightmarish experience. Many worked in the fields while being bombed and shot at.[11] Not surprisingly, productivity began to fall as those who labored under these stressful conditions became increasingly exhausted.

The results were remarkable, although evidence suggests that the official Soviet claim that on August 20 88 percent of the harvest had been collected in areas outside of the war zone (as against 98 percent in 1940)[12] may be high. In his wartime memoirs, Ilya Ehrenburg twice noted that much grain still stood in fields in October.[13] Moreover, in the invaded areas, most of the grain that had been planted in the spring probably was lost.[14] As a consequence, the grain harvest in 1941 was 59 percent of the 1940 total, government procurements were fulfilled by only 80 percent, and there was a bread cereal deficit of about 8,000,000 tons in the country.[15]

This was much better than they did with the harvest of nongrain crops, however. By October 1, they had harvested only 17.1 percent of the sown area of sunflowers, 27.4 percent of the vegetables, 5.7 percent of the potatoes, and 21.6 percent of the grass seeds.[16]

The prewar weakness in the transport system now became worse, creating a general transportation shortage and bottlenecks in both the rail and water networks. Rail facilities were primarily devoted to the movement of soldiers westward and industrial enterprises eastward.[17] Therefore, it was difficult to find the facilities to transport food. By August 1, although 32,731 railroad cars filled with grain had been evacuated, an unspecified amount accumulated at a number of loading points in the western and southern areas of the country, reflecting

[9] *Ukrainskaia*, p. 134.
[10] Ibid., p. 136.
[11] Ibid.
[12] Ibid., p. 137.
[13] Ilya Ehrenburg, *The War: 1941–1945*, Cleveland: World, 1964, pp. 14, 18.
[14] *Foreign Relations of the United States*, 1942, Vol. III, Washington, D.C., 1961, p. 423 (*FRUS*).
[15] *Istoriia*, Vol. 6, p. 67, Arutiunian, p. 35: *FRUS*, 1942, Vol. 3, Washington, D.C., 1961, p. 423.
[16] *Ukrainskaia*, p. 137.
[17] The most detailed telling of this story is Sanford Liberman, "The Evacuation of Industry in the Soviet Union During World War II," *Soviet Studies*, Vol. XXXV, No. 1, January 1983, pp. 90–102.

the inadequacy of the railroad to carry out its multiple responsibilities.[18] A serious effort was also made to use water transport to ship grain. Beginning in July, the Soviet steamship fleet was not only asked to perform its regular duties but, like the rail system, was also called upon to ship soldiers and war material and, when possible, food. In July, 130,000 tons of evacuated cargo was sent from Kiev to the lower Dnepr River by ship. This included 26,500 tons of grain fodder that went from Kiev to Dnepropetrovsk. And about 42,000 tons of grain were sent up river from Kherson. In August the fleet began to take part in the evacuation of the population. On top of this, orders were issued to transport 60,000 tons of grain out of the Don and Kuban areas. Grain was carried on everything from passenger ships to barges that hauled stones. The sense of urgency was great. With the Germans coming ever closer, the only way to ensure getting some of the ships carrying grain to safety was to send them through the Manych Canal, which connected the Don River with the Caspian Sea. It was not built to accommodate large Don steamships, but it did so during the terrifying summer of 1941.[19]

The transportation shortage had a serious negative effect on the ability of the Soviets to ship grain out of the endangered areas. According to the official history of the Ukraine in the war years, between July 1 and October 23, 1941, some 1,667,400 tons of grain and 269,500 tons of grain products were sent out of the Ukraine. The Germans got hold of more than 900,000 tons of grain and grain products.[20] On the assumption that these figures correctly show a total grain harvest in the Ukraine of 2,837,000 tons, this means that the Soviets rescued only about two-thirds of the Ukrainian grain harvest.

The evacuation of livestock and machinery

The second major task in agriculture was to evacuate livestock and agricultural machinery. There were high costs associated with the long cattle drives. The herds diminished dramatically in number over the course of the evacuation. Soviet scholars make a sharp distinction between animals who died and those slaughtered to satisfy meat delivery obligations – for example, they say only 3.5 percent of the livestock of the Orlov oblast died, while 45 percent were delivered

[18] G. A. Kumanev, *Na sluzhbe fronta i tyla*, Moscow, 1976, p. 111.
[19] *Sovetskii rechnoi transport v Velikoi Otechestvennoi Voine*, Moscow, 1981, pp. 46, 63, 64, 70. After the ships were unloaded they were taken apart and used to make war material.
[20] *Ukrainskaia*, p. 273.

to the state, and 2 percent of Volgograd livestock died, while 61 percent were delivered to the state[21] – but the distinction is something of a fiction. A large number of the animals delivered to the state would have died because of the lack of fodder and proper housing. Indeed, many state and collective farms asked to be allowed to cull their herds of old, sick, and unproductive animals and to use these animals to meet their delivery quota for 1941 and put something toward their obligations for 1942.[22]

In the Ukraine, as early as June 29 the party authorities ordered the removal of tractors, cattle, young animals, and horses to the left bank of the Dnepr. The mass evacuation of tractors from the machine-tractor stations (MTS) did not begin until mid-July. Their removal was held up for as long as possible in order to help with the harvest. Reflecting the transportation shortage, livestock and agricultural machinery had to travel on their own accord, unlike the evacuated industrial enterprises, which were sent east by rail.[23] By July 16, the State Defense Committee began to make decisions as to where livestock should go.[24] As things became regularized, the management of the evacuation was given over to the Commissariat of Agriculture (*Narkomzem*) and the Commissariat of State Farms (*Narkomsovkhozy*) of the USSR and to local party, state, and agricultural organizations.[25] The process involved the entire administrative apparatus of the party and of collective farms and the MTS.[26]

There is a striking differential between the rate of success in saving state farm livestock relative to collective farm animals, other than horses. The outcome of the evacuation of collective farms in the Ukraine shows that in 1941 65 percent of the cattle, 92 percent of the sheep, 31 percent of the pigs, and 14 percent of the horses were evacuated. In contrast, the figures for state farm animals show that well over 80 percent of the state farm cattle, almost all sheep and

---

[21] Arutiunian, p. 44.
[22] Ibid., p. 43.
[23] Arutiunian, p. 36.
[24] *Ukrainskaia*, pp. 269–70. For a detailed analysis of the State Defense Committee, see Sanford R. Liberman, "Crisis Management: The Wartime System of Control and Administration," in Susan J. Linz, editor, *The Impact of World War II on the Soviet Union*, Totowa, N.J.: Rowman & Allenheld, 1985, pp. 59–76. A more general discussion of the evacuation can be found in Mark Harrison, *Soviet Planning in Peace and War 1938–1945*, Cambridge: Cambridge University Press, 1985, pp. 63–81.
[25] Likhomanov, p. 68. The commissariats decided which machinery would go and in what order as well as about cattle drives and where animals would go. For day-to-day management of the evacuation in the countryside they created special groups under the *narkomaty* and appointed authorized agents (*upolnomochennye*).
[26] Ibid.

Lithuanian peasants take their cow along with them as they evacuate the battle area. *Source:* National Archives.

goats, two-thirds of the pigs, and 17 percent of the horses were evacuated.[27]

Two kinds of herds were sent to the rear: common herds, combining the animals of both collective and state farms, and individual herds, comprising the livestock of individual collective farmers. In addition, collective farmers in principle were not required to evacuate the animals that belonged to them on a private basis, but the authorities did all they could to see that these animals went with the collective farm herd, promising that they would be returned to the farmers on

[27] Arutiunian, p. 41. The small percentage of horses evacuated from both state and collective farms reflects the fact that so many were confiscated by the Red Army. It is hard to know why such a differential exists between the two. It may reflect one of the following: (1) the traditional favoritism shown to state farms; (2) the relative backwardness of the collective farms and their inability to organize as well as the state farms; and (3) the passive resistance of the peasants – the Ukrainian peasantry warmly greeted the Germans.

arrival. Many farmers were very reluctant to part with their animals; they had to be promised that their animals would be returned to them when they arrived at their destination.[28]

The task undertaken was of heroic proportions, with a sadly unheroic and largely failed ending. The evacuation of collective farms and their herds took months and faced enormous difficulties; roads were in awful condition and there was a major snowfall and freezing temperatures after mid-November 1941. Feeding stations were supposed to have been erected along the route, but in some places these never materialized.[29] The travails of a collective farm in the Sinelnikov raion of the Dnepropetrovsk oblast are illustrative. On August 27 the farmers began a trek to the east with their most valuable goods and their children in cattle-drawn carts, a total of 262 people and roughly 1,200 head of livestock. They lived like nomads, driving their herds for 2½ months and 650 miles until November 11, when they stopped for the winter at a state farm near the city of Elist. On the move again after the winter, they ended up walking another 1,900 miles before they stopped. Such a two-stage evacuation was the common pattern.[30] Therefore, conditions of the evacuation conspired to force the surrender of meat to procurement organizations and the military.[31]

Of the 2,212,800 head of evacuated livestock said to exist in January 1942, only 433,000 or one-fifth remained after a recount.[32] The implications for the Soviet diet were clear. The animals that died or were slaughtered in 1941 and 1942 because of the conditions of the evacuation obviously could not propagate the future herds, and hence the meat supply fell dramatically during the war period. Consequently, the evacuation of livestock, although it succeeded in terms of getting a large number of animals out of the war zone, failed to get herds to the rear in numbers sufficient to answer future meat needs.

The tale of the evacuation of machinery had an even less happy ending, with only about half of the tractors or perhaps less reaching safety in the east, partly because the evacuation of tractors was delayed to keep them working in the fields as long as possible. Bad planning and/or bad execution, however, allowed a large part of the tractor supply on the right bank of the Ukraine to be trapped by the swift-moving motorized German units. The evacuation of tractors from the southwest Ukraine began in mid-July, allowing ample time

[28] Likhomanov, p. 73.
[29] Arutiunian, p. 42.
[30] *Ukrainskaia*, pp. 271–2.
[31] Likhomanov, p. 77.
[32] Ibid.

to move most of the machinery to the east. In Kirovograd, Nikolaev, and Odessa oblasts, areas that were not occupied until early or mid-August, a large part of the MTS's stock fell to the enemy.[33]

In fact, the ill-fated evacuation from the southwestern Ukraine became a chaotic race to cross the Dnepr River and Soviet descriptions of it read like a Hollywood Western, replete with good guys and bad guys. Imagine Soviet tractors being driven furiously toward the river, livestock unaware of the urgency being driven as fast as their terrified masters could move them, bombs falling from the sky, and the Wehrmacht in hot pursuit. Suddenly, the road to the river is sealed off! The results were tragic. A substantial portion of the cattle and 10,000 tractors trying to cross from the right bank to the left never reached their destination because they were trapped by enemy tanks.[34]

The Soviet loss of tractors in the war zone was extremely high, at least half and perhaps as much as 55 percent. In the entire Ukraine, the Soviets tried to evacuate about 50,000 tractors, but succeeded in evacuating only about 20,000.[35] In the chaotic race across the Dnepr River, roughly 10,000 tractors fell into German hands.[36] On the left bank of the Ukraine, where the evacuation of tractors took place between August and October, they readied 16,897 tractors for evacuation, but succeeded in removing only 9,766.[37] And in Belorussia, where there were 9,002 tractors before the war, they only managed to evacuate about 4,000. In addition, an unknown but apparently substantial number of tractors and combines had to be abandoned on the road because of the lack of fuel and the absence of spare parts to repair machines that broke down on the trip.[38]

Scorched earth policies

Stalin did not speak to the nation for nearly two weeks after the invasion, but then in a radio broadcast on July 3, he called for grim sacrifices:

> In case of a forced retreat of Red Army units, . . . the enemy must not be left . . . a single pound of grain. . . . The collective farmers must

---

[33] *Ukrainskaia*, p. 270. Only two MTSs in the Kirovograd and Odessa oblasts were able to move their equipment.
[34] *Ukrainskaia*, p. 270.
[35] Likhomanov, p. 70.
[36] *Ukrainskaia*, p. 270.
[37] Likhomanov, p. 70.
[38] Ibid.

Soviet scorched earth policy. *Source:* National Archives.

drive off all their cattle and turn over their grain to the safe keeping of the state authorities for transportation to the rear. All valuable property, including... grain... that cannot be withdrawn must be destroyed without fail.[39]

In the Ukraine, where Nikita Khrushchev was party secretary, the danger was imminent. On the same day that Stalin spoke, the Ukrainian Party Central Committee and *Sovnarkom* issued a nine-part directive to collective farms, state farms, and the machine tractor stations showing how the scorched earth policy would be applied. The directive called for the "destruction of valuable property which cannot be evacuated" and "the immediate destruction of all combines, harvesters, winnowing machines, and other agricultural machinery" except for those tractors that could cross the Dnepr or be used by the Red Army. The food industry was to destroy all equipment that could

---

[39] *Stalin's War Speeches*, London: Hutchinson, n.d., p. 10.

not be evacuated.[40] The July 3 directive called for grain to be distributed to collective farmers within twenty-four hours. Pork was also supposed to be collected and meat and salt distributed free to farmers, workers in cities, Red Army men, infirmaries, children's homes, hospitals, and schools. In essence, the Ukraine's capacity to produce food in the future was to be destroyed. Existing stocks of food were to be evacuated, distributed to the people, or destroyed. Evacuees were told to take every scrap of food they could carry with them and to destroy whatever they could not carry, even food that might be consumed by their friends and neighbors, in order to keep it from the Germans.[41] When local party and military authorities decided that it was not possible to evacuate any more grain, orders were issued to distribute a part of the remaining grain and destroy the rest, as much as 60,000 tons in Zaporozhe.[42]

There was a ferocity of intent behind Soviet policy. As Moscow radio announced on July 8, "Wherever Hitler advances, he will find nothing but desert and scorched earth."[43] And within its own terms, the policy had many successes. The most tendentious analysis of the Kharkov hunger asserted unequivocally: "There are no stores, no markets, no shops of any kind. All the stores were either destroyed or plundered and robbed on the last days before the retreat of the Soviet army. *The town before the surrender had to be totally destroyed, deserted and emptied of all foodstuffs*" (italics in original).[44] A physician angrily maintained in a letter to the Red Cross, "As you will know from the newspapers, the Red troops are destroying absolutely everything in their retreat, without bothering about what happens to the civilians who remain in the territories occupied by the Germans."[45] An Associated Press writer who spent five days with the Finnish Army in Russia in early August 1941 testified that the Red Army was carrying out with great care the order to destroy everything of value in the villages: "Any abandoned village or town can be spotted long before we reach it by the chimneys standing like so many sentinels amid scenes of desolation. One of the most curious sights are second-story iron stoves left in mid-air, hooked to the chimneys, when the rest of the town burned."[46]

[40] D. F. Grigorovich, *Sovetskaia Ukrainia v gody Velikoi Otechestvennoi Voiny, 1941–1945,* Vol. l, Kiev, 1980, p. 269.
[41] U. G. Cherniavskii, *Voina i prodovol'stvie,* Moscow 1964, p. 65.
[42] Likhomanov, p. 78.
[43] Columbia Broadcasting System Monitoring Reports (CBS), July 8, 1941.
[44] A Citizen of Khakiw (sic), "Lest We Forget: Hunger in Kharkiv (sic) in the Winter of 1941–1942," *The Ukrainian Quarterly,* Vol. IV, No. 1, Winter 1948, p. 73.
[45] CDR, October 4, 1941, letter to M. de Rouge.
[46] *The Evening Citizen* (Ottawa), August 9, 1941, p. 14.

A Soviet Embassy newspaper in London graphically reported that "such grain as could be carried away by railroad was removed from a granary, and the rest was burned. . . . Milkmaids drove cows over fields of wheat and rye, and women with scythes cut down sheaves, while tractors and horse-drawn rollers destroyed standing crops."[47]

The Soviet scorched earth policy was meant to hurt the enemy, but it also hurt the Soviet people. In the words of Mussolini's propagandists:

> The terrible amount of destruction that is being done shows that the Russians entertain no hope for recovering the territory which they have lost. It also shows how they have no pity or consideration for millions of their people, including all men, women and children who have thus prepared to sacrifice in the hope that the destruction will embarrass the Germans and force them, as they are civilized people, to sacrifice some of their own food for the benefit of the starving Russians who have been reduced to starvation by their own callous government.[48]

Approximately 216,000 tons of grain and other agricultural products were destroyed in the Ukraine as part of the scorched earth policy.[49] That amounts to roughly 13.5 pounds of food for every man, woman, and child in the prewar Ukraine.[50]

The evacuation of people

In a relatively short period of time, many people left their homes in the cities of the Ukraine, Belorussia, and Russia for places that were totally unfamiliar. Their lives had been turned upside down. They had to leave their apartments, their furniture, their friends, and their relatives – everything that was familiar and made life secure. Some had to trade whatever valuables they had for train tickets and all were obliged to leave behind most of their belongings. They were uprooted and plunged into an unknown world, and they were forced to rely on the kindness of strangers and the Communist Party.

There were really two evacuations. The first, the official evacuation,

---

[47] *The Evening Citizen* (Ottawa), July 14, 1941, p. 21. The article originally appeared in *Soviet War News*, a publication of the Soviet Embassy in London.
[48] CBS Monitoring Reports, August 14, 1941.
[49] Likhomanov, p. 78.
[50] The official population of the Ukraine was 30,960,221 as of January 17, 1939. If we take a working figure of 32,000,000 and divide it into 432,000,000 pounds of food (216,000 tons), we arrive at 13.5 pounds per person. The population figure is from *The Statesman's Yearbook 1945*, New York: Macmillan, 1945, p. 1229.

was of people who had official permission to leave. It was organized by the government as part of the effort to transfer key economic or social entities to the safety of the east. When such people were from the city and were transferred with their industrial enterprise or educational institution, for example, they usually, but not always, traveled by rail. The official evacuation also included the tractor drivers and those peasants who drove their herds eastward on foot and in the most difficult conditions. The unofficial evacuation consisted of people who moved away from their threatened homes on their own initiative. They traveled by cart, rail, boat, and foot, but one way or another they left. All of the evacuees had to be fed as they traveled east and then after arrival they had to be fed and housed. The process of feeding those who were evacuated was handled rather badly. Although some of the problems that occurred can be attributed to the pressures of the crisis, a number of the difficulties that ensued resulted from the ineptitude of those who planned the evacuation.

How many were evacuated? We will probably never know with precision. The chaotic character of the process is reflected by the wide variation of estimates made during the war, ranging from an estimate by the U.S. Embassy at the beginning of 1942 that contended "that at least twenty million persons have left invaded territory"[51] to a German estimate of 12.5 million evacuees and a very low Soviet estimate of 7.5 to 10 million evacuated from invaded areas.[52] The first serious postwar Soviet effort to calculate the evacuated population, done in 1961 as part of their major effort to write a post-Stalin history of the war, spoke only to the railroad evacuation and thus was incomplete. The figure offered was a total of 10.4 million people who had been evacuated by rail by February 1, 1942, all but 1 million on special trains, the remaining million having traveled by regular passenger train.[53] An estimate of 10½ million is undoubtedly low. It focuses mainly on the official evacuation, although it takes no account of the officially evacuated peasants who walked east with their herds and those who traveled by means other than rail, such as by boat. More important, it does not give sufficient weight to the unofficial evacuation.[54] A better way to judge the magnitude of the evacuation

---

[51] NFAS, U.S. Embassy at Kuibyshev, Despatch No. 468, January 15, 1942.
[52] The International Labour Office estimated that between 9.5 and 12.5 million were evacuated for 1941 and 1942 together. Eugene M. Kulischer, *The Displacement of the Population in Europe*, Montreal: International Labour Office, 1943, pp. 91–2.
[53] *Istoriia Velikoi Otechestvennoi Voiny Sovetskogo Soiuza 1941–1945 (Istoriia)*, Vol. 2, Moscow, 1961, p. 548.
[54] That same 10.4 million figure appeared as recently as 1974 in M. I. Likhomanov, "Razmeshchenie i ispol'zovanie evakuirovannogo naseleniia v vostochnykh raionakh,"

is to look at the increased population in the unoccupied areas as was done recently by British economist Mark Harrison. His crude but defensible estimate puts the total number of evacuees at 16.5 million.[55]

The confusion inherent in wartime made the logistics of moving and feeding all these people difficult at best. The clogged rail system ensured that the trips to safety were extremely long, in most cases many times longer than they would otherwise have been in peacetime. No one could carry enough food to sustain himself or herself on the trip. It appears that only in Kharkov were people issued a food ration before their evacuation. In early October 1941, Ukrainian authorities established a one-time-only ten-day ration of bread for those being evacuated when they turned in their ration card.[56] Otherwise people started off on the trip either with no food at all or a limited amount of food that they themselves had brought. The amount they could bring was limited by the absence of refrigeration facilities on the trains and their own inability to carry very much of anything. Therefore, it was up to the state to feed them and the evacuation authorities set up evacuation points (*evakpunkty*) along the various railroad routes of evacuation where travelers were supposed to receive food and water. The *evakpunkty*, however, often could not fulfill their mission and so most evacuees depended on the peasantry to sell them food along the way.

A Council for the Evacuation had been created on June 24 and the government's policy on the evacuees was first sketched out in a June 27 decree, "On the System of Removal and Placement of People and Valuable Property," which dealt with the organization of transportation for refugees, feeding them while in transit, and getting them to their ultimate destination. The policy was refined on July 5 with the definition of the evacuation base as a place where people were to receive food free of charge and medical assistance, with each base

in *Sovetskii tyl v Velikoi Otechestvennoi Voine*, Vol. 2, Moscow, 1974, p. 183. A very recent figure indicates that 10 million were evacuated by train and another 2 million by boat. See *Narodnoe khoziaistvo SSSR za 70 let*, Moscow, 1987, p. 43. The total of 12 million again excludes the large number of peasants who walked east and the urbanites who went on their own.

[55] Mark Harrison, *Soviet Planning in Peace and War 1938–1945*, Cambridge: Cambridge University Press, 1985, p. 72. Harrison's estimate begins with a 1940 Soviet population of 194.1 million. He says that the Germans occupied territory by November 1941 on which 77.6 million had resided, thus leaving 116.5 million in unoccupied territory. If one assumes that civilian births and deaths cancel each other out and that there were 3 million military deaths in unoccupied areas, then by 1942 the Soviet population would be 113.5 million. But in fact the population was 130 million, suggesting approximately 16.5 million evacuees.

[56] *Sovetskaia Ukrainia v gody Velikoi Otechestvennoi Voiny 1941–1945*, Vol. 1, p. 226.

serving no fewer than one train load or about 1,800 to 2,000 people. After five weeks of preparation, on August 22, 128 evacuation bases were put into operation in all of the largest cities and at the major rail junctions and piers and another 100 large feeding stations (*punkty pitanie*) were set up, each having the capacity to serve 3,000 hot meals a day. The load on each of these evacuation bases was enormous.[57] From mid-August to the end of 1941, the Ivanov evacuation base and feeding station provided food for 481,000 people. Over roughly the same period, the evacuation base at the port of Kineshma on the Volga served 100,000 refugees.[58]

At the end 1941, *Pravda* waxed enthusiastic about the evacuation process in general and the workings of the evacuation bases in particular. One of the many grateful refugees passing through the Ivanov evacuation base was quoted as saying: "Thanks for the good reception and the food. We note the exceptional organization and warm concern for those evacuated."[59] As good as the evacuation bases may have been for those they served, their services were confined only to those who traveled by rail or ship, and that means that millions were categorically excluded, including the peasants who were driving animals and machinery east and those who had left urban war zones on their own initiative. Therefore, the bases did not feed the entire refugee population.

Moreover, the anecdotal evidence from interviews conducted with Soviet émigrés who had been evacuated suggests that there were nowhere near the number of evacuation bases necessary to feed just the population that was sent east in the official evacuation. Such interviews, although not definitive, give alternative descriptions of the operation and can be used to test the Soviet contention that wartime planning met the food needs of those evacuated.

A woman who was twenty-one years old at the start of the war was sent from her birthplace of Kiev with her mother and 2-year-old daughter to Kuibyshev to work in a defense plant. The trip took three to four months traveling by rail and by truck: "There was not enough to eat on the way. I thought we were only going for a month or so and didn't bring enough to trade with the peasants."[60]

A fourteen-year-old boy also was sent out of Kiev with his mother and brother to the city of Salsk, about 80 miles southeast of Rostov-on-Don. The trip, which is but a few hundred miles, took four weeks,

---

[57] Local Soviets also opened milk kitchens for breast-fed children.
[58] *Istoriia*, Vol. 2, Moscow, 1961, pp. 546–7.
[59] *Pravda*, December 18, 1941, p. 1.
[60] Interview of January 30, 1988.

he says, and there were no evacuation points on the trip and no government-supplied food during the evacuation.[61]

Another man's experience was somewhat different. He was evacuated on June 27, 1941, from Riga and spent about twenty-five days on the train that took him to Novosibirsk: "We ate at *evakpunkty* at the big stations. We got some bread and sausage. There were no peasants selling food at this time." He said that there was no chance to bring food from Riga because of the rapid evacuation of the city.[62] His wife was also evacuated to Novosibirsk, but she went from Moscow during the evacuation in October 1941. She ate at the stations, where her family bought food from the peasants. Her family also took food east, having had sufficient notice to organize for the trip: "On the trip we cooked kasha outside the train. There was some milk at the stations. Some borscht to buy from peasants."[63] Another woman was evacuated on August 31 from Leningrad with her mother and sister and they were sent on a one-month journey to Ufa in the Bashkir ASSR. She remembers that some of the evacuation bases had food, some bread and *brynza* (a cheese made from sheep's milk), but they were very dependent on their ability to buy food at stations when they stopped.[64]

One man left with his mother, younger sister, and grandfather from Odessa at the end of August 1941. They spent the next three months traveling to Alma-Ata in Kazakhstan. First they walked nearly 200 miles from Odessa to Zaporozhe: "We had money, actually a substantial amount of money and bought food. We walked from village to village and knocked at the first door we came to. There was plenty of food." From Zaporozhe they took a boat to Dnepropetrovsk: "Then we took trains – many, many trains with many stops before we finally arrived in Alma-Ata." There was a shortage of food on the rest of the trip: "If you could get food, you got it. If you couldn't, you didn't get. We had money and jewelry. You could buy food with money if you had enough. We bought food when the train would stop. But a lot of people didn't have money. So they exchanged whatever possessions they had for money."[65]

Even one of the official evacuation trains filled with children from Leningrad benefited very little from the evacuation base system remembers the doctor who accompanied them. A gynecologist, she was

---

[61] Interview of November 18, 1987.
[62] Interview of September 23, 1986.
[63] Interview of September 23, 1986.
[64] Interview of September 11, 1986.
[65] Interview of August 19, 1986.

drafted to accompany a trainload of 2,700 children that left at the end of August 1941, shortly before the city was besieged. The destination was a village in the Omsk oblast, a trip that under ordinary circumstances would have taken three days but in 1941 took six or seven weeks. The children ranged in age from seven to sixteen years and, like so many others evacuated from Leningrad during this period, went without their parents. Most carried food for the trip, but after three days it began to spoil; the doctor said: "Every day I threw food out." There were evacuation bases along the way, but they could only supply wheat flour and water, which the doctor and her charges took into a field to bake bread: "Sometimes they got a little milk on the trip, but it was not regular. The children were hungry regularly. Sometimes we would pick things in a field, perhaps tomatoes or carrots. But we couldn't wash it properly. There was hepatitis and jaundice on the train."[66] Lice infestation and weight loss were commonplace and there was constant sickness. Five children died from measles on the trip: "I had to put some children into the hospital. I didn't even know where the place was where I left these children."

Even the diplomatic corps found food scarce during its evacuation from Moscow to Kuibyshev in mid-October 1941. As recounted by Sir Stafford Cripps, British ambassador to the Soviet Union from 1940 to 1942, the trip took five days, rather than the customary twenty hours. The Soviet government provided no food for the evacuees and consequently "there was a brisk trade in eggs and milk by peasants on the way." It was not until the third day somewhere outside of Penza that they had their first state-supplied food, a meal consisting of "unappetizing cabbage soup and chunks of black bread."[67]

Those not traveling by rail or boat were almost entirely on their own to find food. One family traveled from Kiev to Kharkov by horse and cart they obtained through their father's enterprise. The trip took a month. On the way they helped themselves to corn, beets, and other crops in the fields and sometimes exchanged clothes for food. Occasionally people even gave them food and a place to sleep; once they stayed at a farm that tamed wild horses. In October, when the Germans began to approach Kharkov, the family moved with other evacuees to the other side of the Don. Housed in a small village, the children were instructed by their mother not to speak Yiddish because of the virulent anti-Semitism of the Don cossacks. After a couple of days, the government provided flat cars to take the evacuees to the

[66] Interview of September 10, 1986.
[67] Gabriel Gorodetsky, *Stafford Cripps' Mission to Moscow, 1940–1942*, Cambridge: Cambridge University Press, 1984, p. 253.

east, 100 people to a car. It was already cold and they built makeshift tents to keep warm. Once again, they relied on the unintentional charity of the peasants, running into the fields whenever the train stopped and taking food.[68]

An émigré and her family also left Kiev, initially traveling by horse and cart to Kharkov and then taking a freight train to Tashkent. Her experience was one of deprivation. On the trip to Kharkov

> There was not enough bread. We went to small towns, but people hid their bread. Bakeries were closed, the stores were closed. . . . At Tashkent there were a lot of [evacuated] people. We didn't have permission to enter Tashkent. My parents went into Tashkent and got apples and bread. They sold some of the apples because by this time we had no more money. My parents stood on line all night to buy some apples so they could sell them to other people.[69]

The impact of the refugees on the receiving cities

The evacuation not only drained the major cities in the western regions of the RSFSR, the Ukraine, and Belorussia of much of their population, it also poured millions of people into cities and towns east of the Urals and into Central Asia. The evacuation placed enormous strains on the receiving cities, some of which were turned instantly into big cities. As the process of industrialization had brought millions of peasants into the traditional major cities of the western part of the country – a net in-migration of 15 million from 1928 to 1940 – the war moved millions of people out of those cities to the less-populated east. Just as the migration in the 1930s had taken place without all of the infrastructure erected to accommodate the new industrial labor force, especially housing, so too in the crisis of the invasion was there insufficient preparation for all the refugees; housing, schools, health facilities, and even food were often missing. A major reason for the lack of preparation was that the government turned its attention to resettling people after it handled other aspects of the evacuation, such as the crucial movement of industrial enterprises. The Council for the Evacuation concentrated on economic problems and how to move property. It was not until September 26, well after the evacuation was underway, that the government began to address the dimensions of the human problem by creating a De-

---

[68] Interview of November 18, 1987.
[69] Interview of March 21, 1988.

partment for the Evacuation of the Population under the administrative supervision of the Council for Evacuation.[70]

To which cities and areas of the country did the refugees go and how many of them went there? As with the overall count of the number of refugees, it is not possible to know with certainty how many people were in a particular place during the war. A large number, over 2 million people according to a Soviet account, were sent to the industrial areas in the Urals. In the spring of 1942 alone, an estimated 7,417,000 people were sent east. About 5,900,000 people were placed in various areas of the RSFSR, and another 2,316,000 were sent to Central Asia.[71] The resettlement process continued in the fall of 1942 and another quarter of a million or so went to Kazakhstan, raising the republic's refugee population to over 800,000. The cities swelled rapidly. As early as the end of 1941, for example, the population of Kuibyshev had increased by 36 percent, that of Omsk by 42 percent, and that of Sverdlovsk by 28 percent.[72] Even more refugees arrived in 1942. In some of the rural areas of the Novosibirsk, Kemerov, and Tomsk oblasts, there were places where the refugees constituted almost half of the population.[73]

There were many places with an unacceptably low food supply because too many people were sent to them. The most dramatic example of the consequent food shortages that we know of took place in Kuibyshev and was reported by members of the diplomatic corps evacuated there in October, when a serious threat to Moscow arose. Several former Soviet citizens who were there at the time tell virtually the same story. A woman evacuated to a defense plant in Kuibyshev in July 1941, worked twelve to fifteen hours a day, living mostly on soup. At times even bread was not available. She said that people starved to death in and around Kuibyshev, especially those who did not work at the defense plant: "People starved *en masse* who worked in small enterprises and in the kolkhozy. Kuibyshev was not prepared for all the people who came."[74]

---

[70] Likhomanov, "Razmeshchenie," pp. 181–2. The new department was headed by a deputy chairman of the RSFSR Sovnarkom and it had several sections on evacuation, job placement, and daily services and a Central Reference Bureau.

[71] In the RSFSR, over 500,000 were placed in the Yaroslavl oblast, 242,000 in Chkalov, over 200,000 in Kuibyshev, 227,000 in Kirov, 255,000 in Novosibirsk, 266,000 in the Tatar ASSR, 425,000 in the Cheliabinsk oblast, and 715,000 in the Sverdlovsk oblast. In Central Asia about 600,000 refugees went to Kazakhstan, 716,000 to Uzbekistan, and 100,000 to Kirgizia. Ibid.

[72] Ibid., pp. 187–8. The population of Kazan went from 401,000 to 515,000, Kuibyshev from 390,000 to 529,000, Sverdlovsk from 425,000 to 544,000, Omsk from 281,000 to 400,000, Tashkent from 585,000 to 660,000.

[73] Ibid., p. 186.

[74] Interview of January 30, 1988.

A man's experience in Kuibyshev was similar: "The hunger was great," he said. A tool and dye maker working in Minsk who evacuated himself two days after the war started, this man got to Kuibyshev in the fall of 1941 and immediately found a job at Stalin Factory No. 1, an aviation plant in the suburb of Bezmianka, which employed some 84,000 workers. When he arrived in the fall there were not ration cards for everyone and the food situation deteriorated after the first of the year in 1942: "In the summer of 1942, there was so much hunger on the assembly lines that there were cases when people fell over from hunger. Some people died on the job. I personally saw two young people die because of hunger." The plant was built in a field where there were nettles and workers were sent to gather them to make a soup for the young workers.[75]

It became clear to the party in the late fall of 1941 that there were serious defects in the evacuation process. The center blamed local authorities as if they were supposed to conjure up food, housing, and unconditional acceptance of the refugees by the local population. On November 25, the Central Committee sent a telegram to party organizations throughout the country pointing out the "erroneous attitudes" taken toward the workers, employees, and collective farmers who had been evacuated, blaming local party officials for the "carelessness" and demanding correction of the problems.[76] In December, *Pravda* complained about "bureaucratism" in the resettlement process: "In several areas of Kazakhstan, for example, [the authorities] were not prepared to receive the evacuated population, and they weren't provided with a place to live."[77]

Pravda's description of "erroneous attitudes" evokes images of refugees greeted with indifference by those whose lives were inconvenienced by their arrival. The satirist Vladimir Voinovich described the first awkward encounter between the sophisticated lady from Leningrad and the country bumpkin from his fictional village of Krasnoye.

> At the beginning of October the population of Krasnoye increased noticeably; evacuees from Leningrad province drove to Krasnoye or perhaps, more accurately, as the locals put it, were driven there. These were pitiful, unfortunate people, mostly old men, old women, and children, driven from their homes, who had spent a week and a half in cattle cars and had, as they told it, been bombed twice and then had spent three days in the open air on the railroad platform in Dolgov waiting to be assigned quarters.

[75] Interview of March 21, 1988.
[76] Likhomanov, "Razmeshchenie," p. 187.
[77] *Pravda*, December 18, 1941, p. 1.

> When the newcomers were dispersed among the village's various huts, Aphrodite Gladishev, who had been assigned a small, dry, but haughty looking woman and her six-year-old grandson, began shouting to the entire village that she wasn't going to let anyone in her house, that the late Kuzma Matveyevich hadn't built the house and put his whole soul into it to let just anyone stay there and grow lice.[78]

By 1942 we can detect a new stage in the evacuation process that recognized that the relocation would be long term, if not permanent. On February 1, 1942, a census was conducted to provide information on the total number of refugees evacuated and where they had been placed.[79] There were several serious imbalances in the distribution of the evacuated population and a census was needed to help rectify the situation. As a result of the February census, the *Sovnarkom* immediately issued an order that required local party officials in the east to make provisions for what they were to regard as the permanent resettlement of these refugees. The authorities were responsible for ensuring that evacuees had a place to live, including the provision of land and building materials.[80] In view of the shortages created by the war, such a goal was wishful thinking. No mention was made of party responsibility for feeding the resettled population.

Yet there was a food shortage that arose from increasing pressure upon a food supply that was not expanding rapidly enough to accommodate so many new arrivals. In the face of the shortage, how did the refugees survive? U.S. intelligence during the war suggests that refugees depended primarily upon local resources, in particular individual and collective gardens. Based on the experiences of the émigrés I interviewed, it appears that the food situation when refugees first arrived at their new homes varied rather widely from place to place and also depended on their job. Overwhelmingly, unless one was in a privileged position, the food situation of the refugees was quite dismal: "The food problems were great, but the population solved the problem without asking for assistance from the Central Government, including a large increase in the area of new production and a 1,500 percent increase in the total area of victory gardens."[81]

---

[78] Vladimir Voinovich, *Pretender to the Throne*, New York: Farrar Straus Giroux, 1979, pp. 225–6. The experience during the evacuation of British children from the cities to the countryside was similar. British farmers looked down upon city children whom they regarded as dirty and vermin ridden.

[79] Likhomanov, "Razmeshchenie," p. 187. I have never seen any indication of what was done with the results of the census.

[80] Kulischer, p. 88.

[81] USSR: Crop Conditions and Production, 1942–1945. Records of the Foreign Agri-

When one woman arrived in Novosibirsk, because she had a factory job, she immediately received a ration card for 400 grams of bread a day, what everyone else received. In addition to her regular ration as a blue-collar worker, she received special rights to milk because the job she held in a chemical factory was considered dangerous. But as her husband recalled, there was "no food in the stores to buy."[82] When another woman arrived in Ufa "there was both plenty of food and it was good. Most of the people [who were from Ufa] had beef because they had their own cattle. We didn't eat nearly as well as they did."[83]

Another man who was evacuated to the Central Asian city of Dushanbe in Tadzhikistan remembered that in March 1942 there were apricot trees beginning to bear fruit and he and others who had been evacuated were so hungry that they started to eat the green fruit. The Tadzhiks ran out of their houses and told them not to eat the green fruit and gave them some food.[84]

A woman who was a young schoolgirl at the time has similar memories of Dushanbe as a city in which there was hunger mixed with plenty. There was "lots of fruit, nuts, plenty of food and no shortage." She also remembers, however, that "a lot of people came to Dushanbe without work. Many were begging on the streets."[85] Her future husband was evacuated to Alma-Ata where the food situation was

> very bad. We stayed with relatives for two weeks and eating wasn't bad then. But then our relatives helped us find a place to live. It was a small house in the suburbs. Our situation got worse. My mother had a job as a bookkeeper after one or two months. We had ration cards from the beginning. Bread was available but it was very heavy bread. Not good bread. All evacuated people had problems with food. The owner of this house grew beets and stored beets and let us eat the beets. Every day it was beets and bread, beets and bread, beets and bread. For two years we ate bread and beets. I don't remember eating butter or meat.[86]

A doctor sent with a military plant to Sverdlovsk was given the regular ration of 400 grams of bread a day and nothing else. Somehow

cultural Service. Record Group 166, National Archives, Washington, D.C. U.S. Embassy at Moscow, observations by a U.S. news correspondent during a trip of late June and early July.
[82] Interviews of September 23, 1986.
[83] Interview of September 11, 1986.
[84] Interview of December 22, 1985.
[85] Interview of August 19, 1986.
[86] Interview of August 19, 1986.

her brother-in-law, who also worked in Sverdlovsk, managed to get some sugar and kasha. They also ate potato skins, when such could be found.[87]

A woman who was evacuated to a small town in the rich agricultural region of the Caucasus remembered that when she arrived with her fellow refugees they were greeted with a feast that had been prepared for them. People had been ordered by the local party committee to have food ready for them. They ate at tables that had been set up in the street. This, however, was a one-time-only gift. She then went to work at age fourteen in an airplane repair plant rather than go to school. Although there was food at the plant – powdered egg, corn bread, yellow kasha, and *mukakha* (the solid remains of sunflower seeds after they have been squeezed of their oil) – supplies were scarce.[88]

Conclusion

An evaluation of the major policies implemented soon after the invasion produces a mixed report card. Probably, the one unqualified success of this frightening period was the mobilization of resources to bring in the 1941 wheat harvest, or what they could, under unimaginably difficult conditions. It is reasonable to argue that the Soviets succeeded in bringing in the harvest because of central planning, not in spite of it. It is hard to contemplate that much more could have been accomplished. In large measure, the scorched earth policies also succeeded, meaning that a great deal of agricultural products were destroyed and a substantial proportion of the agricultural capital stock, including the livestock, was removed from occupied areas. This also left the remaining population quite vulnerable for the future.[89] Third, they moved a large number of people in a relatively short period of time and thereby provided a trained labor force for the enterprises that they also evacuated to the eastern part of the country. Certainly, they would have been unable to produce the necessary war material without the labor force that had given Soviet economy its astonishing growth rates in the 1930s. The authorities moved people without much thought to how they would feed and house them, however. The fact seems clear this problem was low on

[87] Interview of May 21, 1988.
[88] Interview of March 21, 1988.
[89] In the chapter on the occupation, we will argue that some of the scorched earth policies were counterproductive.

the scale of priorities of the leadership, although probably with justification. Unless they rescued the industrial enterprises, the authorities would have had no reason to relocate the workers. The consequences were nevertheless unfavorable for the refugees.

No success can be claimed for the transport system during the evacuation. Its capacity was simply insufficient to handle the load that was placed on it and there was a serious transportation bottleneck. Clearly, no plans had been made to provide the nation with a transportation system that could have managed the movement of people, war material, industrial enterprises, livestock, and agricultural machinery simultaneously. The opportunity cost of the deficient Soviet rail and water transport systems was extremely high.

As Mark Harrison has pointed out, Soviet policies aimed at wartime preparation were designed to meet long-run contingencies. One of the consequences of this time horizon was that there was an absolute shortage of strategic reserves, including food: "Military-economic authorities simultaneously underestimated the likely demands of a defensive war fought out in the depth of the Soviet homeland, and overestimated the capacity of the existing balance of the economy to respond to them."[90]

Several policies of the evacuation were demonstrably unsuccessful. There is no evidence that a detailed contingency plan was available at the time of the invasion. The failure to lay the proper groundwork led inevitably to the poor results – too many people sent to areas where there was not enough food, a substantial number of livestock and machinery lost, and a scorched earth policy that made victims out of the nation's own citizens.

On the other hand, no invasion can be fully prepared for and to expect the Soviet Union to have poured enormous resources into preparing for a response that they believed would not come before they were economically and militarily prepared seems unreasonable. In this light, the ability to move millions of people, bring in a large percentage of the wheat crop, and move substantial numbers of livestock and machinery out of the front areas seems remarkable. The hierarchical model of planning had served the nation well, It was able to mobilize its resources – limited as they were – in a short period of time and at least provide a holding action against a tide that was running heavily against the nation. One may say that the proof of the pudding is in the final result – the Soviet Union won.

[90] Harrison, p. 61.

3   The German occupation

Hard on the heels of the retreating Red Army and the civilian evacuation, the German occupiers took over a huge portion of Soviet territory, encompassing a substantial portion of the population as well as a great deal of the most important cropland and livestock-raising areas of the country. The German occupation lasted only a year or less at its easternmost edge, but further west, where the occupation was more complete, it lasted two years. Estimates of the population in the occupied areas vary between 65 and 77 million people before the invasion. Given an estimated evacuation of 16.5 million, that left some 50 to 60 million to be fed under German occupation.[1] A population equal to about three-fourths of Germany's 1939 population was entirely dependent upon the magnanimity of its occupiers. And the Germans were not generous, so that the civilian population suffered greatly under the occupation, more so than those who lived in the rear during the war.

The Germans never intended to feed the civilian population at any level approaching adequacy and they were well aware of the potential consequences of their plans. This is clear both from preinvasion statements and from the occupation policies. At a May 2, 1941, conference of State Secretaries in Germany regarding the planned invasion, it was stated that: "The war can be continued only if all Armed Forces are fed out of Russia in the third year of the war. . . . There is no doubt that as a result, many millions of people will be starved to death if we take out of the country the things necessary for us."[2] A month

---

[1] Karl Brandt and Associates, *Management of Agriculture and Food in the German-Occupied and Other Areas of Fortress Europe*, Stanford: Stanford University Press, 1953, p. 90; *New York Times*, September 20, 1942, p. 3. Alexander Dallin, *German Rule in Russia 1941–1945*, London: Macmillan, 1957, p. 365, says there were 65 million in the occupied areas.

[2] *Trial of the Major War Criminals Before the International Military Tribunal*, Vol. 3, Nu-

later, on June 1, 1941, only three weeks before the invasion, an unambiguous document, "File of the District Agricultural Leader," containing a set of detailed instructions couched in the form of "12 Commandments for the Behavior of Germans in the East and Their Attitudes towards Russians," was issued as instructions to district agricultural administrators in the occupied areas. The seventh commandment stated: "Do not ask, 'How will this benefit the peasants?' but 'How will it benefit Germany?'" The eleventh commandment, concerning the people of the occupied area, had an even more ruthless ring: "his (Russian) stomach is elastic, therefore – no false pity for him!"[3]

But the local population did not know of German intentions and many welcomed the invaders. In 1941, the western territories of the USSR – especially the Ukraine, nationalistically resentful of Russian domination and brutally collectivized a decade earlier, and the Baltic states, forcibly annexed in 1940 – were seething with actual or potential anti-Soviet sentiment.[4] Many Lithuanians, Latvians, and Estonians at first viewed the Germans as liberators from the recent loss of freedom. In the Ukraine, peasants hoped that the Germans would lift the fetters of the collective farm system from their shoulders. Bitterness, hope, and a large measure of naiveté and self-delusion were expressed in the words of a Ukrainian collective farmer in early 1942: "May the devil take the kolkhozes. Now we are free Ukrainian farmers. Hitler is a good man. He is very shrewd, but he is also good. Whereas Stalin, this evil spirit, may he tear his hair."[5] Although in the Nazi hierarchy of races the Baltic people were viewed as better than the Slavs, who were dismissed as a group only slightly less despicable than Jews and Gypsies, the overriding concern for the German Reich meant that all the Soviet peoples in the occupied areas would be exploited ruthlessly.

In early September 1941, the Germans let the world community know that they felt no responsibility for feeding the civilian population in the huge areas they occupied, citing the Hague conventions on the

remburg, 1947, p. 142. See Vol. 9 for the same statement and Göring's response, pp. 350–2.
[3] *Trial of the Major War Criminals*, Vol. 8, pp. 20–1.
[4] For an excellent insight on the relationship between Germany and Ukrainian nationalists, see John A. Armstrong, *Ukrainian Nationalism, 1939–1945*, New York: Columbia University Press, 1955.
[5] USSR: Crop Conditions and Production, 1942–1945. Records of the Foreign Agricultural Service. Record Group 166, National Archives, Washington, D.C. (NFAS). A Ukrainian collective farmer interviewed by a Swedish journalist, March 17, 1942. Memo from the U.S. Legation in Stockholm.

rights of the occupying power.[6] This was followed in mid-October by Field Marshal Reichenau's chilling order, apparently with Hitler's approval that: "To supply local inhabitants and prisoners of war with food is an act of unnecessary humanity."[7] In the spring of 1942 Molotov told the Soviet people: "The German command has openly ordered their units to condemn the civilian population, children, women, and old people to starvation, to take away from them their last reserves of food and to destroy those products which the . . . German army cannot take away itself."[8]

The Germans never retreated from their position and, indeed, as the pressure on the German food supply tightened, the indifference toward the occupied population of the Soviet Union only increased. Hitler himself said that he would "take the last cow from the Ukraine before the homeland is forced to starve."[9] In May 1943, a high-level German bureaucrat in the East explained that while "the goal is not to take away the last cow, pig, and sheep, . . . the goal cannot always be reached because meat deliveries are necessarily high," and therefore "new mothers and children and even infants have had to go without milk."[10]

The decline of the food supply in the occupied territories

The territory the Germans occupied included some of the richest agricultural land in the Soviet Union, but it produced less food than usual during the occupation and even less of this diminished output was used to feed the local population than under Soviet rule. There were several reasons for this shortfall. First and foremost, there was the drain of significant shipments of crops and livestock to Germany. There was also destruction by both the Germans and Soviets of Soviet agricultural capacity. Finally, general confusion prevailed in agriculture, especially during the first year of the occupation.

[6] *Records of the Department of State Relating to the Internal Affairs of the Soviet Union, 1940–1944* (CDR), September 3, 1941 telegram from Berlin to the State Department; *New York Times*, September 1941, p. 3. No doubt the Germans were citing Article 52 of the 1907 Hague Conventions, which states that: "Requisitions in kind and services shall not be demanded from municipalities or inhabitants except for the needs of the army of occupation." Their actions certainly constituted a liberal interpretation of the convention. See James Brown Scott, editor, *The Hague Conventions and Declarations of 1899 and 1907*, New York: Oxford University Press, 1918, pp. 123, 125.
[7] *Trial of the Major Criminals*, Vol. 7, p. 187.
[8] *Izvestia*, April 28, 1942, p. 1.
[9] Dallin, p. 356.
[10] *Records of the Reich Ministry for the Occupied Eastern Territories, 1941–1945 (Reich)*, T454, Reel 92, EAP 99/434.

Most, but not all, of the food shortfall in the occupied areas can be laid at the door of the Germans. The scorched earth policy of the Soviets – destroying crops as they headed east – and the enormous and rather successful effort to evacuate machinery and animals left the remaining civilian population extremely vulnerable. Whatever military advantages were gained by ensuring that the enemy did not get hold of either food or the equipment and animals that contribute to food production, there can be little question that those who stayed behind suffered serious consequences. Naturally, official Soviet sources have never taken the position that they contributed in any way to the hunger suffered by their own citizens, but this position is held by others, including the Germans defending themselves after the war.[11] In the overall picture, the Soviet evacuation policies constituted a lesser cause of the people's suffering, although it was somewhat important in the first winter of the occupation and in disrupting planting for the next year.

The combination of crop destruction and the demolition and evacuation of machinery by the Soviets between July and October left agriculture in a very poor state. The success of Soviet policies was revealed by Western correspondents who visited the Ukraine in November 1941 and concluded that "normal cultivation of the land or of useful crops would be impossible for the Germans before 1943."[12] It was estimated that the Germans needed 30,000 tractors to organize the 1942 planting because of the diligence of Soviet destruction of agricultural machinery.[13] It appears that most of the machines left behind were not in working condition.[14]

The 1941 and 1942 crops were disasters. The dramatic decline in draft animals meant that planting in the spring fell behind schedule and was not done thoroughly. In addition, the winter was brutal and nearly half of the crop that had been planted in the fall was destroyed by frost.[15] Only 65 percent of the arable land of the Ukraine was planted in 1942.[16] All of this meant that food supplies for Soviet civilians could not reach normal levels for at least two years.

Part of the Soviet scorched earth effort had included attempts to destroy all grain stocks that were not removed, although this proved

[11] See, for example, Göring's self-serving testimony at Nuremburg. *Trial of the Major War Criminals*, Vol. 9, p. 351.
[12] *The Times* (London), November 4, 1941.
[13] NFAS, U.S. Embassy at Stockholm, Despatch No. 141, February 4, 1942.
[14] NFAS, U.S. Embassy at Stockholm, Despatch No. 105, January 28, 1942. Ingersoll said in his newspaper series: "I do not believe that the Germans have inherited much undamaged or usable machinery except on the field of battle."
[15] Brandt and Associates, p. 132.
[16] NFAS, U.S. Embassy at Stockholm, Despatch No. 1023, October 2, 1942.

to be such a difficult task that incompletely burned grain smoldered for long periods even after the occupation began and was rescued.[17] Panzer leader General Heinz Guderian in his memoirs spoke about the ability of the Germans to recover some of the grain from burning silos, which he says they then distributed to the local population.[18] In early September, it was reported that the Germans sent specialists into the occupied areas to salvage what they could of the burning crops and also to employ the local peasantry to bring in whatever was still out in the fields. The Germans used everything from threats to bribes to promises, for instance that peasants could keep their private plots and own more cattle in the future.[19] On the other hand, it did not always require German efforts to salvage grain. At Barvenkovo, a major grain area in the Ukraine, the Soviets tried to burn as much grain as possible before their exodus, but the local population itself salvaged a part of the stores.[20] To the extent that the Germans, needing grain for their armies, and the peasantry, understandably trying to survive, succeeded in salvaging grain and other agricultural products, the Soviet scorched earth policy failed. Ralph Ingersoll, the editor of *PM* magazine, said that he had been told – and himself believed – that the Germans had captured up to 2,000,000 tons of wheat in the Ukraine.[21]

Later, the Germans also used scorched earth tactics. As early as December 24, 1941, as German forces retreated after defeat at the Battle of Moscow, an order to destroy villages was issued by the commander of the 98th German Infantry Division: "Available stocks of hay, straw, food supplies, et cetera, are to be burnt. All stoves in homes should be put out of action by hand grenades so that their further use be made impossible."[22] The civilians who had been made vulnerable by Soviet scorched earth policies at the beginning of the war on the Russian front were again victimized. Even later, as the long German retreat out of the USSR began in 1943, Hitler took a page from Stalin's book. On September 3, 1943, Göring issued an order calling for: (1) the removal of all food and the machinery used by agriculture and the food industry, (2) the destruction of all factories involved in the food industry, either as producers or processors, and (3) the destruction of all bases serving the food industry. German

---

[17] Brandt and Associates, p. 132.
[18] Heinz Guderian, *Panzer Leader*, Washington, D.C.: Zenger Publishing, 1952. Reprinted 1979 by Dutton, p. 249.
[19] *The Times* (London), September 4, 1941, p. 3.
[20] NFAS, U.S. Embassy at Stockholm, Despatch 801, July 7, 1942.
[21] *The Evening Citizen* (Ottawa), October 29, 1941, p. 1.
[22] *Trial of the Major War Criminals*, Vol. 7, p. 184.

records indicate that about 20,000 railroad cars went west filled with food and equipment related to agriculture.[23] The German stratagem would adversely affect both the near-term and long-term capacity of the Soviet population to feed itself.

Ilya Ehrenburg, serving as a war correspondent for *Red Star*, described the aftermath of the German scorched earth stratagem:

> The ruins of the log-houses were still smoldering; a woman was wandering about. We called to her but she did not answer. Later we spent the night in a hut. I folded my military greatcoat under my head, it smelt of smoke. "I shall remember as a last gift this heart-freezing fever, this night which resembles the day, and the sorrowful shadow among the ashes. The smell of burning is as acrid as unhappiness, it will never leave me, it is with me like the ashes of the villages, like the pallid sickly shadow, like the red and black sheaves of the delirious misery of typhus, like the fragment of the dead moon among the new alien silence."

Sickened by the Germans' destruction of fruit trees in the Ukraine in 1943 he wrote of "an hour when my heart turned to water: I saw the orchards of Glukhov and the posthumous fruit of the apple trees cut down by the foe. The leaves trembled. All was empty. We stood awhile and left. Forgive me, great art; we did not save you either."[24]

The destruction carried out by the Germans was often more systematic than the destruction by the Soviets; it was applied over a longer period of time and complemented their policy of squeezing agriculture in the occupied territories for the benefit of the German Reich. First, we can identify outright destruction. One Soviet source says that agriculture was set back ten years in those areas occupied by the Germans, where there was 181 billion rubles in damage done to the kolkhozy, the complete destruction of scientific research institutes, and the removal of valuable seed varieties.[25] The property damage was estimated to include the destruction and looting of 98,000 collective farms, 1,876 state farms, and 2,890 machine and tractor stations,[26] and 137,000 tractors and 49,000 combines were destroyed or taken to Germany.[27]

[23] Brandt and Associates, p. 144.
[24] Ilya Ehrenburg, *The War 1941–1945*, Cleveland: World, 1964, p. 115.
[25] Ia. E. Chadaev, *Ekonomika SSSR v period Velikoi Otechestvennoi Voiny*, Moscow, 1965, p. 344.
[26] *Trial of the Major War Criminals*, Vol. 7, p. 190.
[27] M. I. Likhomanov, *Khoziaistvenno-organizatorskaia rabota partii v derevne v pervyi period Velikoi Otechestvennoi Voiny (1941–1942gg.)*, Leningrad, 1975, pp. 72–3.

Second, large quantities of animals and food were directly appropriated by the Germans. During three years of occupation, they took 7 million horses, 17 million cattle, 20 million pigs, 27 million sheep and goats, 110 million head of domestic fowl,[28] and 6 million tons of grain, 5 million from the Ukraine alone.[29] Large quantities of grain were requisitioned to feed the occupying armies in the Ukraine and the Northern Caucasus, an amount estimated by the British to have included at least 600,000 tons of bread grains to supply the local military.[30] In addition to feeding the occupation armies, 1.8 million tons of grain, an average of 600,000 tons a year, was shipped to Germany.[31]

Third, the Germans took a very high proportion of the harvest from those who grew it and distributed little of it to any part of the local population. Initially, with the exception of what was to be used for food or fodder, the entire output of Soviet farms was subject to delivery to the German authorities, the same system that prevailed in Germany itself. This meant that the Germans not only retained the Soviet compulsory delivery quotas, they also obliged collective farmers to deliver all marketable output above these levels.[32] After a year it was recognized that this policy created a disincentive to produce and the system was in principle modified to introduce fixed quotas for the 1943 crop year, although in practice, quotas were determined by the level of output.[33] In many areas German delivery quotas were said to be twice what they were under the Soviets.[34] According to a May 1943 German report, Russian farmers were expected to turn over 80 percent of their output and were entitled to dispose of the other 20 percent as they saw fit; wealthy farmers could keep 30 percent of their output.[35] The system of German priorities for distributing the food that was procured was as follows: (1) combat troops in the Soviet Union; (2) noncombat German troops in the Soviet Union; (3) troops stationed in Germany; (4) German civilians, (5) the population of the

---

[28] *Istoriia Vtoroi Mirovoi Voiny 1939–1945*, Vol. 12, p. 148; the poultry figure is from *Trial of the Major War Criminals*, Vol. 7, p. 190.
[29] Bohdan Krawchenko, "Soviet Ukraine Under Nazi Occupation, 1941–4," in Yuri Boshyk, editor, *Ukraine During World War II*, Edmonton: University of Alberta Press, 1986, p. 27.
[30] NFAS, "Exploitation of Occupied Russia," February 2, 1943, report of the British Ministry of Economic Warfare.
[31] Brandt and Associates, p. 147.
[32] Ibid., p. 184.
[33] Ibid., pp. 108–9.
[34] Krawchenko, p. 27.
[35] *Reich*, T454, Reel 92, EAP 99/434.

Table 3.1. *Food contributions of the occupied Soviet territories to Germany, July 17, 1941–March 31, 1944 (selected items, in tons unless otherwise stated)*

Commodity	Deliveries to German Army	Distributions to Germany	Total to civilian officials and collaborators in the East	Total
Grain	5,650	1,161	2,341	9,152
Bread grains	2,222	788	2,006	5,016
Pulses and vegetables	302	40	260	602
Hay	1,817	0	691	2,508
Livestock and meat	412	67	85	564
Eggs (thousands)	783	133	162	1,078
Butter	118	21	68	207
Oil seeds and oil	29	726	217	972
Potatoes	2,040	13	1,229	3,282
Sugar	244	62	95	401
Beer (in hectoliters)	1,680	0	807	2,487
Alcohol	182	0	125	307

Sources: Brandt, p. 129; Dallin, p. 373.

occupied countries.[36] German accounts confirm the large amounts of food, particularly grains and potatoes, that were contributed to the German diet by the occupied Soviet territories. The data found in Table 3.1 are largely based on the records of *Zentralhandelsgesellschaft Ost (ZO)* or Central Trading Company for the East, the organization that controlled the entire nutrition economy of the occupied eastern areas.

The German plans for the distribution of the 1943 harvest called for 22 percent of the grain to go to the peasantry, but this is to be compared to the 27 percent that was allocated in 1938 under Soviet procurement policies.[37] Accordingly, an even smaller percentage of a much smaller grain harvest was to feed the peasantry than before. The combination of a severely damaged Soviet agriculture, German procurement policies, and a distribution system that put the civilian population at the end of the queue for food led to a situation in which,

[36] *Trial of the Major War Criminals*, Vol. 4, p. 3.
[37] Dallin, p. 375.

according to a Berlin radio report in October 1942, "one-fourth of the population has very little to eat."[38] It was estimated that the 1942 harvest in the Ukraine and Crimea was 7.5 million tons. If annual per capita rural consumption was set at 225 kilos, somewhat below normal, the population of 26 million would need 5.2 million tons for human consumption plus 2.0 million tons for fodder, leaving a surplus of 0.3 million tons.[39] That would have allowed a peasant to consume about 1,350 grams of bread a day. All reported consumption figures, however, are well below this number because that year the area fed anywhere from 2 to 3 million members of the German military, whose food needs were at least 400,000 to 600,000 tons, with another 600,000 tons going to feed the German and sometimes the Italian civilian population. Therefore, the estimated 300,000-ton surplus that might have existed before the Germans took what they wanted was, in fact, a 700,000- to 900,000-ton deficit. This was the main cause of hunger under the occupation.

A detailed examination of ten distinct administrative areas of the western RSFSR provides a profile of the impact of changing quantities of inputs into agricultural production during the war. The combined population of these areas was 15.7 million at the 1939 census and 11.8 million after liberation, a decline of 25 percent. Table 3.2 lists the factors of production in agriculture and the changes that took place from the period before occupation to liberation in 1943.

The striking thing about these numbers is that in all cases, inputs into agriculture fell by more than the decline in the general population, in some cases by very large amounts. The relative decline in the amount of land sown during this period is probably the most devastating result. Even if all other inputs had remained constant, the fall in sown area alone was sufficient to ensure serious declines in agricultural production and therefore a decline in per capita availability of food for the civilian population. This was all compounded by the startling decline in both the labor and capital inputs.

Such declines were not unusual in the occupied areas. According to a leading Soviet economic planner, after liberation in the Ukraine, only 30 percent of the prewar number of horses remained, and only 39 percent of the tractors and 40 percent of the combines survived the occupation. Similarly, in Belorussia, 39 percent of the horses, 10 percent of the tractors, and 5 percent of the combines existed when

[38] Columbia Broadcasting System Monitoring Reports (CBS), October 12, 1942.
[39] NFAS, "Exploitation of Occupied Russia," February 2, 1943.

Table 3.2. *Inputs into agriculture in ten RSFSR regions before and after occupation*

Factor of production	Before occupation	After liberation	Percent decline
Land			
Sown area (thousands of hectares)	5,253.4	2,072.1	60.6
Labor			
Number of males (aged 16–55) as percent of total population	22.1	11.8	46.6
Capital			
Tractors	52,966	33,910	36
Tractor horsepower (thousands)	1,002.6	611.6	39
Working bulls	358.5	149.1	58.4
Working horses	565.3	159	71.9

Source: Calculated from M. P. Gubenko, "K ekonomicheskoi kharakteristike raionov RSFSR, osvobozhdennykh ot fashistkoi okkupatsii v 1943 g.," *Istoriia SSSR*, Vol. 6, No. 1, 1962, pp. 116, 118–19. The ten regions are oblasts, krais, and autonomous republics.

liberation came.[40] Moreover, the planting of grain fell by 40 percent.[41] Naturally, this affected the recovery of agriculture and therefore the food supply after liberation, but this is a story we will tell later. The absolute decline in food production combined with the German procurement policy had an immediate impact on the civilian population in the occupied area. Indeed, the food supply was very tenuous in all but a few places for most of the war. This was true for both the urban and rural population, although the pattern was somewhat different in the two cases.

Urban diets in the occupied zone

Soviet urbanites were last in line for available food, after the German military and the citizens of the Reich. Moreover, the only

[40] Nikolai A. Voznesensky, *The Economy of the USSR During World War II*, Washington: Public Affairs Press, 1948, p. 31.
[41] *Pravda*, November 2, 1944, p. 3.

Table 3.3. *Weekly adult rations in Tallinn, Estonia (March 1942)*

	Weekly ration (grams)	Calories
Bread	2,000	4,640
Meat	350	530
Butter	100	785
Macaroni	12.5	45
Rolled oats	12.5	50
Groats	25	90

Source: Records of the Reich Ministry for the Occupied Eastern Territories, 1941–1945, T454, Reel 21, EAP 99/54.

Table 3.4. *Ration allowances in Estonia (September 1942, in grams)*

	Bread	Fat	Meat	Sugar
Average civilian	1,700	180	150	100
Prisoner of war	2,600	130	250	110
German civilian	2,350	280	700	280

Source: Records of the Reich Ministry for the Occupied Territories, 1941–1945, T454, Reel 14, EAP 99/7.

Soviet urbanites with the right to an official ration were those who were working for the Germans.[42] A well-organized ration card system was instituted in Latvia, Lithuania, and Estonia, no doubt reflecting the view that the Baltic peoples had a different relationship to the Reich and should be treated better than the Slavs. Although the Baltic peoples were fed better than Slavs, in fact their diets were only marginally better and were at a level that can only be described as appalling, as can be seen in a close examination of the conditions in Estonia. About 450,000 Estonians received ration cards, mostly in the capital city of Tallinn.[43] During 1942 and 1943 (see Tables 3.3 and 3.4), the bread ration fluctuated, but was typically in the range of 1,700 grams a week (243 grams a day), about the same as in Latvia and Lithuania. Early in the year the ration for potatoes was 100 kilograms

---

[42] Brandt and Associates, p. 122.
[43] The discussion on Estonian rations is drawn from *Reich*, T454, Reel 14, EAP 99/7 and Reel 21, EAP 99/54.

a year, roughly 600 grams or a little more than a pound a day, that for meat was 13 kilograms a year, and for fats was 9.4 kilograms a year. These figures can be contrasted to the better rations supplied to the 8,000 German civilians in Estonia, who were entitled to 42 kilograms of meat a year, more than three times the allowance for Estonians, and 15 kilograms of fat a year, virtually twice the Estonian allowance. Estonian civilian rations were also generally below the rations supplied to prisoners of war.

Thus, the basic daily ration in Tallinn in early 1942 amounted to a mere 877 calories. This total could go up by 38 calories a day, to a total of 915, for anybody who actually received the supplemental monthly ration of 198 grams of potatoes, 58 grams of grout sausage, 7 grams of liver pastry, 119 grams of salt, 32 grams of grain coffee, and 129 grams of cod.[44] Six months later, in September 1942, the meager diet of civilians had scarcely improved; rations provided a subminimal 1,069 calories a day. The Germans themselves considered 1,800 calories a day an absolute minimum and knew that in 1937 and 1938 Estonians received 3,353 calories a day.[45] General Commissar Litzmann, who wanted to raise rations, wrote of this situation: "The mood sinks and the enmity against the German empire and the German government [in Estonia] is growing. The ability of workers to perform . . . in areas of the economy necessary to the war is constantly diminishing."[46]

As a consequence of the poor rations, the black market was extremely important in the Baltic republics. The food situation in 1942 was so critical that one high level German official conceded: "It cannot come as a surprise that under such circumstances the black market has reached enormous dimensions."[47] In actuality, there was little food for civilians to buy on the black market, if only because the Germans kept a close watch just to ensure that their own supplies were not endangered. In Estonia, the black market dealt mainly in meat and butter, but farmers also traded with German soldiers for such items as gasoline, schnapps, saccharine, soap, and horseshoes.[48] By 1943, however, the dimensions of the black market were cut back from two directions. First, the Germans began to restrict the participation of German nationals in the black market by an increased police

[44] *Reich*, T454, Reel 21, EAP 99/54.
[45] Ibid.
[46] Ibid., T454, Reel 14, EAP 99/7.
[47] Ibid., T454, Reel 21, EAP 99/54.
[48] Ibid., T454, Reel 14, EAP 99/7.

presence, notably in Tallinn, with the reported result by April 1943 that "a larger part of the population is starving."[49] Second, the population began to run out of money to buy or items to barter on the black market, as was shown by a July 14 report from Riga saying that even relatively well-paid Latvian industrial workers had nothing with which to purchase black market goods.

There was also a rationing system in the cities of the Ukraine, but what this really meant was that the occupiers made the Ukrainians responsible for distributing scarce food to their own people. After the German army took care of its needs and those of *Volksdeutsche* and other supporters, what food remained was allocated to Soviet citizens; this third-class status meant there was never any certainty of how much Soviet citizens would receive in any given period.[50] The responsibility for distributing what food there was to Soviet citizens was assigned to special departments of the municipal administrations, staffed by local residents. The tasks of these departments included determining the amount and coverage of rations, transporting food from outlying areas into the cities, operating bakeries and official food stores, and also supervising private food markets.[51] The limitations of rationing in the Ukraine were compounded by the fact that it was also unsystematic, leaving many uncovered, as in Stalino, where 70,000 of the 248,000 residents were without a ration card, and in Rostov, where it was estimated that two-thirds of the population received no food from the Germans.[52]

In Kiev, which was occupied from mid-September 1941 to early November 1943, the food situation was extremely bad, although the accounts vary in describing *how* bad. U.S. correspondents visiting Kiev in late 1943 shortly after the city was liberated reported that the bread ration during the occupation was 200 grams a day for workers and 100 grams for dependents,[53] amounts well below the ration in the Baltics. A recent study comes to the bleaker conclusion that at the end of the occupation, food rations in Kiev were less than 30 percent of the minimum required.[54] The worst figures come from an article published in *Pravda* on November 8, two days after the city

[49] Ibid., T454, Reel 21, EAP 99/54.
[50] Brandt and Associates, pp. 122–3.
[51] NFAS, U.S. Embassy at Stockholm, Despatch No. 2678, January 12, 1944.
[52] Edgar M. Howell, *The Soviet Partisan Movement 1941–1945*, Washington, D.C.: Department of the Army, 1956, p. 105.
[53] U.S. Department of State, *Foreign Relations of the United States*, 1943, Vol. III, p. 605.
[54] Krawchenko, p. 27. If we use the 1,800-calories figure that we earlier cited as the German's minimum standard, then the bread ration would be 540 calories.

was liberated, which said that workers had a *weekly* ration of 300 grams of bread "made from leftover millet."[55]

But we do not have detailed German documentation about rations in occupied Kiev, which we do for Estonia. Nor did the controlled press in the Ukraine report amounts of rations during the German occupation,[56] although indirect confirmation of how hard times were come from internal German documents that report that there was not enough straw for horses and cattle because people were using it to heat their houses and fuel their stoves.[57] As an alternative to such information it is worth quoting from A. Anatoli's émigré version of his *Babi Yar*, which describes the first winter of occupation, 1941 and 1942. He speaks of the bread to which German-issued ration cards entitled workers and dependents (at a rate of about a pound a week for workers and half a pound for dependents):

> It was an ersatz bread: very crumbly and dry, with a crust like cardboard covered with millet husks. It was baked from some flour substitute made from maize tops, millet husks, barley and horse-chestnuts. It was gritty to eat and had a bitter-sweet taste. It was difficult to digest, but, of course, I treasured it, dividing my [dependent's ration of] half pound up into seven pieces, just over an ounce a day – never touching my next day's ration.[58]

As bad as the food situation was in Kiev, it was much worse in Kharkov, which was occupied from late October 1941 to mid-February 1943 and then after a month's reprieve, occupied from mid-March until late August 1943. Kharkov's is a grim story, although again one marked by some discrepancies as to what happened in the city.

The worst period was the first winter of occupation and the year 1942. Kharkov was a city "without electric lights, without streetcars, water supply and sewers, [and] hundreds and thousands died from hunger, cold, and the sickness and exhaustion associated with them, in particular the Kharkov intelligentsia."[59] By March 1942 there were reports of backyard graves for those who died of starvation[60] – "For

[55] *Pravda*, November 8, 1943, p. 3.
[56] NFAS, U.S. Embassy at Stockholm, Despatch No. 2678, January 12, 1944.
[57] *Reich*, Reel 18, EAP 99/35. The report sarcastically remarked that, "The horses and cattle are lamenting their situation."
[58] A. Anatoli (Kuznetsov), *Babi Yar*, New York: Pocket Books, 1971, pp. 180, 185.
[59] *Pravda*, August 28, 1943, p. 3.
[60] CBS, March 25, 1942.

Table 3.5. *Death rates in Kharkov 1942–1943 (per 1,000)*

	1941	1942
November	20	—
December	26	—
January	—	48
February	—	65
March	—	76
April	—	98
May	—	80
June	—	60
July	—	65
August	—	40
September	—	36
October	—	30

Source: "Lest We Forget: Hunger in Kharkiv [sic] in the Winter 1941–1942," *The Ukrainian Quarterly*, Vol. 4, No. 1, 1948, p. 75.

months dead bodies lay in the basements of homes. They were buried in courtyards by the hundreds and buried in graves without coffins."[61]

A city of some 850,000 at the time of the 1939 census, Kharkov's population had fallen to 450,000 by December 1941 and had declined further to 200,000 by the time the Germans left in February 1943.[62] We can explain much of the decrease in population, first by official and unofficial evacuation of large numbers of people to the rear, then by the slaughter of 14,000 Jews by the Germans, and finally by the sending of forced labor, including about 100,000 children and adolescents, to Germany.[63] This still leaves a large number unaccounted for – the people who starved to death. In the prior decade the death rate in the city had been 11 to 13 per 1,000, but it rose sharply to catastrophic levels in 1942, peaking in the spring, as is shown in Table 3.5.

What should we take to be the total number of Kharkov residents who died of hunger? Shortly after the war, strongly anti-Soviet Ukrainian émigrés charged that 20,000 died of hunger in 1942 alone.[64] A more recent and more scholarly account estimates that in the entire period of the occupation 70,000 to 80,000 died of hunger and mal-

[61] *Pravda*, August 28, 1943, p. 3.
[62] Krawchenko, p. 27.
[63] *La Prensa* (Buenos Aires), February 25, 1943, p. 5.
[64] A Citizen of Kharkiw, p. 76.

nutrition.[65] The Soviet press, however, did not use such high figures after the liberation, which is odd in view of the potential for swaying popular opinion, and data in recent Soviet historical works are not high either. Also, it is hard to explain why death from starvation should have been so much more widespread than elsewhere. My own estimate is that the deaths in Kharkov were at least 30,000 (20,000 in the year 1942 plus half of that figure for the months at the end of 1941 and in early 1943), amounting to about 10 percent of an estimated population of 300,000 in 1942 and possibly going as high as 27 percent of the population if 80,000 died from hunger.

Other urban centers also experienced deprivations, but each case was different. Occupied Odessa was described as a city "starving," without drinking water, soap, or medicine.[66] In the Belorussian city of Minsk, on the other hand, workers received a ration of two kilograms or slightly more than four pounds of bread a week and their dependents received 800 grams or about a pound and three-quarters of bread a week.[67] And in the old Russian city of Rzhev on the Volga, where the Germans were trying to reestablish the operations of a wood factory, there were only two stores, neither sold food to the civilian population, and only Germans could shop in the stores that did sell food. Instead the Germans would feed their Russian workers "rotten potatoes and only now and then give them a meager bread ration." A small girl was reportedly killed for violating the 7 P.M. curfew to beg for a piece of bread on the street.[68]

Even when urban residents did not suffer the horrible starvation of Kharkov, their rations were simply not adequate, particularly for those doing hard work. Their need for other sources of food drove prices way up on the illegal and semilegal food markets, despite German efforts to control prices at ludicrously low levels (Table 3.6). Evidence of how unrealistic the fixed prices were can be seen in the July 1943 decision of the Simferopol municipal authorities to sell bread in their official stores at prices many times higher than the fixed prices, although they still remained well below the prices on the collective farm markets. In the private market, good white bread cost 60 rubles a kilogram, whereas the official German price was 45 rubles. The prices for barley bread were 35 rubles and 25 rubles a kilo in the two

[65] Krawchenko, p. 27. The figure of 70,000 also appeared in a 1943 foreign newspaper story. *La prensa* (Buenos Aires), February 25, 1943, p. 5.
[66] *Izvestia*, April 9, 1944.
[67] NFAS, U.S. Embassy at Moscow, July 13, 1944.
[68] I. Shvankov, "V Verkhov'iakh Volgi," *Eto bylo na Kalinskom fronte*, Moscow, 1985, p. 59. Originally published in *Proletarskaia pravda*, June 28, 1942.

Table 3.6. *Food prices fixed by July 2, 1942, Reichskommisar decree (in rubles per kilogram)*

Rye flour	1.3
Wheat flour	1.6
Corn meal	1.3
Millet porridge	1.3
Barley porridge	2.0
Peas	3.0
Beans	3.1
Lentils	2.5
White sugar	5.0
Table salt	0.2

Source: NFAS, U.S. Embassy at Stockholm, Despatch No. 1023, October 2, 1942. The decree was originally published in the *Krakauer Zeitung*.

outlets, respectively.[69] Moreover, a Swedish newspaperman visiting Kiev in February 1942, before the decree fixing food prices, reported the prevalence of barter within the food distribution system. He reported that one sack of potatoes cost one winter overcoat and a saucepan would exchange for a few grams of butter. Where a cash market still existed, nominal prices were extremely high, as in a Kiev market where he observed one potato selling for one ruble at the same time as the daily wage was ten rubles.[70]

Rural diets

It is not possible to compare precisely the diets of Soviet peasants during the occupation with those of their urban counterparts, but we can say that hunger was no stranger to the villages. Further, we can say that from the peasants' point of view the regime in the countryside differed little from the days when the Soviets ruled. The Germans used a system of calculating work days and in kind payments to collective farmers that was virtually identical to the prewar Soviet system of *trudodni*. In the village of Shipitski, 15 miles from Kiev, the Germans paid ordinary workers 100 grams of barley per labor day with a maximum of 3 kilograms per month and paid brigade leaders 5 kilograms a month.[71]

[69] NFAS, U.S. Embassy at Stockholm, Despatch No. 2678, January 12, 1944.
[70] NFAS, U.S. Embassy at Stockholm, Despatch No. 141, February 5, 1942. Based on an article published in *Aftonbladet*, February 2, 1942.
[71] NFAS, U.S. Embassy at Moscow, November 13, 1944.

What did make the rural situation different from that in the cities was that the Germans allowed the peasantry to keep a part of their grain as a maximum ration. At the beginning of the occupation the German authorities set the ration at 11 kilograms of grain a month for working peasants, with 8 kilograms a month for dependents,[72] but in 1942 when the first harvest under German rule was collected they cut the ration for working peasants to 10 kilos a month. The ration of 10 kilos, providing about 333 grams or about two-thirds of a pound of bread a day, was only about 60 percent of the already low 16.4 kilos a month these same peasants had consumed under Soviet rule.[73] Even if the ration was evenly distributed, it would barely provide for a marginal existence. Not all villages grew bread grain, however, and so many did not have enough. Last, the Germans often went well beyond the stated demands on the peasants. "In our village," a peasant said, "the Hitlerites played the master for more than ten months. They took away all the grain, potatoes, livestock and poultry of the village inhabitants."[74]

The result was hunger, sickness, and even death in the countryside where the food was grown. A doctor who remained in occupied territory after the invasion wrote in October 1941 to the Red Cross in Geneva about the peasants in his district. "These people are in a generally bad physical condition: almost all the children have rickets and are undernourished. . . . Food is getting more and more scarce."[75] In the village of Vlasov in the Kalinin oblast 250 died during the winter of 1941 and 1942.[76] And things became worse in the course of 1942. "Terrible hunger ensued. Many peasants starved to death. Hearts broke when small children died," said *Izvestia*'s account.[77] And hunger stalked the shtetls of the Ukraine as well. In one about 90 miles from Odessa, where the population of under 2,000 was increased by 200 refugees, "more people died from hunger than died from the war. About 100 people died of starvation during the war. . . . The Jews bought food for money, clothes, and gold from the peasants. Not even everybody had potatoes. We made soup from potato skins."[78]

As bad as the rural situation was, it could have been even worse had there not been passive resistance on the part of the peasantry and German rewards to cooperative farmers. There had been a con-

---

[72] *Pravda*, November 2, 1943, p. 3.
[73] Brandt and Associates, p. 127.
[74] *Izvestia*, September 5, 1942, p. 1.
[75] CDR, October 4, 1941, letter sent to Norman Davis of the American Red Cross by M. B. de Rouge, Secretaire General de la Ligue des Sociétés de la Croix-Rouge.
[76] *Izvestia*, September 1, 1942, p. 1.
[77] Ibid.
[78] Interview of October 1, 1986.

siderable amount of hoarding even before the German takeover. When the Germans occupied the Ukraine, it was believed that only 20 to 30 percent of the seed stock necessary for the spring 1942 planting would be available. As it turned out, there was a good deal more, in some cases up to 95 percent of the normal requirement because of what peasants had withheld from Soviet procurement agencies.[79] The peasants also withheld from the Germans, killing some of their livestock, salting the meat, and then burying it. Grain was similarly buried.[80] Those peasants regarded as cooperative were rewarded with the right to enlarge their private plot and to maintain some livestock.[81] As of mid–1942, the German press reported that there were 222,000 hectares of market garden plot enlargements in the southern Ukraine and that in the entire Ukraine these private plots amounted to 5 percent of the republic's arable land.[82] Those peasants who did such things as collaborate against the partisans or who helped rescue grain during the early period of the occupation were the recipients of garden enlargements.

Partisans

The partisans, the bands of underground guerillas who operated behind enemy lines blowing up rail lines, bridges, and storehouses of food and ammunition and killing Germans and collaborators, lived in ways that bore little relation to the way they lived before the invasion. They numbered about 30,000 as of January 1, 1942, and at their height in the summer of 1943 their numbers reached about 200,000.[83] Although the partisans were supplied with weapons by the Soviet Air Force after 1941, only such food items as sugar, salt, and coffee were parachuted in,[84] and so they had to fight not only the Germans, but also hunger.

Food was an abiding concern and often an obsession. The partisans lived on sparse rations drawn from the land, the staples being unmilled grain, horsemeat, and potatoes,[85] and on occasion this fare

---

[79] NFAS, U.S. Embassy at Stockholm, Despatch No. 851, July 29, 1942.
[80] A Fyodorov, *The Underground Committee Carries On*, Moscow: Foreign Languages, 1952, pp. 95, 98.
[81] Ibid.
[82] NFAS, U.S. Embassy at Stockholm, Despatch 846, July 28, 1942.
[83] Earl Ziemke, "Composition and Morale of the Partisan Movement," in John A. Armstrong, editor, *Soviet Partisans in World War II*, Madison: The University of Wisconsin Press, 1964, p. 151.
[84] Ziemke, p. 158; Howell, p. 85.
[85] Ziemke, p. 159.

Russian partisan milks a cow to help feed members of her detachment. *Source:* National Archives.

would be supplemented by bread or a cow donated or extracted from a village.[86] Sometimes there would be ample food for stretches of time and then there would be a long period of severe deprivation.[87] In fact, the partisans were almost totally dependent on local sources of food and both charity and conscription had their place in their battle to eat. Popular culture of the 1970s treated with sympathy the life of the partisans, for example, *Sotnikov*, the 1975 novel by Vasil Bykov and the 1972 film *Proverka na Dorogakh* (*Trial on the Road*), in which the premise is the effort of a partisan unit to steal a train bearing food expropriated from the local villagers and destined for Germany.[88]

---

[86] Jack Nusan Porter, editor, *Jewish Partisans: A Documentary of Jewish Resistance in the Soviet Union During World War II*, Vol. I, Washington, D.C.: University Press of America, 1982, pp. 159–60.

[87] Ziemke, p. 159.

[88] Vasil Bykov, *Sotnikov*, Moscow, 1975, esp. pp. 132, 134–6, 140. This novel begins with two partisans on a mission to find and bring back food for the partisans with

Soviet partisans in enemy's rear talking to collective farmers. *Source:* National Archives.

There was charity in the substantial peasant support for partisans. For instance, there is the way that a few village women, in the face of great danger, baked bread for partisans on the Kalinin front. The partisans stole wheat from the German warehouse in Kozlovo, about 50 miles from Kalinin, took it to the village where the women worked all night to grind it into flour and then bake the bread. The partisans ordered twenty loaves but, at the beginning at least, the women were only able to supply eight loaves a night.[89] A German officer complained that "the population slaughters [their cows] to prevent our

whom they fought. Searching for food was a dangerous enterprise because of the German presence in and near the villages and because of the collaborators within villages. There is a poignant moment when the two talk of the absence of fresh bread in their lives. Raibak says, "'Yesterday out in the marsh I dozed off and dreamed of bread. A warm loaf under my coat. Then I woke up and found it was the warmth from the fire. What a let-down!' 'It's hardly surprising you dream about it,' Sotnikov agreed. 'After a week on boiled rye.'"

[89] V. Kirillov, "Evdokia," *Eto bylo na Kalinskom fronte,* Moscow, 1985, p. 139. These women risked being shot or hanged if they were caught aiding partisans; Howell, p. 120.

getting them and gives the meat to the partisans."[90] In the village of Kholmy, four peasant cottages were hiding places for dried bread, corned beef, and clothing for partisans, risky business because the Germans knew well that people buried things under the floor of their houses.[91]

The partisans also relied on confiscation of food as a major source of supply. Among partisans, "'to organize' meant taking from the villagers. To accomplish this a group of armed partisans would go out and, in a show of strength, would obtain food, fuel, matches, house and kitchen utensils, and more."[92] In one large partisan unit, part of the training involved teaching new recruits from urban areas how to steal potatoes from peasants' fields.[93] As the size of their force grew in 1942, and especially as winter approached, partisans were increasingly driven to raid civilian food stocks to feed themselves. The storage of food for future use was accomplished in the Chernigov region, about 80 miles from Kiev, by building about 200 dumps to store food:

> The typical dump was an excavation three meters deep and some thirty to forty meters square. The walls were reinforced with heavy logs. . . . Such a dump – actually a sturdily built underground ware-house – was roofed with logs, covered with earth and levelled to the surrounding surface, [then covered] with turf or moss and plant[ed] with bushes or small trees on it.[94]

Horses were especially needed. The seizure of animals, often rationalized by the argument that the Germans would take them anyway,[95] got so out of hand that it created great peasant animosity toward the partisans. We can get some sense of partisan strong-arm methods in the order of the partisan central command: appropriation of food and animals was to take place only during the day and only after negotiation with village authorities; everything taken was to be signed for; anyone caught stealing food at night was subject to being shot.[96]

Partisan units were sometimes complex organizations with civilian family camps including women, old men, and children as part of the

[90] Fyodorov, p. 321.
[91] Ibid., pp. 103, 115.
[92] Porter, Vol. II, p. 98.
[93] Porter, Vol, II, p. 101.
[94] Fyodorov, pp. 25–6.
[95] Ibid., p. 360.
[96] Howell, p. 175.

Table 3.7. *German procurement deficits (1941–1942)*

	Belorussia		Baltic states and northwest Russia	
	Percent	Tons	Percent	Tons
Meat	65	16,000	40	1,200
Grain	60	55,000	40	20,000
Lard	55	1,700	16	340

Source: Edward M. Howell, *The Soviet Partisan Movement 1941–1944*, Washington, D.C.: Department of the Army, 1956, p. 114.

community, and sometimes they lived relatively well.[97] They created their own agricultural production units, herding cattle, processing milk and meat. Such a complicated production unit could only exist where it had secured the areas and often a camp would have to move when the Germans threatened. In addition, though, they also had to confiscate food from the fields and gardens of peasants, sometimes assassinating peasants in order to do so.[98]

What kind of an impact did the partisans have on the food supply in the occupied areas? The Germans would have us believe that their impact was momentous.[99] The Germans admitted to huge procurement deficits in the agricultural year June 1941 to May 1942 in Belorussia and sizable ones in the Baltic states and northwest Russia (Table 3.7). All these losses were attributed to the partisans, although it is inconceivable that so few could have wreaked so much havoc. The deficits are also likely to have been the result of unrealistically high German quotas to begin with, Russian scorched earth policies, and peasants hiding food. Having said all of that, it appears that the partisans were fairly effective in their raids in the villages. That means that in Robin Hood fashion, they denied food to the Germans, but it also means they took food from civilians from whom the Germans were taking food and ironically, therefore, the partisans also stole from the poor.

[97] Porter, Vol. II, pp. 79–80.
[98] Ibid.
[99] Howell, p. 114.

The Jewish population

The Germans saved a special brand of cruelty for Soviet Jews, of whom about 1.5 million perished. As badly as the Nazis treated all their subjects, the Jews were treated worse. Before the Germans annihilated the Jewish population, food was used as a weapon to inflict deprivation and great suffering upon the population forced into ghettos or locked in the shtetls. The Jews were systematically denied access to food, and were allowed to eat less as a matter of explicit policy.

Although there was not perfect consistency in the policies in areas with Jewish populations, there was a relatively uniform pattern of German practices that differentiated their treatment of Jews from the non-Jewish population of the occupied areas. First, Jews were either totally forbidden from going to the market or could go there for only an extremely limited period during the day. In the Ukrainian city of Berdichev, Jews were allowed to buy food in the market, but only after 6 P.M., by which time there was virtually nothing left. In the town of Brailov, Jews were allowed to go to the market for ten minutes a day, at the sound of a whistle. In Glubokoye, at first they were allowed two hours a day in the market, but after a while, even that privilege was removed altogether.[100] Second, when allowed to go to the market, they were restricted as to what they could buy. In the small Ukrainian city of Khmelnik, Jews were forbidden to buy anything at the market except potatoes and peas. In another town Jews could not buy butter, meat, eggs, or milk. Later, they were forbidden to buy berries, fruits, or fats, upon pain of death. In Riga, Jews could not buy food in the stores where Germans and Letts shopped.[101] Third, Jews who worked outside the ghetto were not allowed contact with the peasants, effectively eliminating the possibility of buying food and bringing it back.

The denial of contact with the peasantry and strict prohibitions against leaving the ghetto allowed the Germans to control the food intake of Jews and to starve them slowly with pitifully meager rations. In Chernovitsy, Jews were given 100 grams of bread and a "thin unsalted pea soup" once a day. In the Minsk ghetto, Jews were de-

[100] Ilya Ehrenburg and Vasily Grossman, editors, *The Black Book* (E & G), New York: Holocaust Publications, 1981, pp. 16, 44, 188. On occasion, the Germans enjoyed blowing the whistle after three or four minutes and making the Jews leave the market and then blowing the whistle again, allowing them to reenter the market area.
[101] E & G, pp. 28, 188, 190, 302, 329.

scribed as literally having to eat garbage from German kitchens, scavenging potato skins to cook as pancakes or to bake to make a pudding. And in Brest, there were Jewish ration cards for 150 grams of bread a day.[102] Ghetto workers did not fare much better. In Lvov, 100 grams of bread was the daily payment to workers, and even that was occasionally sold by the workers' bosses. In Minsk, workers received 300 grams of bread a day and "a murky water called soup." Borisov ghetto workers received only 150 grams of bread a day.[103] Such miserable rations led to chronic hunger, diseases associated with malnutrition, and death by starvation.

Jewish resistance to such systematic food deprivation took many forms. Ghetto Jews looked for an opportunity to have contact with non-Jews because the latter had more food than did Jews. In Minsk, Jewish children begged for bread outside the ghetto walls despite knowing that if they were caught they would be taken to the Jewish cemetery and shot.[104] The prohibition against Jews having contact with peasants did not prevent a good deal of smuggling, although both Jew and non-Jew risked death.[105] Jews who had been successful in hiding clothing and jewelry from the Germans exchanged these items for food.[106] In Minsk there were some who managed to elude the German guards and go periodically into eastern Poland to bring food back into the ghetto.[107] In the Vilna ghetto, where the Germans let in very little food, there was substantial smuggling, despite the fact that death was the punishment if one was caught smuggling or selling even a kilo of sugar. The Jewish resistance organization in Vilna officially set up its own food department to bring food into the starving ghetto.[108]

For most Jews, the Germans were not the only enemy. Many Ukrainians, Russians, Lithuanians, and others willingly cooperated in the extermination of Soviet Jews during the war. Sometimes long-standing anti-Semitism was sufficient incentive to torture and kill Jews, but in case it was not, the Germans paid a premium for Jews turned in by Ukrainians. In one place the Germans paid 16 kilograms of salt, a liter of kerosene, and 20 boxes of matches for every Jew

[102] Ibid, pp. 101, 157, 215.
[103] Ibid., pp. 110, 148, 361.
[104] Ibid., pp. 172–3.
[105] Porter, Vol. I, p. 54.
[106] Porter, Vol. II, p. 235.
[107] NFAS, U.S. Embassy at Moscow, July 13, 1944.
[108] *Partisans of Vilna*, a 1986 film directed by Josh Waletzky and distributed by European Classica. The United Partisan Organization was known by its Yiddish initials, FPO.

Table 3.8. *Food rations of normal consumers in occupied countries and Germany about April 1942 (in grams per week)*

Country	Bread and flour	Cereals	Potatoes	Sugar	Meat and meat products	Liquid milk	Egg (pieces)
Germany	2,000	150	2,500	225	300	0	0.5[a]
France	1,925[b]	nil	930	115	180	0	[c]
Netherlands	1,800	160	3,750	250	225	0	[d]
Government General:							
(Poles)	1,490	[c]	2,500	100	130	0	[c]
Slovakia	1,670	[c]	[d]	250	300	[c]	[c]

[a] Rations changed according to supply.
[b] Prefects may have imposed temporary reductions of rations.
[c] No information.
[d] Unrationed.
Source: League of Nations, *Wartime Rationing and Consumption*, Geneva, 1942, pp. 20–25.

killed.[109] In another part of the Ukraine, three murdered Jews were exchanged for 30 kilograms of salt.[110] Not surprisingly, due to the combined efforts of Germany and local collaborators, relatively few Jews survived to tell the tale of the occupation.

Conclusion

There is no doubt that the civilian population of the German occupied areas in the Soviet Union suffered enormous food deprivation. Their situation was quite different from and worse than the occupied countries in Western Europe (Table 3.8). As might be expected, rations were highest in Germany, and for the first four years of the war the Germans ate better than the peoples of the occupied countries, although later in the war, especially in 1944 and 1945, the food situation in Germany would

[109] Porter, Vol. I, p. 22.
[110] Porter, Vol. II, p. 139.

deteriorate quite seriously.[111] The food situation in Western Europe was in many ways quite desperate, and Germany's wholesale expropriation of food was the fundamental cause of the plight of the occupied countries, although the situation was somewhat exacerbated by the mildly successful British blockade of continental Europe that began in late 1940. At the beginning of 1943, it was reported that many Belgians were getting 800 to 900 calories a day instead of the 2,700 calories they had been consuming before the war.[112] The Dutch caloric intake fell to about 1,600 a day during the war and remained at that low level until October 1944.[113] French caloric consumption was about 1,500 a day in occupied areas where black markets operated and less in the cities where the black market did not exist.[114] Yet it should be noted that, meager as they might have been, rations existed in the occupied countries for most of the food categories. In the Soviet Union, the only food that was systematically rationed was bread; although there were occasional special distributions of other kinds of food, only bread was guaranteed. In that sense, the Soviet Union was quite different from and certainly worse off than other countries.

It is also plausible to argue that the suffering under the occupation was worse than for those in the rear. Even if one doubted the Soviet figures we have at our disposal, because of their incentive to paint the German cruelties in the very worst light, the German data on nutrition confirm the wretched food conditions under the occupation.

Last, there appears to have been a great deal of unevenness in the distribution of food in the occupied areas. The peasantry in the occupied areas, unlike their counterparts in the unoccupied zones, seem to have eaten better than their urban counterparts. The German administrators seemed less able than the Soviet authorities to keep a tight hold on the peasantry. We are quite sure the peasants were able to hoard food, but we cannot know this with precision because we are at the mercy of statistical problems.

---

[111] One would not know this from the complaining by ordinary German citizens in 1941, who for the first time in late summer had to cope with shortages of vegetables, fruits, and potatoes. At the end of the year the meat and sausage ration was cut from 16 ounces a week to 13 ounces. The decrease was attributed to the campaign in the Soviet Union; by then food imports had fallen. See Max Seydewitz, *Civil Life in Wartime Germany*, New York: Viking, 1945, pp. 108–9. Seydewitz was a former member of the Reichstag. In the early years, the Germans benefited from their own agriculture and the appropriation of food from other countries, including the Soviet Union and France.
[112] *The Times* (London), January 29, 1943, p. 5.
[113] Brandt and Associates, p. 419.
[114] Robert O. Paxton, *Vichy France: Old Guard and New Order, 1940–1944*, New York: Knopf, 1972, p. 360.

How did civilians survive in the occupied areas? There is certainly no single reason, but rather a combination of several factors of which two were the most important. First, there was an indomitable will to survive, toughened by the trials of history. Hardship was not a new phenomenon; only the names of the rulers changed – Russian tsars, Soviet commissars, and German meisters. Second, working urbanites and peasants received rations that allowed them at least a minimum diet. These I believe to be the two main sources of survival. In addition, there was some concourse between peasant and urbanite to provide additional sustenance for the city dweller. Free market activity was not great, but neither was it nonexistent. Moreover, the peasantry likely had some food stored away from before the war and was probably able to hoard food and seed during the occupation. The peasantry was well practiced at deceiving others and Germany's success in stripping away food and livestock could not have been perfect despite its ruthlessness. The peasant simply had too much wile to allow all of his food to pass through his fingers.

If there had not been additional ways for Soviet civilians to get food, however, the number who starved would have been much greater. Indeed, there was starvation in Kharkov and Kiev during the first winter and spring of the occupation. A highly propagandistic pamphlet produced by the U.S. wartime fund-raising organization, Russian War Relief, Inc., quoted an eyewitness estimate of 5 to 15 million civilian deaths of starvation and disease in occupied areas.[115] There is no supporting evidence for this estimate. Moreover, the suspiciously large gap of 10 million does not inspire confidence. Certainly, there does not appear to have been mass starvation after the calamities in the Ukraine. That this did not happen suggests that despite German contempt for and indifference toward the Soviet people, they could not afford to starve the entire population. And so with the minimum of food and the maximum of courage, the population survived.

[115] *Russia Fights Famine: A Russian War Relief Report*, New York, n.p., n.d. (probably 1943).

4 Producing food for the unoccupied USSR: the factors of production

Even in the unoccupied parts of the USSR, the war greatly altered the way food was produced in the Soviet Union. Everyone lived in the short run. In the initial crisis of 1941, the best land was occupied by the Germans, the best capital was destroyed or taken over by the Red Army, and the best labor was hastily drafted. The initial crisis was followed, therefore, by a more deep-seated crisis in which there was a shortage of all inputs and the war disrupted the mix of land, capital, and labor, turning the process of food production virtually upside down at both farm and national levels. In theory, the centralized planned economy of the USSR that had been created at the end of the 1920s should have provided the government with a particularly effective instrument to deal with both crises. In fact, this was only partly true. The story of the food economy during the war is one of disorder rather than order, of hand-to-mouth solutions and, especially, of a staggering and uneconomical degree of substitution of one kind of input for another. Many of the substitutions were not obvious and show local ingenuity and initiative as well as the dire straits in which the nation found itself.

In every sector we can see a similar pattern. The initial crisis of 1941 was met with emergency measures and showed the government abandoning central economic power to localities. The next year, 1942, was probably the worst in terms of production and feeding the population. War production starved the civilian economy; ambitious programs to solve the food supply problems created by the invasion were announced, but in fact the government continued to allow wide economic autonomy to localities; and the harvest was disastrously low, providing no relief for the end of the year or the winter of 1942 and 1943. However, 1942 also was the year that the government began to recreate the policies and means to reestablish central economic control. In 1943, as the Red Army began to expel the Germans from the RSFSR and parts of the Ukraine, the government was able to move more deliberately to regularize its methods of dealing with the problems of food supply and to impose greater control over localities. By 1944, as even more territory was liberated from German occupation and the Red Army began to move into Eastern Europe, we can note an extension of central control and the beginning of the shift of resources away from war production and back into providing for the starved civilian economy, but not always immediately into providing food for starving civilians.

Land

The most intractable problem in Soviet food production was adjusting to the loss of vast stretches of rich agricultural land to the German invaders. In effect, it was an insoluble problem. Labor and machinery could be evacuated or, within limitations, satisfactory substitutions found, but the choice lands that the Germans had conquered were lost and there simply was no good substitute. Specific crops were affected differently; only 59 percent of the grain acreage, 40 percent of the sunflower seed acreage, 10 percent of the sugar beets, and 46 percent of potato land were untouched by military activity.[1] Losses in the Ukraine, the Northern Caucasus, and the Rostov oblast diminished the total sown area by one-third or more during the first years of the war. In 1940, sown acreage of grains had been 110.4 million hectares; this fell to a low of 67.3 million hectares in 1942, about 60 percent of the prewar total, and even in 1945, only 85 million hectares were planted.[2]

Massive shifts toward the east took place. In comparison with 1940 (when the base was fairly low), 1942 sowings in Siberia increased by 44 percent, in the Urals by 37 percent, in the far east by 30 percent, and in Central Asia and Kazakhstan by 32 percent.[3] As a result, in the unoccupied areas of the country sown acreage increased by nearly four million hectares.[4]

[1] U. G. Cherniavskii, *Voina i prodovol'stvie*, Moscow: 1964, p. 38. The base is land sown in 1939.
[2] T. I. Shilagin, *Narodnoe khoziaistvo SSSR v period Velikikoi Otechestvennoi Voiny*, Moscow, 1960, p. 197.
[3] Ibid., p. 201.
[4] Nikolai A. Voznesensky, *The Economy of the USSR During World War II*, Washington, D.C.: Public Affairs Press, 1948, p. 50. Kazakhstan is a good example of the effort

These efforts could not compensate for the loss of the nation's most fertile lands, and grain yield per hectare decreased. In 1940, the yield was 950 pounds per hectare, but that fell by about half in 1942 and 1943.[5] Other factors, such as the decline in the use of machinery and fertilizer, contributed to this decline in output (see the next section), but the essential cause was the loss of huge stretches of the best agricultural land to the Germans.

Capital

In the retreat from the western lands, the Soviets suffered great losses of agricultural machinery. This was devastating precisely because when the war started the process of food production in the Soviet Union had only begun to climb out of the dark ages. In 1932 only 22 percent of agriculture had been mechanized.[6] Mechanization had risen rapidly thereafter, and Soviet estimates are that 53 percent of the field work in kolkhozy was done by tractors in 1940, with a 1941 goal of 57 percent.[7] If one takes the four basic functions of plowing, sowing, harvesting, and threshing, then in 1938, 68 percent of the work was done mechanically, the rest either manually or with horses. Mechanized agriculture had become important and the war dealt a severe blow to production capability.

Once the war began, mechanization fell precipitously. In 1940 there had been about 483,000 tractors and 153,000 combines doing agricultural work. About 180,000 of these tractors were left in areas that were occupied by the Germans and the remaining 300,000 or so were in unoccupied areas.[8] Soviet accounts say that 111,846 tractors and 44,781 combines were destroyed in occupied territory, although it is not always clear whether this was done by the Germans or by the Soviets themselves.[9] In addition, tractors were conscripted from agriculture for

made to shift grain production. From 1932 to 1940, the Soviets increased the number of hectares sown to grains from 4,496,000 to 5,834,000, but in the two-year period from 1940 to 1942, the sown grain area went from the latter figure to 6,869,000 hectares. *Sotsialisticheskoe sel'skoe khoziaistvo*, p. 23.

[5] *Istoriia Velikoi Otechestvennoi Voiny Sovetskogo Soiuza 1941–1945 (Istoriia)*, Vol. 6, p. 68.
[6] USSR: Crop Conditions and Production, 1942–1945. Records of the Foreign Agricultural Service (NFAS). Record Group 166, National Archives, Washington, D.C. U.S. Embassy at London, No. 9382, June 1, 1943.
[7] M. Moiseev, "O sisteme mashin v sel'skom khoziaistve," *Sotsialisticheskoe sel'skoe khoziaistvo*, January 1941, pp. 34–5.
[8] This is based on a wartime interview with the chief of the Machine Division of the Commissariat of Agriculture. See NFAS, U.S. Embassy at Moscow, probably an October 1943 memo.
[9] Iu. V. Arutiunian, *Sel'skogo khoziaistvo SSSR v 1929–1957gg.*, Moscow, 1960, p. 66.

Table 4.1. *Production of agricultural machinery (1940 to 1944)*

	1940	1941	1942	1943	1944
Tractors	18,467	6,556	435	416	1,833
Tractor plows	29,317	12,567	727	1,754	2,435
Horse-drawn plows	33,800	17,100	—	31,900	22,700
Grain-seeding tractors	17,200	8,700	—	—	—
Horse-drawn grain seeders	4,518	5,214	—	62	1,037
Combines	11,408	4,794	—	—	127

Source: Iu. V. Arutiunian, *Sovetskoe krest'ianstvo v gody Velikoi Otechestvennoi Voiny*, Moscow, 1963, p. 273.

use in the Red Army in numbers that the Soviets treated as a military secret, but that wartime U.S. intelligence estimated to be 300,000 in 1941 and another 100,000 in 1942.[10] In the fall of 1944 the U.S. Embassy in Moscow estimated that there were no more than 260,000 tractors in the entire country, 75,000 in the areas liberated from occupation areas and 185,000 in the unoccupied areas.[11] The results showed in how fieldwork was done. For the 1942 harvest, only 20 percent of the nearly 51 million hectares of grain crops was cut by combines, the rest being done with either simple machines or by hand with sickles and scythes.[12] In 1944, only 29 percent of the winter sowing, 50 percent of fall plowing, and 20 percent of the grain harvesting were done by machine.[13]

The war brought the production of tractors and other farm machinery to a virtual standstill (Table 4.1) for two reasons. The tractor factories were either destroyed, as at Stalingrad, or, more important, they were converted to military production. The severely damaged tractor factory in Leningrad was moved to Cheliabinsk and was converted to tank production. The damaged Kharkov plant was also evacuated and reestablished in the Altai krai to produce tanks.[14] No threshers were produced in 1942 and 1943.[15]

Consequently, the Soviet tractor inventory was aging. Soviet accounts say that two-thirds of the tractors were eight to nine years old

[10] NFAS, October 1943 memo.
[11] NFAS, U.S. Embassy at Moscow, No. 102, September 27, 1944.
[12] M. I. Likhomanov, *Khoziaistvenno-organizatorskaia rabota partii v derevne v pervyi period Velikoi Otechestvennoi Voiny (1941–1942gg.)*, Leningrad, 1975, p. 130; *Istoriia*, Vol. 2, p. 518.
[13] *Istoriia*, Vol. 5, p. 389.
[14] NFAS, October 1943 memo from Wheeler to Michael; U.S. Embassy at Moscow, No. 102, September 27, 1944.
[15] *Moscow News*, February 10, 1945.

when the war started[16] and a wartime U.S. estimate was that before the war the average age of Soviet tractors in the field was ten years.[17] There was almost no production for three years, from mid–1941 to mid–1944, and thus the Soviets were either working with an older and less effective stock of tractors or with fewer tractors as aging survivors broke down. In 1943, on average, one tractor plowed only 182 hectares, about 44 percent of the 1940 figure of 411 hectares.[18]

Tractor production began to recover only in the middle of 1944. The Stalingrad Tractor Plant did not begin to produce again until June 17, 1944, a date chosen to commemorate its fourteenth anniversary; the Svobodny farm machinery plant did not start producing threshers and parts until the beginning of 1945; and the tractor plant in Kharkov did not produce tractors again until the very end of the war because it was producing spare parts.[19] Even then recovery was slow, a sign of how severely the capacity to produce agricultural machinery had diminished. A February 1944 decree included a plan for the production of 5,500 tractors in 1944, three times what was actually produced, and a grandiose 27,000 tractors in 1945, when in fact they actually only manufactured 7,700.[20]

The Soviets used four approaches in their efforts to solve machinery shortages. First, and especially in the early years, horse-drawn equipment or manual tools were substituted for machines. Second, non-agricultural personnel were mobilized to repair equipment. Third, intensive use was made of the surviving and aging machinery. Fourth, mass-mobilization campaigns such as the collection of scrap metal served to create enthusiasm and discipline in the countryside. Only toward the end of the war could industrial capacity be mobilized to diminish the stark shortages of machinery.

The spare parts and repair problem

The loss of agricultural machinery was compounded by the loss of capacity to keep the remaining machines in good working

[16] *Istoriia*, Vol. 3, p. 182.
[17] NFAS, U.S. Embassy at Moscow, No. 102, September 27, 1944.
[18] Arutiunian, *Sel'skogo khoziaistvo*, p. 92; Naum Jasny, *The Socialized Agriculture of the USSR*, Stanford: Stanford University Press, 1949, p. 288.
[19] NFAS, U.S. Embassy at Moscow, Report No. 635, July 3, 1944; NFAS, U.S. Embassy at Moscow, Report No. 1394, January 15, 1945; *Moscow News*, February 10, 1945.
[20] February 18, 1944 resolution, "On the construction of tractor factories and the development of production capacities for the production of tractors for agriculture," in *Direktivy KPSS i sovetskogo pravitel'stva po khoziaistvennym voprosam*, Moscow, 1957, p. 818; *Istoriia Vtoroi Mirovoi Voiny 1939–1945*, Vol. 11, Moscow 1980, p. 340.

order. Overall, the supply of spare parts for tractors fell during the war period to 5 to 10 percent of the prewar level.[21] During the first two and a half years of the war, no spare parts were produced. By the end of 1943, 16.5 percent of the tractors and 28 percent of the combines on the state farms did not work because of the absence of spare parts.[22] Because the factories that ordinarily supplied these parts were producing military goods, local organs had to scrounge for spare parts. A major campaign was launched to secure capital inputs, a task often assigned to the Komsomol units. As early as the beginning of 1942 Komsomol members in the Stalingrad area began "collecting metal, instruments, and parts on the roads, in village streets, and in the kolkhoz fields."[23] On February 18, 1942, the Sverdlovsk oblast committee issued a resolution on collecting spare parts, instruments, and various materials for MTS, and for state and collective farms. The Komsomol organizations were supposed to collect unused parts, parts needing repair, and scrap metal to repair tractors and other agricultural machinery. By February 23, the oblast's branch of sel'khozsnab (agricultural supply) was to organize the collection and further distribution of these parts and materials to the MTS and state farms.[24] The members of the Komsomol were credited with collecting and fixing 65 million rubles worth of spare parts in 1942 and 1943.[25]

As might be expected, the level of completion of machinery repair work around the country was slow and very uneven. By 1944 *Pravda* was conducting a campaign of criticism. An April 1944 *Pravda* article criticized the fact that only 86 percent of the Akmolinsk oblast's tractors had been repaired and that only 20 percent of the 42 MTS had finished the repair plan,[26] and a June article noted that in Altai, only 206 of 7,300 combines had been repaired as of June for the 1944 harvest.[27] As late as the beginning of 1945, the Sakhalin oblast reported that only 27 percent of its tractor repairs had been done.[28] Even when repair personnel had parts to work with, these were fabricated from lesser quality materials; instead of alloy steel, parts

---

[21] Arutiunian, Sel'skogo khoziaistvo, p. 82.

[22] N. E. Zelenin, "Sovkhozy SSSR v gody voiny," in Sovetskii tyl v Velikoi Otechestvennoi voine, Moscow, 1974, p. 201.

[23] Arutiunian, Sovetskoe krest'ianstvo v gody Velikoi Otechestvennoi Voiny, Moscow, 1963, p. 133.

[24] Vse Dlia Fronta!, Sverdlovsk, 1985, p. 209. It should be noted that although the resolution ordered collecting from collective farms, there was no provision for giving them anything in return.

[25] Istoriia, Vol. 3, p. 182.

[26] Pravda, April 7, 1944, p. 3.

[27] Pravda, June 18, 1944, p. 2.

[28] NFAS, U.S. Consulate at Vladivostok, No. 1, March 1945.

were made from ordinary steel, plastic, and even wood, and bronze was substituted for iron.[29]

One problem was that the war claimed many of the repairmen who had worked in the MTS, thereby reducing the level of technical knowledge in the countryside. The two related solutions called on urban areas to make up the shortfall. Mechanics were brought in from the cities to do repair work on equipment they had likely never before seen.[30] In a second version of this process in 1944, a patron relationship (*shefskaia rabota*) was developed between a factory or factories in a particular area and the MTS repair shops or state farms in that area. In Moscow, where this process apparently first began, 160 industrial enterprises did some tractor repair work and produced some spare parts. In the Sverdlovsk oblast, the Urals Machinery Plant (*Uralmash-zavod*) supplied the MTS in the area with spare parts and instruments and loaned some skilled workers to the MTS to repair tractors.[31] Such relationships suggest the inherent inadequacy of attempts by farms to jerry-build parts and machines as they were forced to do under the great restrictions of the war.

Not until 1944 were spare parts again manufactured because it was recognized that the 1943 agricultural failures stemmed from the inability of the MTS to do its job because of their absence. A special resolution of March 14, 1944, put forth a plan for the production of 65.3 million rubles of spare parts.[32] Even plants involved in military production were pushed to manufacture spare parts.[33]

The fuel shortage

The shortage of oil supplies made itself felt quickly in the food economy. Before the war, agriculture had used 66 percent of the Soviet consumption of kerosene, 70 percent of the diesel fuel, 33 percent of the gasoline, 69 percent of the motor oil, and 76 percent of the diesel lubricants. In 1942, the amount of kerosene, auto fuel, and diesel fuel in agriculture had fallen to 40 percent of the 1940 level.[34] Such diminished supplies affected both collective and state farms, although it appears to have been worse for collective farms and the MTS that

[29] *Istoriia*, Vol. 2, p. 515.
[30] *Istoriia*, Vol. 3, p. 184.
[31] *Istoriia*, Vol. 4, p. 599.
[32] *Direktivy*, p. 828.
[33] NFAS, U.S. Embassy at Moscow, No. 102, September 27, 1944.
[34] *Istoriia*, Vol. 2, p. 515.

serviced them. A June 20, 1942, resolution, "On the saving and elimination of squandering of fuel in the MTS and sovkhozy," required a 10 percent reduction in fuel and oil use in 1942 over the already low 1941 level.[35] In 1940 the MTS and collective farms had received 4,248,000 tons of oil fuels, but in 1942 they were only allocated 1,252,000 tons,[36] and fuel supplies for tractors dropped by 48 percent.[37] As a consequence, the amount of fuel per tractor fell by nearly half, from 8.4 tons in 1940 to 4.7 tons in 1942.[38] The state farms fared better. Their use of fuel per hectare, which was 17.6 kilograms in 1940, never went below 16.8 kilograms in 1942 and in 1943 was slightly higher than the prewar figure.[39]

Shortages existed everywhere. In 1942 most of the fuel bases in western Siberia did not have machine oil and as of April 1942, the Siberian MTS network had only 44 percent of the kerosene and 56 percent of the gasoline it needed.[40] In other areas, the shortage of gasoline was worse than that of kerosene and as a result, a substantial number of combines were converted to kerosene. Even so, the fuel shortage was so bad that many combines were either hooked up to a tractor or were pulled by horses.[41]

One of the major ways of dealing with shortages was by substituting solid for liquid fuels. Soon after the war began, an article in a major Soviet agriculture journal proposed the use of firewood, peat, coal, straw, boon (which is the woody portion of flax), and also natural gas. Preliminary calculations showed that 10 to 15 percent of all tractor work could be done with firewood, but this would require 5 to 7.5 million cubic meters of firewood in the MTS system and a supply sufficient to allow wood to dry so that it could be efficiently burned.[42] The conversion process began later in the year. In 1942, 7,730 wheel tractors and all 11,861 gas generator tractors in the MTS were converted to solid fuels. The MTS hired mechanics whose sole responsibility was to convert tractor engines to solid fuel consumption.[43] Because the conver-

[35] I. I. Vinogradov, *Politotdely MTS i sovkhozov v gody Velikoi Otechestvennoi Voiny (1941–1943gg)*, Leningrad, 1976, p. 107.
[36] Arutiunian, *Sovetskoe krest'ianstvo*, p. 139.
[37] Ibid., p. 82.
[38] Ibid., p. 139.
[39] Ibid., p. 141.
[40] Ibid., p. 139.
[41] Ia. E. Chadaev, *Ekonomika SSSR v period Velikoi Otechestvennoi Voiny*, Moscow, 1965, p. 334.
[42] M. Vanier, "Maksimal'nogo sokratit' raskhod zhidkogo topliva," *Sotsialisticheskoe sel'skoe khoziaistvo*, July–August, 1941, nos. 7–8, p. 29.
[43] Vinogradov, p. 109.

sion to a solid fuel capacity was easier said than done, the necessity to develop a simplified, universal, gas-generating machine was broached early in 1942,[44] and on November 28, 1942, a special order was issued that stipulated that all oil-driven engines were to be converted to gas-driven capacity.[45]

There was a great deal of ingenuity demonstrated at the local level to cope with the oil shortage, although none of the innovations could be as productive as what they replaced. In one MTS in the Sverdlovsk oblast, turpentine was produced as a starting fuel for tractors and automobiles; in Uzbekistan, MTS and state farms used *mazut*, normally a heating fuel, for crankcase oil.[46] In general, oil was recycled, and there was a sizable substitution of grease made from local materials for oil-based grease.[47]

The substitution of animals for machinery

Having lost such a large part of their mechanical power, it was only logical for the Soviets to revert partially to less sophisticated methods of producing food, that is, the use of animal power. The number of working animals in the countryside, however, was itself diminished; by the end of 1943, the amount of working livestock in the collective farms was only 58 percent of the prewar level.[48] There was an obvious pecking order in the pattern of substitution. Horses were the next best thing to a machine, bulls came after horses, and cows were the last resort.

The use of horses was itself constrained by the significant fall in their numbers. At the beginning of 1941, there had been 20.8 million horses, but five years later, there were only 10.7 million.[49] During the early months of the war, 1,251,000 collective farm horses were appropriated by the army at a nearly confiscatory price.[50] In western Siberia, about 167,000 horses, or roughly 25 percent of the total in the region, were taken by the army in the

[44] *Sotsialisticheskoe sel'skoe khoziaistvo*, January, 1942, p. 12.
[45] Arutiunian, *Sovetskoe krest'ianstvo*, p. 141.
[46] *Istoriia*, Vol. 2, p. 515.
[47] Chadaev, p. 334.
[48] Arutiunian, *Sovetskoe krest'ianstvo*, p. 145.
[49] Ibid., p. 425.
[50] Vinogradov, p. 12. Although the Red Army would buy the best horses for 700 rubles and the government would pay 1,500 rubles for horses for other uses, the free market price of a horse was said to be a staggering 12,000 rubles. See Henry Wallace, *Soviet Asia Mission*, New York: Reynal & Hitchcock, 1946, p. 114.

second half of 1941. The consequence of the decrease in the stock of horses was extensive use of cows for fieldwork and hauling, despite serious costs to food production because cows were only about one-third as productive as horses.[51] The use of animals other than horses was especially high at harvest time, and privately owned animals as well as those in the socialist sector had to be used to meet collective farm quotas. A furious pace was imposed from the moment the 1942 harvest began, including a five-day delivery quota that was exacted from every collective and state farm, meaning that every animal had to be mobilized for field and road.[52] In western Siberia in 1942, the combination of the decline in the number of machines and the inability to repair the machines that were available forced the use of about 270,000 cows in the fields, or about half of all collective farm herds.[53]

The use of cows for draft power also meant a tradeoff between the productivity of the animal as a beast of burden and as a milker. There were efforts to make cows with a low milk yield (i.e., one-half the average yield of the herd) the primary candidates for fieldwork, to use productive cows much more selectively, and to avoid putting a cow into the field during the first two months after calving.[54] In fact, it appears that pregnant cows had to be used up until two to three months before birth and to be put back to work a month and a half after birth.[55] In Krasnodar, where there were said to be about 500,000 cows, most were used as draft animals as well as for milking. One observer wrote in the fall of 1944: "Practically all of the cultivation, truck-gardening and hauling are being done with cows. It was a common sight to see a woman leading a cow that was pulling a cart loaded with about twelve poods of goods."[56] Cows were used for both short- and long-distance hauling. In the Shapinsk raion cows hauled produce to the railroad station, which was about 20 miles from the farm; a one-day trip for horses, such a trip took a cow three days.[57]

---

[51] L. Furman, "Ob ispol'zovanii korov na sel'skokhoziaistvennykh rabotakh," *Sotsialisticheskoe sel'skoe khoziaistvo*, March–April, 1943, p. 25.
[52] *Istoriia*, Vol. 2, p. 520. Farmers were awarded one labor day if their cow was used to haul produce a minimum of two kilometers.
[53] Likhomanov, p. 57.
[54] A. Malafeev and V. Milovanov, "Perestrit' zhivotnovodstvo na voennyi lad," *Sotsialisticheskoe sel'skoe khoziaistvo*, September 1941, p. 33.
[55] Furman, p. 24.
[56] NFAS, U.S. Embassy at Moscow, Report No. 920, September 7, 1944. Twelve poods equal 433 pounds.
[57] Furman, p. 24.

Shortages of fodder and fertilizer

The output of meat and dairy products was further constrained by a substantial decline in the availability of fodder, a decline worsened by the inability of the transport system to deliver fodder to deficit areas. The major way in which the problem was treated was by substituting coarse and succulent feeds, particularly silage, for higher-quality feed concentrates.[58] In 1940, such concentrates had constituted more than 13 percent of the diet of a milk cow, but by 1942 that figure had fallen to 2.2 percent and in 1943 it was virtually zero. Before the war, potatoes had been used as livestock feed, particularly for pigs, but with the decline in the food supply for civilians, all potatoes went to human consumption.[59]

Farms did everything imaginable to solve the feed shortage. Instead of grains or potatoes, animals were fed military garbage and unused food by-products[60] and in some places, wild grasses, weeds, vegetable leaves, corn cobs, or scraps from beet production.[61] Another effort involved winter pasturing of Central Asian animals in the desert and semiarid areas of the rear and the steppe.[62] The need both to conserve and alter the composition of fodder became a popular issue.[63] In the name of conservation, one article even advocated that winter feeding be tailored with individual rations for animals.[64]

There is no doubt that the quantity and quality of livestock herds fell because of the shortfall in quality feed. Indeed, after the poor harvest of 1942, the minimum weight at which pigs were to be delivered was lowered for both state and collective farms, a clear concession to the shortage of feed.[65] It is difficult to assess definitively the impact that the fodder shortage had on livestock breeding because of the other factors bearing on breeding as well as the general confusion of the war. Farms that did the best at

[58] Chadaev, p. 366.
[59] Arutiunian, *Sovetskoe krest'ianstvo*, pp. 177–8.
[60] A. Malafeev and V. Milovanov, "Perestroit' zhivotnovodstvo na voennyi lad," *Sotsialisticheskoe sel'skoe khoziaistvo*, September 1941, p. 29.
[61] Chadaev, p. 361.
[62] Shilagin, p. 207; Chadaev, p. 362. In 1942 and 1943 about 3 million animals or 27 percent of the collective farm herds of Kazakhstan were in winter pastures. *Istoriia*, Vol. 2, p. 522.
[63] See, for example, the article in *Pravda*, December 19, 1941, p. 3, entitled, "To Judiciously and Economically Use Fodder."
[64] *Pravda*, August 11, 1942, p. 3.
[65] Arutiunian, *Sovetskoe krest'ianstvo*, p. 179.

breeding animals during the war already had a solid forage base. Those without such a base faced shortage and the need to grow substitute feeds, such as melons.[66]

Parallel to the fodder shortage was the drop in fertilizer production during the war to one-third of the prewar level.[67] Here part of the problem was the very limited role fertilizer of *any* kind played in Soviet agriculture. A campaign of the late 1930s sought nothing more sophisticated than to get farmers to use peat.[68] There were high aspirations for the use of chemical fertilizers, although mostly for industrial crops rather than food production and the Third Five-Year Plan called for annual production of 5,868,000 tons. Even in 1938, however, before the war began to interrupt the plan, production of chemical fertilizer was only 2,610,000 tons. During the war, commercial fertilizer production virtually fell to zero,[69] and the amount that went to agriculture reached a wartime low of 79,000 tons in 1943, rose to 181,000 tons in 1944, and only to 624,000 tons in 1945.[70] The weakness of the transport system made the shortage of fertilizer worse. During most of the war, the only source of phosphorite, the raw material for phosphate fertilizers, was the Khibiny deposits in the Murmansk oblast, almost 2,500 miles from Central Asia, whose agriculture was in desperate need of fertilizer.[71] In the face of great shortage, emphasis was placed on applying local fertilizer sources, particularly manure, to the fields. This was constrained by the sharp decrease in livestock and the lack of transportation to haul manure to the fields. In addition, both the collective and state farm leadership seemed unwilling to recognize the importance of fertilizers.[72] The failure to supply or use fertilizer only intensified the depletion of the land brought on by the methods of overfarming required by the war.

[66] Chadaev, p. 361.
[67] V. S. Tel'pukhovskii, *Velikaia Otechestvennaia Voina Sovetskogo Soiuza, 1941–1945*, Moscow, 1959, p. 505.
[68] Naum Jasny, *The Socialized Agriculture of the USSR*, Stanford: Stanford University Press, 1949, p. 500. Although the amounts used in the prewar period are uncertain, there were substantial declines in its application during the war.
[69] Ibid., pp. 495–6, 498. Only 4 percent of chemical fertilizers were used in potato and vegetable production; the rest were used on industrial crops.
[70] *Istoriia*, Vol. 4, p. 598; Vol. 5, p. 388.
[71] NFAS, U.S. Embassy at Moscow, No. 524, June 2, 1944.
[72] NFAS, U.S. Consulate at Vladivostok, No. 1, March 1945. There were also exhortations early in the war to persuade state farms to use local reserves of fertilizer, particularly phosphorous. See Z. Miriasov, "O rasschirennom primenenii fosforitnoi muki," *Sotsialisticheskoe sel'skoe khoziaistvo*, July–August 1941, No. 7–8, p. 63.

Labor – men

The immediate effect of the war was to reduce the number of able-bodied males available in the collective farms of the nonoccupied areas of the country. Their numbers fell from 8.6 million at the beginning of 1941 to 5.9 million a year later and kept plummeting to 3.6 million at the beginning of 1943 and only 2.3 million in 1944.[73] That is, by the end of 1943, over two-thirds of the prewar able-bodied male population had gone off to war.[74] Most went into the army, but several hundred thousand also went to work in defense plants as well.[75] Either way, the draft swept up the most skilled cadres in the countryside. Most of the machine operators entered the Red Army. In 1936, 56 percent of the tractor drivers, 43 percent of the combine operators, and about 60 percent of the assistants to the combine operators had been under the age of 25, and it was from this age group that the Soviets drafted the bulk of those who would drive military vehicles during the war.[76] Quite early in the war 60 to 70 percent of the kolkhoz chairmen and brigadiers and close to 90 percent of the machine operators were drafted.[77]

In general, the attempt to solve the agricultural labor problem was based upon the idea of pouring as much labor as possible into the countryside to compensate for the loss of the most productive component of the labor force, namely, adult males. It was an effort consistent with the broader strategy of extensive economic development under which the prewar five-year plans operated. Notwithstanding the great strides that had been made in mechanizing agricultural work, Soviet agriculture on the eve of the war remained a highly labor intensive operation.[78] Whereas it took one man-day to produce an acre of wheat in the U.S. at that time, it took 2.5 to 3.6 man-days to produce an acre of wheat in the Soviet Union.[79] During the war, agricultural production became even more labor intensive because of the destruction of the stock of agricultural equipment and the loss of skilled machine operators.

[73] Arutiunian, *Sovetskoe krest'ianstvo*, p. 66.
[74] V. T. Aniskov, "Kolkhoznaia derevnia v 1941–1945gg," in *Sovetskii tyl v Velikoi Otechestvennoi Voine*, Vol. 2, Moscow, 1974, p. 193.
[75] Likhomanov, p. 80.
[76] Arutiunian, *Sel'skogo khoziaistvo*, p. 66.
[77] Aniskov, p. 196.
[78] For example, although 30 percent of spring plowing was mechanized in 1934, 75 percent was mechanized in 1938. The planting of fall crops went from 34.5 percent mechanized to 72 percent. Ibid., p. 64.
[79] Lazar Volin, *A Survey of Soviet Russian Agriculture*, Washington D.C., n.p., 1951, pp. 33–34.

The labor-intensive nature of agriculture obliged the Soviets to find replacements for draft-age men.[80] The main source of replacement labor was farm women. Additionally, adolescents, old people, rural inhabitants not living on collective farms, children of all ages, and urbanites of assorted stripes all became essential to filling the vacuum. In spite of heroic efforts, the gap was never fully closed.

Labor – women

In 1940, women constituted 56 percent of the kolkhoz labor force, but that rose to 73 percent by 1943, remaining at about that level in 1944.[81] Moreover, because women did the least valued work on the farm before the war, they earned only 38 percent of the labor days, but by 1943 when they not only did the back-breaking field work, milked the cows, and slopped the hogs, but also filled the more important agricultural administrative jobs, they earned 70 percent of the total number of work days.[82]

Because machine operators were virtually all men before the war, their departure to the army and industry radically altered the labor force that drove the machinery. Over the course of the war, two million machine operators, 75 percent of whom were women, were trained for the collective farms. In 1940, only 4 percent of the tractor drivers and 6 percent of the combine operators had been women, but as early as 1942, women accounted for about 45 percent of such machine operators,[83] and by 1944, 81 percent of the tractor drivers and 62 percent of the combine operators were women.[84]

Women also moved into administrative positions, although men were still represented in such managerial positions well out of pro-

[80] There was a substantial amount of disguised unemployment in the countryside. One Soviet economist estimated in 1938 that collective farms in the Ukraine could afford to let 1 million out of 7.3 million people go to industry. But this is, of course, much less than the enormous number that left to participate in the war effort. See Jasny, p. 396.
[81] Likhomanov, p. 81. Cherniavskii (p. 44) says that 76 percent of the 1944 kolkhoz labor force was female.
[82] *Bolshevik*, No. 5, 1945, translated in NFAS, U.S. Embassy at Moscow, Economic Information No. 22, May 1945. This continued into 1944, when women earned 71 percent of the labor days. Wallace, p. 225.
[83] Likhomanov, p. 88.
[84] Tel'pukhovskii, p. 301. Much the same pattern held in the state farms, although at a lower level; on September 1, 1944, women accounted for 60 percent of all machine operators. Chadaev, p. 365.

portion to their numbers in the wartime civilian labor force. Although 2.6 percent of the collective farm heads had been women in 1940, women occupied 12 percent of these posts in 1944.[85] The increase in women managers was, however, only an emergency response and was reversed even before the end of the war.[86]

The burden of physical labor that farm women bore during the war was overwhelming, because they had to replace both the men and machines that were taken away or could not be repaired when they broke down. A U.S. observer watched 33 women harvesting wheat in the Volga region with no man in sight and doing all the work by hand, with the exception of one thresher.[87] Or we can grasp what it meant from a popular novel about a Siberian village as a woman reminisces at the celebration honoring the return of her husband from the front:

> It was hard on us, too, . . . Right, girls, it was hard? I hate to think about it. The work in the kolkhoz – all right, that's our own work. But as soon as we harvested the grain – there was the snow and the logging to do. I'll remember that logging until the day I die. No roads, the horses are overworked and can't haul the lumber. And there's no way not to do it: we were the working front, aid for our menfolk. The first years we even left little babies. . . . And the ones without children or with older kids – they were never excused. . . . You haul up the lumber, all those cubic meters of wood, and pull them up with you into the sleds. And you keep the ropes and pole with you all the time. Sometimes you fall into a snowbank – and then the women have to pull out the sled.[88]

The general mobilization of labor

The shortage of labor growing out of the draft of able-bodied males not only led to a rise in the importance of women, but to a general mobilization of the entire population not otherwise employed in farm work. At the beginning of the new agricultural year, on April 17, 1942, a special resolution allowed the recruit-

[85] Aniskov, p. 197.
[86] The proportion of women in leadership positions began to decline in 1945 and this continued until 1947 and 1948, when the distribution of men and women in these positions was about the same as it had been before the war started. Arutiunian, *Sovetskoe krest'ianstvo*, p. 289.
[87] U.S. Department of State, *Foreign Relations of the United States, 1942*, Vol. III, Washington, D.C., 1961, p. 454.
[88] Valentin Rasputin, *Live and Remember*, New York: Macmillan, 1978, p. 73.

ment for summer work in the countryside of the following groups: able-bodied urbanites not working in industry or transportation, certain categories of white-collar employees, students in the sixth to tenth classes, and students in the *tekhnikums* and institutions of higher education (*vuzy*).[89] The number of urbanites involved in agriculture was not trivial; in 1942 3 million worked in the harvest and in 1943, 2.7 million worked in the spring and fall.[90] In some places, urbanites were absolutely crucial. In the Yaroslavl oblast in 1943, for example, 17 percent of the labor days were earned by urbanites.[91]

Some of the urbanites had already received training in agriculture. In December 1941, a course was developed for teaching agricultural techniques to white-collar workers, middle-school students, and *vuzy* students. In 1941, there were about 25,000 student tractor drivers and 16,000 combine operators who had taken short courses that had been developed in the cities in response to the invasion crisis. By 1942, 64 percent of the senior-level students took courses in agriculture.[92] Beginning with 1943, work quotas were set for urbanites sent to the countryside. Adults had an obligation of 40 to 50 workdays on collective farms and 50 to 60 workdays on state farms; student norms were about 20 to 30 days on collective farms and state farms. After the work quota was met, urbanites could go home.[93]

In addition to mobilizing urbanites for agricultural labor, elements of the rural population were also mobilized. A decree issued on January 9, 1943, aimed at mobilizing collective farmers and the rural population not employed in industry or transportation to train them as machine operators or to do repair work on farm machinery.[94] State farm directors were given the right to mobilize the entire able-bodied population, including adolescents who were 14 years old. Students from the area industrial and railroad schools were conscripted to repair agricultural machinery.[95]

[89] Likhomanov, pp. 83–4. These mobilized workers were paid the same as the collective farmers, state farm workers, and MTS employees and were to receive 50 percent of their regular salaries during their stint in the countryside. Students who were at the end of their education were exempt from the mobilization. Lazar Volin, "German Invasion and Russian Agriculture," *Russian Review*, Vol. 3–4, November 1943, p. 83; *Istoriia*, Vol. 2, p. 531.

[90] *Istoriia*, Vol. 2, p. 531; Vol. 3, p. 188.

[91] *Istoriia*, p. 188.

[92] Arutiunian, *Sovetskoe krest'ianstvo*, pp. 110–11.

[93] NFAS, U.S. Embassy at Moscow, Report No. 196, July 26, 1943.

[94] *Direktivy*, pp. 744–6.

[95] Zelenin, p. 203.

Children

There was also a significant use of children and adolescents, aged 12 to 16. Indeed, by 1944, this age group comprised 17 percent of all collective farm workers. The komsomol leadership was assigned major responsibility for this mobilization.[96] Campaigns were organized, for example, *voskreseniki*, which were Sundays on which large numbers of students would work, and *dekadniki*, which were ten-day campaigns for bringing in the grain.[97]

Children were used during both the planting and harvest seasons, usually in ways that reflected a sense of great urgency. In the hungry harvest of 1942, schoolchildren were sent into already harvested fields in the morning before school, the boys with baskets, the girls with bags tied around their waists, to work for about an hour filling their sacks with grain that had not been collected on the first pass through the fields.[98] Children were often part of a harvesting team in grain fields, serving as gleaners. After the cutters, threshers, and bundlers had been through the field, two or three children would rake and pick up whatever grain had been left in the field.[99] Tons of grain were said to have been harvested in this way, although some examples invite disbelief, as for instance the claim that in the Sverdlovsk oblast, 50,000 Pioneers and schoolchildren picked up almost 22,000 tons of grain![100]

After a chaotic mobilization of city children in 1941, it was decided that training was needed because the children had demonstrated wholesale ignorance of what happens on a farm and how to use farm equipment. A plan was developed by the Commissariat of Agriculture in preparation for the 1942 spring planting. It visualized schoolchildren taking eight hours a week of training in agriculture, the youngest children being taught how to cultivate vegetables, berries, and fruit, children aged 12 to 14 being taught how to handle simple tools and how to care for animals, and 14-year-olds being instructed on how to operate tractors and combines.[101] The plan that was actually implemented during the 1941 to 1942 school year, however, was less ambitious. Agricultural training was introduced for two hours a week for schoolchildren aged 11 to 13 and for students aged 14 to 16 for

[96] *Istoriia*, Vol. 4, p. 598.
[97] *Pravda*, September 9, 1944, p. 2.
[98] *Pravda*, September 21, 1942, p. 3.
[99] Vinogradov, p. 113.
[100] Ibid., p. 115. If true, this would mean that each of 50,000 children personally gathered close to half a ton of grain.
[101] *The New York Times*, January 7, 1942, p. 6.

two hours a week. According to the data of thirty-six RSFSR oblasts, during 1942 schools trained 148,000 tractor drivers, about 29,000 combine operators, and 7,500 drivers, in addition to the students who were trained to do ordinary fieldwork.[102] Despite the numbers trained, the program was not regarded as helpful because it was too general and did not have a "clear professional character."[103]

In addition to providing training, the schools also became organizers of labor. For the entire four years of the war, some 14.5 million students and more than 500,000 teachers worked in the countryside,[104] including 500,000 middle-school students and 50,000 students in higher education.[105] In 1942 in the RSFSR, 3,970,866 younger students and 181,344 teachers worked on collective and state farms, putting in 139.3 million labor days, or an average of 40 labor days apiece.[106] Students and teachers did everything from bundling sheaves and collecting straw and grain as they did in Sverdlovsk[107] to taking major responsibility for gathering in wild plants for eating and medicinal purposes. In the summer of 1942, they collected 22,627 tons of oak bark (used as a healing tea) and 4,866 tons of medicinal plants and prepared 20,074 tons of pickled mushrooms and 770 tons of dry mushrooms.[108]

The war made children grow up fast; they had to become adults before their time. As one émigré said matter of factly: "The day the war started, my childhood ended."[109] Right from the beginning, children were moved to new situations where they had to take on responsible tasks, including the operation of tractors and combines.[110] A man originally from Kiev was twice sent to work on a kolkhoz before he was old enough to be drafted. The second time he was assigned to a farm where he lived in a single room inhabited by three families and was made responsible for the care of the bulls. He was to take them out to the fields and bring them in again.[111]

[102] S. A. Chernik, *Sovetskaia shkola v gody Velikoi Otechestvennoi Voiny*, Moscow, 1975, p. 98.
[103] Ibid., p. 97. The curriculum was not centrally determined. Local officials decided what was to be taught to fit local needs.
[104] Ibid., p. 103.
[105] Likhomanov, p. 84.
[106] Chernik, p. 99.
[107] *Vse dlia fronta!*, p. 210.
[108] Chernik, p. 107.
[109] Interview of August 19, 1986.
[110] Columbia Broadcasting System Monitoring Reports, August 20, 1941.
[111] Interview of November 18, 1987. One day he and another child were caught in a violent tornado and could not tell where they were: "We were very frightened. We were frightened and cold. The bulls had become used to me and so I could get close to them and I warmed myself with their body warmth. I can still remember the feeling."

Increasing labor-intensive production in agriculture

The attempt to replace the labor of farmers taken into the Red Army not only meant increased participation by other groups, but also that everybody worked more. Data from seventeen oblasts in 1944 showed that the work load was anywhere from 40 to 75 percent higher per worker than it had been in 1940. Agricultural work also became more labor intensive. In 1940, the MTS had accomplished 82 percent of the plowing and 50 percent of the sowing and harvesting, but by 1943, 47 percent of the plowing, 70 percent of the sowing, and 80 percent of the harvesting were done by the farmers. The increase in the labor intensiveness of production was especially great in the growing of potatoes and vegetables and in livestock breeding, where the amount of work per farmer increased 40 to 50 percent over the prewar figure.[112]

The participation rate in agricultural work on collective farms by men and women, which was already 97.9 percent and 95.5 percent, respectively, in 1939, was even higher during the war.[113] A minimum labor-day obligation had been introduced in 1939 to reduce the amount of time farmers spent working on their private plots.[114] Outside of the cotton-growing regions, adults on collective farms were obliged to work at least 60 or 80 labor days, depending on the region of the country.

Soon after the war began, the minimums were raised by half or more and new ones were established for adolescents. In February 1942, the minimum obligation was raised to 120 days in the major agricultural regions and 100 labor days in the remaining areas,[115] and local authorities could increase or decrease the number of labor days by up to 20 percent.[116] A minimum of 50 workdays was instituted for children between the ages of 12 and 16 living on collective farms.[117] The number of labor days per able-bodied farmer went from 187 days in 1940 to 238 in 1942,[118] but most of the growth took place among

His voice broke at this point, his eyes glazed over with tears, and he got up and began to pace back and forth.

[112] *Bol'shevik*, No. 5, 1945, U.S. Embassy at Moscow, Economic Information, No. 221, May 1945.

[113] I. Merinov, "Trudovye resursy kolkhozov i ikh ispol'zovanie," *Sotsialisticheskoe sel'skoe khoziaistvo*, March 1941, No. 3, p. 16.

[114] Volin, "German Invasion," p. 84.

[115] Arutiunian, *Sovetskoe krest'ianstvo*, pp. 76–7.

[116] *The New York Times*, April 18, 1942, p. 6.

[117] Chadaev, p. 339.

[118] *Istoriia*, Vol. 2, p. 524. This figure is apparently a weighted average of the work done by able-bodied men, able-bodied women, the aged, and adolescents. The figures

women and adolescents. The number of labor days worked by women increased by 31 percent from 1940 to 1944 (193 labor days to 252); among youths the increase was 39 percent for the same period (74 to 103).[119] In the unoccupied areas, the total number of labor days in 1942 was 2.5 percent higher than in 1941, in spite of the massive decline in the work force,[120] and in the collective farms of Siberia in 1942 the number was the same as in 1940, despite the fact that the Siberian kolkhoz labor force had decreased by 40 percent.[121]

Along with the increased work minimums went veiled threats, such as that uttered in April 1942 by President Kalinin, who said, "This is no time when we can afford the luxury of laziness or lack of discipline. Under the skin of the lazy man may hide an enemy of collectivization."[122] Those who did not meet the minimum work requirement were punished and a small percentage (0.6 percent) of the violators were even expelled from the collective farms.[123]

Training machine operators

Drafting the bulk of the machine operators may well have served the national military effort, but it stripped the countryside bare of many of its most skilled personnel, a situation made worse as the most-experienced tractor drivers who remained were trained to be mechanics and leaders of tractor brigades.[124] As a result, the Soviets were forced to undertake a mass training program of machine operators for groups who during peacetime had performed much less demanding tasks.

During the first two months of the war, the MTS trained some 198,000 tractor drivers and 48,000 combine operators, 175,000 of whom were women.[125] The rush was on. In 1944, 282,000 tractor

are consistent with Volin's prewar data. He said that in the Ukraine and Belorussia, the number of labor days worked in 1937 was 188 and 204, respectively. See "The 'New Agrarian Order' in Nazi-Invaded Russia," *Foreign Agriculture*, Vol. 7, No. 4, April 1943, p. 78.

[119] Arutiunian, *Sovetskoe krest'ianstvo*, p. 84.
[120] *Istoriia*, Vol. 2, p. 524.
[121] Aniskov, p. 194.
[122] *The New York Times*, April 10, 1942, p. 10.
[123] Arutiunian, *Sovetskoe krest'ianstvo*, p. 83. In areas where the minimum requirement was 100 labor days, 3.9 percent of the inhabitants did not fulfill the requirement and 15.2 percent of them were expelled from the kolkhoz. In the areas where the requirement was 120 days, 12.2 percent of the inhabitants did not satisfy the obligation and 5 percent of them were expelled from their village.
[124] *Istoriia*, Vol. 3, p. 182.
[125] *Istoriia*, Vol. 2, p. 164.

drivers and 53,000 combine operators were trained in MTS courses and in the regular agricultural schools. As a result of all this training, the number of machine operators increased from 391,000 on July 1, 1943, to 600,000 on July 1, 1944.[126] Although the effort to train people was great, the outcome was less than satisfactory.

There were MTS training programs for women and young men ineligible for the draft, and there were schools for mechanics and agricultural schools. The training period was shortened from the usual four to five months for tractor drivers to twenty-five days and from five to six months for combine operators to thirty-five days. There were full-time and part-time courses and students went to school twelve hours a day.[127] In the desperate days of 1941, the training period might be even shorter. In the Sverdlovsk oblast, on July 2, the party and MTS leadership were given responsibility for identifying which women and young males had previously taken machine operator courses and these people were to be given ten days retraining and then used as tractor drivers and combine operators.[128] The short courses were also the training staple on the state farms. It was not until 1944 that the training of machine operators was resumed in the regular schools.[129]

The pressure to get drivers into machines rapidly meant they were inadequately trained, accounting for a large part of the decline in productivity. Students often did not receive proper educational materials and many students never received the opportunity to drive a tractor during their training. As a result, they spent the first days of spring planting getting de facto on-the-job training and in the process did not get the job done, wasted precious fuel, and damaged machinery.[130] So many of the new machine operators were inexperienced and were often so unskilled that they left as much as seventy-five pounds a hectare in the fields,[131] hence the need to send schoolchildren into the fields to reap what machine operators missed. The new operators also did not know how to take care of their machines properly, in part because they did not really know very much about the construction of their machine,[132] which meant that tractors and com-

[126] *Istoriia*, Vol. 4, p. 598.
[127] Arutiunian, *Sovetskoe krest'ianstvo*, pp. 30–1.
[128] *Vse dlia fronta!*, p. 204.
[129] Zelenin, p. 203.
[130] April 9, 1943 resolution, "On the Training of Tractor Drivers, Combine Operators, Mechanics and Brigadiers of Tractor Brigades for the MTS and the State Farms," in *Direktivy*, p. 744.
[131] *Pravda*, August 1, 1942, p. 1.
[132] *Sotsialisticheskoe sel'skoe khoziaistvo*, March–April, Nos. 3–4, 1943, p. 22; *Istoriia*, Vol. 3, p. 183.

bines were out of commission for sustained periods of time.[133] There was a wartime saying, "Tractors were to the field what tanks were to battle" (*traktor v pole – chto tank v boliu*).[134] If soldiers had done their jobs as poorly as the tractor drivers did theirs, the Soviet Union might not have won the war.[135] This kind of inadequate training of machine operators, mechanics, and tractor brigadiers went on for almost two years. On April 9, 1943, a resolution was issued that addressed the problems of educating these groups.

There were other problems in the program to train machine operators. In some instances, there was a serious gap between the orders from Moscow and what was done by local officials. The instructions from the USSR *Sovnarkom* and *Narkomzem* were that all tractors were to operate 20 hours a day, which obviously required two drivers a day, but in Azerbaidzhan, contrary to instruction, the number of tractor drivers trained to drive a particular tractor was 2,000 less than the requirement and so there were only enough drivers for one shift.[136] There was also a lot of on-the-job training. New tractor drivers and combine operators were trained right in the field.[137] In addition to the formal courses of study, industrial workers received on-the-job training in how to drive a tractor or a combine. In 1942, over 50,000 tractor drivers and 5,000 combine operators were trained in this way.[138]

Yet the real problem was not the shortage of trained drivers, but rather the shortage of equipment. A large number of tractor drivers and combine operators were being trained each year of the war, despite the fact that there were virtually no tractors being produced and the dearth of machines did not begin to decrease until 1945. In 1940, 18,100 new tractors were delivered to the MTS. In 1941, however, the number fell to 6,300, in 1942 new deliveries numbered a mere 400 and in 1943 only 500. The production of combines, threshing machines, and other automatic machinery was absolutely nonexistent during the war.[139]

Consequently, it appears that too many tractor drivers were trained. Table 4.2 shows the official figures for the number of tractor drivers and combine operators who were trained during the war and the

---

[133] It did not help that repair facilities were themselves in terrible condition, often without roofed buildings in which to do the work. Ibid.

[134] *Istoriia*, Vol. 3, p. 184.

[135] The February 1944 band-aid tactic creating medals designating one as "Best Tractor Driver" or "Best Combine Operator of the State Farm" or "Excellent MTS Mechanic" could not overcome the built-in limitations. *Istoriia*, Vol. 4, p. 600.

[136] Likhomanov, pp. 87–8.

[137] *Istoriia*, Vol. 2, p. 524.

[138] Likhomanov, p. 89.

[139] Arutiunian, *Sovetskoe khoziaistvo*, p. 132.

Table 4.2. *The number of machine operators trained and the number of machines in operation (1940 to 1945)*

	Tractor drivers trained	Number of tractors	Combine operators trained	Number of combines
1940	285,021		41,600	
1941[a]	438,000	435,253	75,603	153,353
	207,700		48,803	
1942	354,202	259,207	54,200	102,124
1943[b]	276,600		42,000	
1944	233,000		33,000	
1945	230,200	327,271	26,000	125,627
Total (1941–1945)	1,816,823		272,103	
Total (excluding short courses)	1,609,123		223,293	

[a]The data for 1941 include 256,503 machine operators trained in short courses.
[b]The data from 1943 are given only for the rear regions, without the northern Caucasus and the Ukraine.
Sources: Iu. V. Arutiunian, *Sel'skogo khoziaistvo SSSR v 1929–1957gg*, Moscow, 1960, p. 78; T. I. Shilagin, *Narodnoe khoziaistvo SSSR v period Velikoi Otechest-vennoi Voiny*, Moscow, 1960, p. 211.

number of machines present in the MTS during this period. The imbalance is dramatic; six times as many drivers were trained as tractors were produced. Even recognizing that many of the newly trained tractor and combine drivers were males who expected to be drafted, it seems clear that the ratio of drivers to machines *rose* during the war.

The explanation for the increasing gap between the number of machines and the number of drivers lies in the low skill level of the drivers who were trained during the war and the need to work the existing machinery so intensively. The effort to run two tractors for twenty hours a day was achieved by the preparation of large numbers of poorly trained people. If the Soviets did not treat agricultural workers, particularly women, as a free good, they certainly implicitly assigned them a low value. This was not done because of the massive number of able-bodied men who went to the front, but precisely because it was the only way the government believed that it could cope with this enormous shortfall.

Labor productivity

During the war more people worked harder, the sown acreage in the collective farms of the unoccupied areas increased, and the total number of labor days worked during the war was virtually the same as it had been in the prewar period, despite a 13.8 percent decline in the number of people working the land.[140] Yet productivity declined. Estimates vary as to the degree of the decline. One estimate is that labor productivity during the war fell by 40 percent on collective and state farms.[141] Another Soviet economist suggests that in terms of able-bodied men equivalence, the labor force actually fell not by 13.8 percent, but by 24.4 percent, because of the low productivity of adolescents, old people, and nonable-bodied workers.[142] The average output of a woman was about one-half that of a man, and the productivity of a teenager and senior citizen was 33 to 40 percent that of a man.[143] Certainly this gets at a major factor. The attempt to substitute for the men who went to the front assumed heroic proportions. It was a solution born of necessity and crafted out of the interstices of life in every corner of the country. The effort narrowed, but could not possibly close, the gap between need and capacity.

Conclusion

The war did enormous damage to the food economy of the USSR. It forced the nation to use the resources best suited to agriculture to fight the war and to use what was left over to grow food. The constraints were enormous and the options limited; the central government was unable to produce both for the war and for the agricultural sector. It implicitly expected the food economy to accept second-best and third-best solutions and to find ways of handling their shortages with the use of local resources. It was only out of necessity and resourcefulness at the local level that food production went on.

[140] Relative to 1940, the number of labor days worked in 1941 was 97.7 percent, in 1942 it was 100.7 percent, and in 1943 it was 90.5 percent. Aniskov, p. 195.
[141] Ibid., p. 196.
[142] Cherniavskii, p. 44.
[143] Arutiunian, *Sovetskoe krest'ianstvo*, p. 69.

5   Local food sources

The striking decline in the capacity of the nation to produce food combined with the priority given to winning the war led almost logically to the adoption of a policy in which local production and distribution of food was the centerpiece. There was an intentional shift from the prewar policy of reliance on the central distribution of food to a wartime policy of substantially greater reliance on local food supplies. In view of the emergency brought about by the war and of the commitment to a command model in economic planning, such a policy shift is surprising. One would have expected the Soviet Union to accentuate further the use of its central planning institutions under these conditions. Instead, central planning was rejected when it came to feeding the civilian population. This change in food supply policy was the consequence of the inability of the Soviet Union's central apparatus to fight a war against the Germans, to mobilize armaments centrally, to feed the armed forces from centralized sources, and at the same time to feed the civilian population. They therefore turned to local sources to solve the food problem. The payoff for the state was that it could concentrate its resources on feeding the Red Army and could husband scarce railroad capacity, while keeping the population minimally fed. Only in the case of bread was there complete central responsibility for feeding the population.

The transportation of food was a major aspect of the central government's problem because of the shortage of railroad capacity. The highest priority for the railroad system was to move soldiers and war materiel. The wartime demands on the rail system were immense and it could not meet them. During the summer and fall of 1941, the railroads carried 291 divisions, 94 brigades and 2 million draftees to the front.[1] The inability of the railroad system to function properly

---

[1] *Current Digest of the Soviet Press*, Vol. 38, No. 26, July 30, 1986, p. 9. Originally in *Pravda*, June 30, 1986, p. 7.

in the delivery of food became evident quite early in the war. The commissariat in charge of transportation reported on July 29, 1941, that grain shipments had been carried out unsatisfactorily. The July plan was to ship 26,910 railway cars with food during a 27-day period. Instead, only 20,224 cars were moved.[2] The most extreme expression of the shortage of rail facilities to ship food was present in the July 4, 1941, revised plan. It was decided to reduce the transportation of all foodstuffs, with the exception of grain.[3] The scarcity of food in Vladivostok was attributed to the transportation shortage, as well as the reallocation of civilian supplies to the army.[4] While the railroad was the primary means for transporting food, particularly over long distances, the capacity to bring food to the urban areas was also diminished by the mobilization of horses and trucks for military purposes.[5]

The railroad problems persisted throughout the war. The Soviet rail system absolutely lacked the capacity to transport perishable items such as fresh meat and vegetables. Grain could be transported as could canned food, although these went to the Red Army.[6] Refrigerated railroad cars were extremely scarce even in 1944, and goods such as fish were shipped in special vans (*teplushki*), which were packed with ice.[7] The absence of railroad facilities often led to food wasting away rather than being sent to where it would be consumed. In mid-1944, Ukrainian sugar beets spoiled or were shipped with delays because of the absence of transportation facilities. Nor was it viewed as justifiable to ship sugar beets as fodder because of the high water content and the space they took up in railroad cars.[8] The shortage of rail facilities led to a general lack of imported feed in the unoccupied areas and, as a result, there was a considerable slaughter of livestock.[9]

With grain in short supply, during the war potatoes and vegetables – particularly cabbages – became more important. Indeed, "potatoes were the second bread."[10] Special shipping problems emerged be-

---

[2] I. V. Kovalev, *Transport v Velikoi Otechestvennoi Voine (1941–1945gg.)*, Moscow, 1981.
[3] U. G. Cherniavskii, *Voina i prodovol'stvie*, Moscow, 1964, p. 66.
[4] USSR: Crop Conditions and Production, 1942–1945. Records of the Foreign Agricultural Service. Record Group 166, National Archives, Washington, D.C. (NFAS), U.S. Consulate at Vladivostok, February 12, 1942.
[5] *Foreign Relations of the United States*, Washington, D.C., 1941, Vol. I, p. 636.
[6] U.S. Department of Agriculture Archives – World War II files (DOA), "Russian Food Mission and Purchasing Committee" file, October 22, 1943.
[7] K. S. Karol, *Between Two Worlds*, New York: Henry Holt, 1986, p. 254.
[8] *Pravda*, June 26, 1944, p. 2.
[9] *The Financial Post* (Toronto), May 8, 1943, p. 17.
[10] Ia. E. Chadaev, *Ekonomika SSSR v period Velikoi Otechestvennoi Voiny*, Moscow, 1965, p. 358.

cause it was inefficient to ship potatoes and cabbages by rail, as the cars could only be partially filled.[11] The implications are clear. If potatoes could not be shipped because there was a shortage of rail facilities, it must mean that a number of areas had to substitute local food sources, especially for potatoes and vegetables, which were planted in all available plots of land, especially in the cities. This policy was reasonably successful, but persistent transportation shortages meant there were gluts in some areas and shortages elsewhere. One author claims that urban areas had a surplus of potatoes and vegetables, so much so that in 1944 the supply of these two items was almost 2.5 times the railroad capacity to transport them.[12] On the other hand, in respect to shipping food from the nonurban to urban areas, the author estimates that to do this adequately the railroad system needed 720,000 more cars than were available.[13] Therefore, the development of private gardens and subsidiary farms attached to state enterprises, and ultimately, reliance on private sources was not only justified by the need to make up for food shortfalls, but also to relieve the strain placed on the rail and water transportation systems.

There were three facets to the local food supply, each representing a different degree of government control and responsibility. First, there was food coming from the private plots of the collective farmers, which was sold on the collective farm markets. Second were the subsidiary farms affiliated with state industrial enterprises. Although in formal terms these farms were under the aegis of the state, in fundamental ways, they were strictly under local control. Finally, there was the development of vast numbers of private and collective gardens in urban areas.

In apparent recognition of the severe constraints it faced, a decision to shift the responsibility for feeding the civilian population away from the state was made at an early juncture. On July 19, less than a month after the war had started and the day after rationing was introduced, a front page *Pravda* story enunciated the principle of local autonomy: "Each factory, each city – is its own food base.... Now before the local organization stands the extremely important task: In every possible way to expand local food resources."[14] It is here that the principle of local autonomy was first articulated.

[11] Potatoes used 35 to 85 percent of the capacity of a rail car, whereas fresh cabbages used between 35 and 60 percent. Cherniavskii, pp. 189–90.
[12] Ibid., p. 190.
[13] Ibid., pp. 190–1.
[14] *Pravda*, July 19, 1941, p. 1. Subsidiary farms, the catching of fish in local waters, and organizing the feeding of pigs by local cafeterias (*stolovye*) were all options suggested by *Pravda*.

Table 5.1. *Sources of food supply for the USSR urban population (in percent of total calories)*

Food source	All products			All products, except bread and flour		
	1942	1943	1944	1942	1943	1944
State retail stocks	78.5	73.0	68.0	46.4	40.3	39.8
Subsidiary farms associated with state enterprises	3.4	4.2	4.5	9.3	10.4	9.0
Decentralized procurements	1.0	0.8	0.6	2.8	2.2	1.1
Private plots of the urban population	8.0	9.4	12.4	22.6	24.0	25.3
Collective farm market	9.1	12.6	14.5	18.9	23.1	24.8

Source: U. G. Cherniavskii, *Voina i prodovol'stvie*, Moscow, 1964, p. 186.

This theme became a linchpin of food policy and would be repeated in the public press.[15] If there were ever any doubts about local initiative having to assert itself, they were dispelled by the March 3, 1942, letter to *Pravda* attributed to the workers and employees of the Saratov Lenin Plant. The letter stated that they understood that the state would not be able to supply vegetables and potatoes completely or to provide meat and milk to a significant degree: "In wartime it is impossible to receive everything from central stocks."[16] Earlier, at the end of September 1941, a radio broadcast directed at farmers about preparing for the winter included the following with regard to the care and feeding of cattle: "A special feature of the current year is the fact that collective farmers do not wait for assistance from outside [the village] but act on their own initiative to obtain all essentials locally."[17] Local areas were also encouraged to develop their own seed stocks and not to depend on central supplies.[18] The campaign to shift part of the burden for feeding the population was underway.

The decreasing dependence of the urban population on state supplied food is evident from Table 5.1. The only food that state supplies guaranteed through the ration system was bread. It should be noted that the data are given in caloric terms, which tend to exaggerate the

[15] See, for example, *Pravda*, March 3, 1942, p. 3. The words were almost the same in this article. Indeed, the article title was "Each Enterprise Is Its Own Food Base."
[16] *Pravda*, March 3, 1942, p. 3.
[17] Columbia Broadcasting System Monitoring Reports (CBS), September 26, 1941.
[18] "Zadachi oveshchevodstva v vostochnykh raionakh soiuza," *Sotsialisticheskoe sel'skoe khoziaistvo*, January 1942, p. 18.

role of the state because of the proportion of food consumption that was associated with bread. If we were able to count vitamins, it would likely give a different picture. In any case, the data show that the proportion of the caloric intake of the population provided by state retail sources fell from slightly more than three-fourths in 1942, to about two-thirds of the caloric intake in 1944. Unfortunately, there is no comparable figure for the prewar period to serve as a benchmark.

We turn now to an examination of the three ways in which the nation used local forms of production to compensate for the diminished role of state-supplied food.

Private plots in the countryside

The peasants' private plots served three purposes. First, they fed the peasantry itself. Second, food was sold to the nonagricultural population on the collective farm market. Third, the peasants provided food to the massive numbers of people who were being evacuated or were evacuating themselves, particularly during the first months after the invasion.

The private plot was not new. Created in 1934 as a concession to the peasantry in the wake of the bitter response to collectivization, the private plot had already become an important source of food for the population and income for the peasant. In the years just before the war, private plot agriculture had been under attack. In 1938 and 1939, a minicrusade was carried out against private farming, explicitly restricting the size of the plot and the size of the livestock herd and implicitly limiting the amount of time spent on the private plot by introducing a compulsory minimum number of days that had to be worked in the socialist sector.[19] The role of the private plot became more important during the war, however, when each collective farm was asked to deliver even more food to feed the army, a subject we explore in the next chapter.

In the chaotic period of 1941 after the war began, local sales by peasants were particularly important to the large number of people from the western regions of the USSR who were either evacuated by the state or evacuated themselves, especially in view of the inadequacy of the system of evacuation points along the evacuation routes.

The private plot primarily served two purposes. The first was as a

[19] Lazar Volin, *A Survey of Soviet Russian Agriculture*, Washington, D.C., 1951, p. 82; Volin, "German Invasion and Russian Agriculture," *Russian Review*, November 1943, p. 82.

Table 5.2. *Average daily payment of grain and potatoes to collective farmers (in grams)*

	1940	1943	1945
Grain	550	180	190
Potatoes	330	110	70

Source: Iu. V. Arutiunian, *Sovetskoe krest'ianstvo v gody Velikoi Otechestvennoi Voiny*, Moscow, 1963, p. 335.

major source of food for the peasantry. Prior to the war, 90 percent of the grains and 30 percent of the potatoes the peasants ate had come from the socialist sector of agriculture. During the war the dramatic decline in food availability fell heavily upon the peasantry. As can be seen in Table 5.2, in 1943, grain and potato consumption by collective farmers was about one-third of the prewar figure and overall the situation was even worse in 1945, amounting to a "glassful of grain and one potato" a day.[20] Beyond that there was little in the way of food available to peasants from the socialist sector. Even in 1945, which was not the worst year for the peasantry, the combination of cash income and inkind payments of grain and potatoes met only half the collective farmers' total food needs.[21] The peasant food supply declined as the state squeezed out more for the army and industrial workers. Therefore, the private plot took on great importance and government policy was relaxed to allow private agriculture to flourish.

Second, because the collective farmer could not grow bread grains and did not receive sufficient supplies of them in payment for collective farm work, it was necessary for him to take other foods to the collective farm market to trade for grain. This usually meant exchanging potatoes, vegetables, milk, and meat for bread. In the RSFSR, of production on private plots, approximately 5 to 6 percent of the grains and potatoes, 9 percent of the vegetables, and 10 percent of the milk was taken to the collective farm market for sale. In some republics, such as the Turkmen and Uzbek republics, this figure was even larger, with about 15 to 17 percent of the potatoes going to the collective farm market; in Azerbaidzhan, 23 percent of the milk was sold on the free market.[22]

[20] Iu. V. Arutiunian, *Sovetskoe krest'ianstvo v gody Velikoi Otechestvennoi Voiny*, Moscow, 1963, p. 335.
[21] Ibid., p. 345.
[22] Ibid., p. 347.

Table 5.3. *Deliveries and sales of livestock in 1940 and 1943 (percent of total)*

	Cattle		Pigs		Sheep and Goats	
	1940	1943	1940	1943	1940	1943
Obligatory meat deliveries	62.9	84.1	20.9	30.5	44.2	79.2
Sold to state purchasing agents and cooperatives	19.4	8.2	2.0	4.3	17.1	9.2
Sold to collective farmers	4.8	3.6	39.5	42.9	9.3	2.7
Sold on the collective farm market	12.9	4.1	37.6	22.3	29.4	8.9

Source: Iu. V. Arutiunian, *Sovetskoe krest'ianstvo v gody Velikoi Otechestvennoi Voiny*, Moscow, 1963, p. 203.

Private plots also became important for state farmers during the war. In 1941, 16,400 hectares were planted in kitchen gardens, but by 1945 the area sown had increased by about 50 percent, to 24,600 hectares, about two-thirds of which was used to plant potatoes and the rest for vegetables and groats.[23]

Finally, the collective farm market was an important part of the food supply system to the general population during the war, although the amount of food it offered declined and what was sold differed from the years before the war. How important were these markets? Before the war, in 1940, the collective farm market accounted for 20.2 percent of the retail turnover of all foods[24] and was especially important as a source of meat. As Table 5.3 shows, in 1940, 13 percent of the cattle, 38 percent of the pigs, and 30 percent of the sheep and goats were sold on the free market. By 1943, obligatory deliveries left much less in the hands of the peasantry. As a result, cattle sales on the collective farm market dropped to one-third of their prewar level, the sale of pigs dropped by almost 40 percent, and the sale of sheep and goats dropped to a little less than one-third of 1940 sales.

For other kinds of foods, the collective farm market remained extremely important. Before the war, the urban population had bought one-half of its milk, one-third of its potatoes, vegetables, and meat products, and one-fifth of its flour (excluding baked bread) on the collective farm market. In 1944, when food was still in short supply,

[23] N. E. Zelenin, "Sovkhozy SSSR v gody voiny," in *Sovetskii tyl v Velikoi Otechestvennoi Voine*, Moscow, 1974, pp. 205–6.
[24] *Istoriia*, Vol. 2, p. 553.

the urban population bought 40 percent of its butter and potatoes, 33 percent of its meat products, and 20 percent of its milk and vegetables in the free market.[25] Consequently, although there was a dramatic decline in the absolute availability of food, in relative terms the collective farm market remained an important source of food for urbanites.

Subsidiary farms

The idea of a subsidiary farm (*podsobnyi khoziaistvo*) associated with an industrial enterprise was not a totally new concept. Just prior to the war, there had been some movement in the direction of developing such farms. Indeed, before the war the sown area of subsidiary farms was already 1.4 million hectares. But the war gave impetus to their development. On April 7, 1942, at the beginning of the new crop year, an important joint party and government resolution put forward a number of ways to expand food production, one of which was to give local organs the right to give all empty land in both urban and rural areas to enterprises for growing food and raising livestock to feed the workers from their organizations. Collective farms were not allowed to have unused plots and nonagricultural enterprises were temporarily permitted to use such plots for growing food.[26] In 1943, 3.2 million hectares were sown in these subsidiary farms, about 3 percent of total sown area,[27] and by the end of the war, the area sown was about 5 million hectares.[28]

The industrial commissariats were given the best land. By the end of 1942, they had 25 percent of all the subsidiary farms, including 60 percent that planted potatoes and vegetables and 60 percent of the pigs, more than half of the large horned cattle, and 40 percent of the poultry.[29] Data on the amount of potatoes, vegetables, and melons produced on subsidiary farms in 1944 show substantial differences between the commissariats. Output ranged from 124 kilograms per worker in the Construction Commissariat to 138 kilograms in the Chemical Commissariat to 181 kilograms in the Ferrous Metallurgy Commissariat.[30] It is unclear whether these differences reflected dif-

[25] Cherniavskii, p. 152.
[26] April 7, 1942 resolution, "On the division of the land for subsidiary farms and for gardens of workers and white collar workers," in *Direktivy*, Moscow, 1957, p. 723.
[27] Chadaev, p. 368.
[28] *Istoriia*, Vol. 5, p. 391.
[29] Cherniavskii, p. 134.
[30] Ibid., p. 146.

ferential resource endowment or the priority assigned to the industry in the war effort.

The growth of subsidiary farming in some places was quite staggering. The city of Irkutsk had 45 subsidiary farms in 1941, but 110 in 1942, and in the oblast as a whole, each of the more than 400 enterprises in the oblast had a farm by the time the 1942 spring planting began. The largest farm had a sown area of over 1,000 hectares.[31]

These farms became important – in some areas of the country even decisive – sources of food for the urban population, despite the fact that they were such a relatively small proportion of the total sown area. By the end of the war, the proportion of potatoes and vegetables that came from the subsidiary farms was 38 percent and 59 percent, respectively.[32] In their first year of operation the subsidiary farms under the official auspices of forty-five commissariats produced 360,000 tons of potatoes, 400,000 tons of vegetables, 32,000 tons of meat, 60,000 tons of fish, 108,300 tons of milk, 420 tons of honey, and 3.1 million eggs.[33] From 1942 to 1945, the subsidiary farms increased their potato production 3.7 times, vegetable production 5.4 times, and milk production 2.5 times.[34]

The land for subsidiary farms was placed under the supervision of a newly created organ, the *ors (otdel rabochego snabzheniia)* or Department of Worker Supply.[35] This department was created in February 1942 in the largest enterprises of the defense, coal, chemical, and ferrous metallurgical industries. The fundamental purpose of the *orsy,* who were under the supervisory control of the deputy director of the enterprise, was to administer the rationing system. By the end of the war, 48 percent of those receiving rations obtained them through an *ors.* The number of *orsy* increased and by the end of 1942 there were some 2,000. By January 1945 there were about 7,000 *orsy.* The second

---

[31] *Pravda,* May 21, 1942, p. 3.
[32] *Istoriia,* Vol. 5, Moscow 1963, p. 391. There were even subsidiary farms organized by the military on active duty starting in 1943. By the end of the year there were about 5,000 such subsidiary farms with a total sown area of about 298,000 hectares. At the beginning of the war, the military had about 19,500 hectares. These plots produced 517,700 tons of potatoes and vegetables, more than 2,000 tons of meat, about 6,000 tons of fish, and an unknown amount of milk, eggs, mushrooms, and greens. See *Tyl sovetskikh vooruzhennykh sil v Velikoi Otechestvennoi Voine,* Moscow, 1977, p. 207.
[33] *Istoriia,* Vol. 2, p. 555.
[34] Cherniavskii, p. 137.
[35] Ironically, the land used for these farms, which came from the so-called *Glavuros (glavnye upravlenie rabochego snabzheniia ministerstva),* had been taken away from the enterprises in the 1930s and was returned only after the war started. Cherniavskii, p. 134.

major function of the *orsy* was to increase the food supply above state supplies.[36] To that end they were not only responsible for the development of previously unused land, but they also had 550 state farms transferred to their control. From 1942 to 1945, the output of potatoes grew by 3.7 times, the production of vegetables by 5.4 times, and milk by 2.5 times in the subsidiary farms under the control of the *orsy* in 45 ministries.[37]

There were several variants of subsidiary farms that operated during this period. One variant involved the merger of a number of industrial firms with nearby state farms. In Novosibirsk, over a hundred industrial enterprises created subsidiary farms in 1942. The largest were given seven dairy and vegetable state farms in their vicinity.[38] A second variant involved starting a subsidiary farm and purchasing agricultural equipment by the enterprise to handle the farming. A plant evacuated to Siberia in August 1941 started a subsidiary farm the following spring. It had 300 hectares and it purchased 15 horses, a tractor, and farm implements to work the land, although it is not clear from whom they purchased these inputs.[39] Still a third variant was one in which factory managers contracted on their own with local state and collective farms, for example, to deliver seedlings.[40]

Even the military was provided with land for subsidiary agriculture. In 1942 the navy used 240 hectares in blockaded Sevastopol to grow vegetables. Land was also given to the navy in Leningrad during the war.[41] In 1944, the Red Army harvested about 8.7 million tons of potatoes and vegetables, increased the size of their livestock herds by 71,000 head, and caught about 16.5 million pounds of fish. These subsidiary agricultural operations were partly used to supplement military rations and partly to meet planned rations.[42]

It is overwhelmingly apparent that enterprises were on their own as regards obtaining capital inputs for their agricultural production. Many of the enterprises in Irkutsk had to manufacture all the agricultural tools they needed, using scrap metal and unused machine parts.[43] The Lenin Saratov factory repaired all of its farm equipment.[44]

[36] Cherniavskii, pp. 100–1; *Istoriia*, Vol. 2, p. 554.
[37] Cherniavskii, p. 137.
[38] *Pravda*, May 8, 1942, p. 3.
[39] *Pravda*, April 23, 1942, p. 3.
[40] *Pravda*, April 10, 1942, p. 3.
[41] *Opyt sovetskoi meditsiny v Velikoi Otechestvennoi Voine 1941–1945gg.*, Vol. 33, Moscow, 1955, p. 200.
[42] NFAS, U.S. Embassy at Moscow, Despatch No. 1540, March 8, 1945.
[43] *Pravda*, May 21, 1942, p. 3.
[44] *Pravda*, March 3, 1942, p. 3.

Probably the greatest difficulties were faced by subsidiary enterprises that were developed in regions that were climatically hostile
to agriculture and that had been heavily dependent before the war
on imports from traditional agricultural areas. In the Baku area, for
instance, there was a substantial increase in the number of agricultural
enterprises, in spite of the serious shortage of fresh water. The problem of watering vegetable gardens was solved by the laborious task
of digging wells, virtually all of them at least 150 to 200 meters deep.[45]

Despite these multiple handicaps, their operations were held to a
remarkably high standard as the scapegoat mentality of Stalinist pol-
itics insinuated itself in the food economy of the country. At a conference in January 1943, the acknowledged lower yield per hectare of
subsidiary farms relative to collective farm productivity was described
as "intolerable and disgraceful." Rather than recognizing the lack of
resources on these farms, the conference chose to blame their poor
performance on the people on the farms.[46] The press blamed managers for many problems. One set of complaints was that managers
were not giving enough serious attention to the subsidiary farms.
Others were accused of trying to grab as much land as possible for
their enterprises without being sufficiently concerned with whether
the additional land would be well used.[47] Yet there were also frequent
complaints in the press that factory managers and workers were devoting too much time to subsidiary farms.[48]

Notwithstanding the criticism, the subsidiary farm was regarded
as an appropriate prototype to follow. On October 18, 1942, the Central Committee and USSR Sovnarkom issued a joint resolution entitled
"On Measures for the Further Development of Subsidiary Farms of
Industrial Peoples Commissariats."[49] The upshot of the resolution was
that the industrial commissariats (narkomaty) had done such a splendid
job of creating their own food base for their employees that the leadership wanted them to expand their operations. In the spring of 1942,
the subsidiary farms of twenty-eight industrial commissariats had

[45] NFAS, U.S. Embassy at Moscow, Despatch 209, February 24, 1944.
[46] Daily Report of Foreign Radio Broadcasts, January 13, 1943. This was not a problem
that would go away. Low productivity abided with a large number of subsidiary farms.
For example, in 1944, out of 22,000 hectares planted to potatoes and vegetables in
Moscow, 5,900 of them had never been cultivated as of July 10. NFAS, U.S. Embassy
at Moscow, Despatch No. 724, July 26, 1944, from Izvestia, July 19, 1944.
[47] Pravda, April 10, 1942.
[48] DOA, "Russian Food Mission and Purchasing Committee" file. October 22, 1943,
letter from Lester Pearson to Mordecai Ezekiel.
[49] Printed in Direktivy, pp. 734–43.

sown 818,000 hectares, of which 150,000 were devoted to potatoes and 88,000 to vegetables. These farms also raised an unspecified amount of livestock. There must have been serious constraints on the amount of livestock these farms raised because of the feed shortage, and enterprises were told to do better at recycling the garbage from factory cafeterias and the wastes at food enterprises.

The state's expectations of the subsidiary enterprises rose in 1943. It wanted the industrial commissariats to increase sowings to 1,016,300 hectares, and the industrial plants and their farms became responsible for providing all the seeds for potatoes and vegetables. The factory and farm directors were also supposed to supply a minimum of twenty tons of local fertilizer for each hectare that was to be planted, which meant recycling manure, peat, and urban garbage. An ambitious livestock plan was also established. As of January 1944, the subsidiary farms were supposed to have 610,600 pigs, 311,100 large horned cattle, 857,000 poultry, and 101,400 beehives.

An incentive system was introduced, modest as it was, for people to raise livestock for the subsidiary farm. A contract system was developed whereby if manual and white-collar workers would sell young animals to the subsidiary farms, they would receive not only the state procurement price, which was low, but also the monetary equivalent of from five to ten centners of fodder, depending on the quality of the animal. Presumably, this would enable workers to feed animals they were raising for themselves. In fact, at the end of 1943, there were reportedly 400,000 head of cattle, 500,000 pigs, and 400,000 sheep and goats on the subsidiary farms. Thirty industrial commissariats planted 1,328,500 hectares in 1943.[50]

The output from the subsidiary farms was distributed in the following way: the state organization (be it an industrial enterprise or an educational institution) was entitled to 50 percent of the meat, grain, and fish; 100 percent of all other products, such as potatoes; and all dairy and poultry products above the ration card allowances. It could then distribute this surplus to the workers.[51]

The subsidiary farms were a hybrid of private and public involvement in operating locally within the framework of a state organization to supplement worker diets. The final form of local food production, private gardening, operated outside of an institutional format, but also involved a mix of public support for private effort.

[50] Arutiunian, p. 171.
[51] Cherniavskii, p. 133.

Individual and collective gardening

The war made farmers out of urbanites who had either never had to grow their own food or who had left such practices behind in their former lives as rural peasants. The Soviet Union was not the only country where private gardening took place during the war. There were Victory Gardens in the United States and allotment gardens in Great Britain. In the Soviet Union, however, what urbanites grew on their own little plot of land was often the difference between having very little to eat and having an adequate amount.

Private gardening by Soviet urbanites did not begin with the war, but the war stimulated its extraordinary expansion.[52] On March 1, 1942, President Kalinin said:

> It is necessary to speak about the planting of potatoes and vegetables. It is unnecessary to prove the importance of the potato in the national diet. This year the significance of the potato will be even greater. To the sown area of the state plan, it is necessary to significantly increase individual plantings of potatoes. Workers in settlements, railroad workers at stations, rest homes, sick people, . . . should add an additional amount of products to their own diets from their own gardens. It is necessary to propagandize widely and in every possible way to encourage workers, especially those in small cities, to develop collective and individual gardens.[53]

Two days later, a party resolution called for the mass development of vegetable gardening among workers and employees under the direction of the All-Union Central Council of Trade Unions and local trade union organs, which were to create vegetable garden commissions under local trade union and party committees. Most dramatically, workers were given the right to receive and work plots for a period of five to seven years and enterprises did not have the right to take the land away from them.[54] A month later the important joint resolution of April 7, 1942, designated for gardening land parcels in

---

[52] In 1940 the gardens of the nonagricultural population accounted for 3.5 percent of all land planted in potatoes and vegetables which, along with melons, accounted for 80 percent of what urbanites planted. Cherniavskii, p. 137.

[53] *Pravda*, March 1, 1942, p. 2. As late as the spring of 1944, the infamous geneticist, T. D. Lysenko, was urging an expansion of potatoes and vegetables in the gardens of workers and employees. See *Pravda*, April 13, 1944, p. 2.

[54] Cherniavskii, p. 139.

and around cities and settlements and land not being used on collective farms.[55]

By the spring of 1943 private urban gardening had emerged as a more systematic part of national policy and in essence the party took an extremely active part in promoting private economic activity. On March 11, 1943, a trade union resolution assigned 100,000 trade union activists to work in the vegetable garden commissions. A committee formed under the central trade union organization was responsible for encouraging cooperation between individual and collective gardening.[56] The city soviets formed agricultural departments to manage livestock breeding and poultry raising, as well as vegetable gardening.[57] They were also responsible for distributing land to the workers.[58]

The party's formalized support for private agriculture in the cities was a strong vote for local autonomy. Moreover, there was both implicit and explicit subsidization of these private endeavors. Trade unions had to distribute garden tools and to ensure that workers had access to vegetable seeds through the republican, oblast, and krai stocks.[59] By the 1944 harvest, the number of trains going to the suburbs of the city was increased to assist the 212,500 citizens of Kuibyshev who had gardens.[60] In 1944, after touring Central Asia and Siberia, U.S. Vice-President Henry Wallace described the private gardens in Komsomolsk, where there were 8,000 acres devoted to gardens. The land must have been marginal, because about 1,200 larch stumps per acre had to be cleared before planting could take place. One thousand of the acres were spaded by hand, but the other 7,000 were plowed by tractors that must have been supplied by the state.[61]

The shortage of food was matched by a shortage of inputs for gardening. The participation of the state, for all its good intentions, was never able to provide the level of inputs needed to make the private gardens as successful as they could have been. As a consequence, local resourcefulness was required to compensate for the shortage of inputs. For instance, in 1942, no mineral fertilizer was available, so gardeners were allotted part of the ashes from their

[55] Direktivy, p. 723.
[56] Cherniavskii, p. 140.
[57] Ibid., pp. 139–40.
[58] DOA, "Russian Food Mission and Purchasing Committee" file, October 22, 1943.
[59] Pravda, March 15, 1943; Istoriia, Vol. 2, p. 555.
[60] Pravda, September 28, 1944, p. 1.
[61] Henry A. Wallace, Soviet Asia Mission, New York: Reynal & Hitchcock, 1946, pp. 94–5.

Table 5.4. *Development of individual and collective gardening among the Soviet nonagricultural population during World War II*

Year	Number of households (millions)	Sown area (thousands of hectares)	Total harvest (thousands of tons)	Yield per garden (kg)
1942	5.0	500	2,000	400
1943	11.8	796	5,492	465
1944	16.5	1,415	9,836	596
1945	18.5	—	1,000 (est.)[62]	—

Source: 1942–1944 – U. G. Cherniavskii, *Voina i prodovol'stvie*, Moscow, 1964, p. 141; 1945 – Ia. E. Chadaev, *Ekonomika SSSR v period Velikoi Otechestvennoi Voiny*, Moscow, 1965, p. 368.

apartment block. By 1943, some mineral fertilizer became available and its distribution was supervised by the trade unions.[63] Basic farm tools like spades, rakes, and hoes were not readily available and were therefore often fabricated from scrap metal in school workshops and in consumer goods enterprises.[64] Seeds constituted the most serious bottleneck for gardeners. One estimate was that twice as much land could have been planted had the seeds been available. In Moscow, the Park of Culture was converted into a nursery and children saved potato eyes and tuber tops to be used as seed.[65] It was in some ways a noble patchwork process to eke out a margin of survival.

As Table 5.4 shows, private gardening soared. The number of gardens more than tripled between 1942 and 1944 and the amount of food taken from each garden increased by 50 percent, from 400 kilograms to 600 kilograms. About 80 percent of the garden output in 1943 was potatoes and the rest was other vegetables.[66] In 1942, almost one-third of all urbanites either had their own garden or participated in a collective garden.[67] A Canadian diplomat described a typical spring Sunday in 1943 in Kuibyshev in this way: "Each Sunday morning during the month of May the streets of Kuibyshev were full of

[62] DOA, "Russian Food Mission and Purchasing Committee" file, October 22, 1943.
[63] U.S. Department of State Decimal File, 1940–1944. Document No. 550.AD 1/1007, *Russia Fights Famine: A Russian War Relief Report*, New York, d.p. probably 1943, p. 10; CBS, March 15, 1943.
[64] *Russia Fights Famine*, p. 10; *Pravda*, March 15, 1943, p. 1.
[65] *Russia Fights Famine*, p. 10.
[66] *Rabotnitsa*, January 1944, no. 1, p. 19.
[67] Cherniavskii, p. 142.

men, women and children carrying spades and other tools and pro-
ceeding to the railway station, the Volga ferry or the streetcar stops
to go out to their allotments."[68] According to U.S. press reports, it
was hoped that output in 1944 would exceed the 1943 level by 25
percent;[69] in fact, actual production increases well exceeded this
target.

From one end of the country to the other, local residents were using
overwhelmingly local resources to meet local food needs. Roughly
one-fourth of potato consumption and one-tenth of vegetable consumption in urban areas came from the output of gardens.[70] In Stalingrad, in the spring after the war began, 95,000 families applied for
land for gardens in 1942, twice the number of a year before.[71] The
increase in applications for land rose in meteoric fashion all over the
country. People coveted a piece of land to grow food. In Siberia, there
was great dependence on the gardens, particularly in the outlying
villages where the gardens were the main source of vitamins.[72]
Emigrés remember their family gardens; one woman described the
importance of her family's garden in Novosibirsk: "We grew potatoes,
cabbages, carrots, and onions. The garden was very helpful for our
family. It fed our family."[73] Another woman's family did not do so
well with their garden: "In the spring [of 1942 in Chernikovsk] my
mother tried to grow a garden. But she was completely a city person
and really didn't know how to do this. She tried to grow potatoes in
a garden. She paid people to take care of the garden but they treated
the garden very badly and we received nothing. Also the garden was
far away from the plant; it took my mother an hour to get to the
garden. Finally, in the second summer we had potatoes."[74]

There were, however, substantial differences in the level of involvement in gardening throughout the country. One critical deter-
minant was city size, with larger cities having proportionally fewer
gardens. Moscow provides an excellent example of the inherent limitations on gardening. In 1942, only one-seventh of Moscow's population was engaged in gardening at a time when the average for the
country's urban population was about one-third. In addition, the

---

[68] *Life*, March 27, 1944, p. 72.
[69] The 1945 figure suggests a very small gain in output in spite of a large increase in
the number of gardeners. This apparent anomaly may be due to the fact that the data
are drawn from two different sources and they may be using different methods of
estimating output.
[70] Cherniavskii, p. 138.
[71] *Pravda*, April 10, 1942, p. 3.
[72] Wallace, p. 95.
[73] Interview of September 23, 1986.
[74] Interview of June 18, 1988.

average size per garden plot in Moscow was about 170 square meters or about one-third less than the average for the country as a whole. As a consequence the per capita output of potatoes and vegetables in Moscow was about eleven kilograms against a national figure of forty-five kilograms.[75] Muscovites had not gardened much before the war and their relative inability to garden during the war was surely determined in part by the limited free space of a crowded, major industrial city. Moscow was also an example of a city that could not totally depend on its own resources, as planners wanted. Seeds, for example, had to be brought into the city. In the spring of 1942, about 80 tons of seeds were brought in from Gorky for the individual gardens of Muscovites.[76] On the other hand, urbanites in Kemerovo in western Siberia had gardens averaging 1,040 square meters; more than half the population had a garden. As a result, the average Kemerovo citizen had 194 kilograms of potatoes and vegetables. It was not for lack of effort that Muscovites were unable to benefit substantially from the gardening movement. In 1943, 300,000 or 40 percent of them were involved in gardening, almost triple the number involved in 1942 and about the same proportion as the country as a whole. Per capita production remained substantially lower than the rest of the country, however: 38 kilograms as against the average of 64 kilograms for the rest of the country.[77]

There was a direct correlation between the proportion of the urban population participating in gardening and the per capita consumption of potatoes; in those areas where per capita consumption of potatoes was lower than the average for the USSR, we find uniformly that there was a lower level of participation of the urban population in gardening. Although it is hard to separate cause and effect, it is likely that people participated in gardening when it was easier to grow potatoes and not likely that a high level of participation led to a high level of potato production.[78]

There were a variety of ways in which people were encouraged to garden. The popular women's magazine *Rabotnitsa* on more than one occasion published gardening instructions in a very detailed form. In mid–1943, for example, the magazine published step-by-step instructions for urbanites on how to take care of potatoes they had planted:

---

[75] *Life*, March 27, 1944, p. 72.
[76] *Pravda*, June 4, 1942, p. 4.
[77] Cherniavskii, p. 147; *Pravda*, March 15, 1943, p. 1.
[78] Cherniavskii, p. 148.

The care of potatoes requires the complete destruction of weeds and the maintenance of the soil in a loose and moist state. The first loosening is done after the shoots reach a height of 8–10 centimeters. The loosening of the rows and interrow cultivation and weeding is done 3–4 times, until the crust forms and weeds appear.

The first hilling is started when the tops reach 15–16 centimeters. During the summer potatoes are hilled 2–3 times. It is advisable to do the first hilling before the flowering.

On poorly fertilized land, where the planting is relatively slow, it is necessary to fertilize potatoes. In this case for each part of manure you need 4–5 parts of water. Each 1–2 groups of potatoes should receive a kilogram of the solution. The first time fertilization of the plants is done is after the appearance of shoots and the second in 3–4 weeks after the first fertilization.[79]

Whether it was through necessity or instruction, the urban population quickly learned that it was in their interest to do as much as possible for themselves. To a large degree they depended on themselves to provide dietary staples.

Conclusion

The war made clear a number of things about the Soviet system. First, it was incapable of fighting several battles simultaneously. It could not fight the Germans at the same time that it fought the food supply issue. After coming to that conclusion, however, the response was swift. The regime quickly decided that local forces would have to assume responsibility for what had been the province of the state since the 1930s. For the time being, it was every locality for itself. The subsidiary farms under the state enterprises, the victory gardens of urbanites and state farmers, and the private plots throughout the country were all different forms of the same strategy, namely, to oblige the civilian population to rely upon itself. It was a logical policy. In 1941, the population was barely a decade distant from the days of the New Economic Policy, when privatization of agriculture was the rule.

The appropriation of major food areas by the Germans was the major cause of the food shortage. Nevertheless, it is equally true that

[79] *Rabotnitsa,* June–July 1943, Nos. 6–7, p. 16. Other instructional pieces appeared in *Rabotnitsa.* An article in the June–July 1944 issue talked about weeding, how and when to apply mineral fertilizer, how to take care of the garden during the summer, etc.

Soviet central planning system, once it decided that winning the war came before all else, simply did not have the apparatus or the capacity to feed its civilian population. Without local initiative, there would not have been as many survivors.

6 The first priority: feeding the armed forces

With food in short supply, choices had to be made about how to distribute it. Wartime created the necessity in the USSR, as it did in other belligerent nations, for government control of scarce resources, especially food. During the war the armed forces and especially the Red Army, on whom the survival of the nation depended, were the most important groups to feed. There was a disastrous period at the beginning of the war marked by retreat and defeat when the food supply for elements of the military was totally inadequate. But the problems did not fully disappear even after the period of confused retreat ended toward the end of 1941. An analysis of the food situation for the armed forces provides insight into the irreducible problems of Soviet wartime food supply, because any failures in providing for these groups did not result from low priority. There are really two issues. The first is the general adequacy of food supplies. That is, was there enough food to feed the military? The second question has to do with the efficiency with which food was distributed to troops. The evidence is that the organizational difficulties were very serious at the beginning of the war and, as will be seen later, remained so through Stalingrad and beyond.

The military was responsible for feeding large numbers of people, even in 1941, and the number of individuals in the armed forces grew dramatically once the war began. There were about 4.2 million members of the armed forces at the start of the war and by 1942 this number had grown to 10.9 million. The military grew in strength to 11.2 million in 1944 and 11.6 million in 1945.[1] Each increase in the armed forces

[1] I am using the numbers of the total armed forces supplied by P. V. Sokolov, *Voenno-ekonomicheskie voprosy v kurse politekonomii*, Moscow, 1968, p. 215. George Deborin, *Secrets of the Second World War*, Moscow, 1971, p. 272, said that the number on active

meant a concomitant rise in the pressure on the food supply, which moved from low-priority civilian status to a high-priority military status.

It is the contention of this chapter that the central allocation mechanism was not even able to provide a stable food supply for its top priority, the nation's armed forces, and not just in the chaotic earliest period of the war. As a consequence, even the army had to turn to local sources of food. Ultimately, the diet of Soviet soldiers was a mixture of food produced and distributed by the state, U.S. Lend-Lease food, and food commandeered from local sources, with the latter two sources becoming increasingly important as the war progressed.

Disaster in 1941

The Red Army's retreat on all fronts at the beginning of the war and the confusion associated with that process, so costly in lives and territory, also severely damaged the ability to feed the troops. There were huge losses of cooking equipment, enough to supply 100 artillery divisions, compounded by the absence of reserve equipment.[2] By November, only 30 to 40 percent of the army units were equipped with mobile kitchens and there was a shortage of thermoses, making the goal of providing soldiers with two hot meals a day a pipe dream.[3]

The rapid advance of the Germans was matched by a decline in army food supplies. At the beginning of October there was a supply of at least fifteen days of food for the Red Army defending the road to Moscow. But as the Germans approached and the army retreated, food had to be abandoned. As of November 5, there were twenty-

duty peaked at 6,442,000 on July 1, 1943. U.S. intelligence said there were 10.5 million military support personnel as of March 31, 1943. USSR Crop Conditions and Production, 1942–1945. Records of the Foreign Agricultural Service. Record Group 166, National Archives, Washington, D.C. (NFAS). October 2, 1944, memorandum from Louis Michael to the ambassador. I am not inclined to accept the higher U.S. figure in view of the limited knowledge of troop strength that existed during the war.

[2] These losses included damage to 7,740 mobile kitchens, the loss of almost 400 stoves, and 3,700 twelve-liter thermoses. *Tyl sovetskikh vooruzhennykh sil v Velikoi Otechestvennoi Voine (Tyl)*, Moscow, 1977, pp. 190, 192.

[3] *Tyl*, p. 194. Quite independent of the issue of equipment loss was the problem of the suitability of the equipment for functioning in the field. The mobile kitchens had to be redesigned so that they would serve 300 people, instead of 180 as before, in order that the number of kitchens could be reduced by 30 to 40 percent. Battlefield conditions also showed that the stoves that baked bread were far too heavy and had to be replaced with more mobile units. Equipment that could better adapt to local bakeries was also used.

three days' rations of cereals, fifteen days of sugar, twelve days of salt and tobacco, ten days of flour and bread, eight days of fats, and three and one-half days of meat and fish. For some units, the situation was even worse. The 5th Army had only four days worth of flour, three days of cereal grains, four days of sugar, and a day's worth of salt.[4] The 10th Reserve Army of about 100,000 men reported shortages of food, clothing, and weaponry in both October and November.[5]

One of the main problems during the summer and fall of 1941 was the serious lack of cohesive organization in supplying food to combat troops. There was no central machinery in the early months to co-ordinate food supplies and several food agencies were involved. So much attention was paid to evacuating food to the rear that the bureaucracy failed to get adequate provisions to the front. Food needed to feed the soldiers was being evacuated from Moscow to the rear, and then some had to be shipped back to the west. Stocks were available from commercial sources, state reserves, central food warehouses of the Food Supply Administration (*Uprodsnab*) of the Soviet Army, and the Moscow military district. All these agencies had food at their disposal, but there was so much disorganization that they could not get the process coordinated.[6] As a consequence, the supply of food to the military warehouses and ultimately to the front was extremely uneven.[7]

The troops at the front suffered greatly. A particularly grisly example was the encirclement in October of troops in the bogs of the Vyazma region on the main road from Smolensk to Moscow. A German radio description in late October emphasized the hunger of the Soviet troops. "One cannot imagine how army could continue in these bogs. . . . At first few prisoners. Circle became smaller, prisoners began increase. . . . Shots. . . . Equipment found everywhere . . . then began surrender by thousands, human wrecks, expecting to be shot, emaciated with hunger, wild-eyed. Accounts of suffering unimaginable, after first days nothing to eat, ate dead horses. Worst was planes constantly above them. Still duck when hear planes . . . wounded left to die. In woods, find gnawed bones of horses."[8] In the bloody battle

---

[4] Ibid., p. 193.
[5] Mark Harrison, *Soviet Planning in Peace and War 1938–1945*, Cambridge: Cambridge University Press, 1985, p. 91.
[6] *Tyl*, p. 192.
[7] *Tyl*, p. 189.
[8] Columbia Broadcasting System Monitoring Reports (CBS), October 23, 1941. A radio report from Manchukuo a week later quoted a deserting Russian officer as saying that, "Soviet forces are suffering from extreme shortages of food and winter clothing." CBS Monitoring Reports, October 30, 1941.

for Kalinin, guarding the northwesterly approach to Moscow, the 235th Infantry Regiment, which had a 50 percent casualty rate, had no hot food for twelve days and they were eating only 200 grams of bread a day.[9]

Even behind the battle lines it is not at all clear that the soldiers were regularly supplied with adequate food. A man who served during the Moscow campaign as a lieutenant in an army unit where he was one of 300 officers remembers there was only enough food in the warehouse to feed 100 of them. The other 200 officers were given ration cards and therefore had to get their food like ordinary civilians.[10]

Feeding the military

As always, the regime turned to the peasantry to meet the needs of the expanded Red Army and make up for the lost food. A great sense of urgency about the need to deliver food to the armed forces was almost immediately established. The campaign to extract food from the peasantry took on many forms, but there could be no mistaking what the leadership expected. A *Pravda* article of November 5, 1941, called for more meat and butter for the Red Army.[11] Later that month *Pravda* announced enthusiastically: "Collective farmers live now with one thought, with one aspiration – to give to the front as much food as it can."[12]

Obligatory deliveries during the war years took a higher percentage of grain output than they did before the war. In 1940, 18.5 percent of collective farm grain production was subject to obligatory delivery; that figure kept rising and reached 21.7 percent in 1943. A substantial part of this additional burden was the result of a July 11, 1942, decree that obliged collective farms to deliver 2.4 million tons of grain for the Red Army above the original compulsory delivery quota.[13] All of

[9] Ibid., November 13, 1941.
[10] Interview of October 28, 1986.
[11] *Pravda*, November 5, 1941, p. 3. Because the evidence is so overwhelming that the first months of the war brought serious food shortages for the army, it is impossible to accept as typical *Life* photographer Margaret Bourke-White's October report of soldiers in Moscow eating "their huge meals of cabbage soup, meat, potatoes, cucumbers, milk and stewed cherries." *Life*, October 27, 1941, p. 28. I am inclined to believe that the dining hall was Potemkinized for a prominent visiting U.S. journalist.
[12] *Pravda*, November 23, 1941, p. 2.
[13] Lazar Volin, "German Invasion and Russian Agriculture," *Russian Review*, Vol. 3–4, November 1943, p. 80. Originally, the order was only supposed to apply to the 1942 crop, but collections under the aegis of this fund went on until at least the early postwar period. Naum Jasny, *The Socialized Agriculture of the USSR*, Stanford: Stanford University Press, 1949, p. 374.

this came out of a diminished total agricultural output. And in 1942, the rhythm of the harvest was changed to accommodate the sense of urgency. Grain was taken every day to the procurement points. Every collective and state farm had to meet a five-day quota.[14] Sometimes the pressure on farmers to give included thinly veiled threats. A radio broadcast from Khabarovsk in the spring of 1943 chastised several Amur districts for falling behind with the spring sowing: "[A]n indifferent attitude towards spring sowing inevitably results in a poor harvest. In turn it acts as a brake on the Red Army's fighting effort and is equivalent to treason."[15]

On top of the increased obligatory deliveries, the state extracted amounts of produce from the peasants through special funds to which the collective farms "donated" crops. The first was the Defense Fund, created in the fall of 1941. Collective farmers were asked to donate a certain portion of field crops and livestock for the army. Only 0.2 percent of grain output went to the Defense Fund and it never got above 0.4 percent.[16] The November 16, 1941, issue of *Pravda* reported on a collective farm meeting in Khabarovsk at which one of the twenty farmers who spoke proclaimed that, "We should let Comrade Stalin know that the Far Eastern collectives do not complain, in order to completely destroy the German bandits. I will personally give to the Defense Fund six poods of grain, two pigs, 300 rubles and three hens."[17] During the first six months of the war, the Defense Fund collected 21,501 tons of grain, 11,780 tons of poultry and livestock, 10,310 tons of milk and other dairy products, and 5,685 tons of potatoes and other root vegetables.[18] There was also a constant campaign in 1942 for collective farmers to plant part of their land for the Defense Fund.[19]

Other funds were created later, the most important being the Red Army Fund, which operated much like the Defense Fund. The Red Army Fund eventually dominated the campaigns as the war progressed. The crusade in the countryside continued throughout the war. A major theme for the 1944 harvest was that collective farmers

---

[14] *Istoriia Velikoi Otechestvennoi Voiny Sovetskogo Soiuza 1941–1945*, Vol. 2, Moscow, 1961, p. 520. If farmers used their own cows to cart potatoes and vegetables at least two kilometers to market they were rewarded with in-kind payments of food.
[15] *Daily Report of Foreign Radio Broadcasts*, June 4, 1943.
[16] Iu. V. Arutiunian, *Sovetskoe krest'ianstvo v gody Velikoi Otechestvennoi Voiny*, Moscow, 1963, p. 201.
[17] *Pravda*, November 16, 1941, p. 2. A pood equals 36.11 pounds.
[18] *Sotsialisticheskoe sel'skoe khoziaistvo*, January 1942, p. 6.
[19] See, for example, the articles in *Pravda* of May 25, 1942, and June 1, 1942, reporting pledges to plant some 15,000 hectares for the Defense Fund.

all over the country pledged to give grain to the Red Army Fund above and beyond their obligations. On October 12, 1944, the Saratov collective farmers pledged to give 9,000 tons of grain above the planned deliveries to the Red Army Fund by November 1. The collective farmers of the Gorky oblast and Kirov oblast each pledged the same amount by November 5.[20] The collective farmers of the Kalinin oblast pledged 26,000 tons of potatoes and vegetables to the fund by November 10 and the farms of the Vladimir oblast pledged 16,000 tons by November 10.[21] There was also the Fund for the Health of the Defenders of the Motherland, a venue for milk to be donated. This fund provided some 23 million liters of milk as of January 1, 1944.[22]

The funds allowed the state to acquire a larger percentage of collective farm production above the already increased obligatory state delivery quotas. In 1942 the Defense and Red Army Funds together provided an additional 4.5 percent of collective farm grain production, and in 1943 the figure rose to 7.0 percent. The same was true of potatoes. Whereas obligatory deliveries took 17.2 percent of collective farm production in 1939, in 1943 the comparable figure was 24.8 percent. The total amount of kolkhoz potato production delivered and sold to the state went from 23.6 percent in 1939 to 31.5 percent in 1943.[23] Whereas in 1940, the military took 9 percent of gross agricultural output, in 1942, its share was 24 percent.[24] In addition, the favored status of the army invariably allowed it to buy the pick of the wheat, the best horses, and first-quality potatoes and vegetables.[25] It was also a privilege that extended to processed food; virtually all of the canned meats were designated for the armed forces.[26]

The campaign to get the peasantry to contribute more to the war effort relied on various kinds of theatricality to capture attention. The writer Kornei Chukovskii depicted a 1943 collective farm meeting as if it were a religious revival. He described how people lined up and stepped forward one at a time to speak about how much they would

---

[20] *Pravda*, October 13, 1944, p. 1.
[21] *Pravda*, October 26, 1944, p. 2. Similar announcements of pledges can be found in the October 16, 20, 21, and 23 issues of *Pravda*.
[22] *Pravda*, January 14, 1944, p. 1. See also *Pravda*, July 30, 1943, p. 2.
[23] Arutiunian, p. 201.
[24] Harrison, p. 152.
[25] Wallace, p. 114; *Pravda*, August 26, 1942, p. 1.
[26] U.S. Department of Agriculture Archives – World War II files (DOA), "Russian Food Mission and Purchasing Committee" file, October 22, 1943, from Lester B. Pearson to Mordecai Ezekiel. In a factory that produced a canned macaroni and meat dish earmarked exclusively for the front, the broth leftover from the cooking was divided among the workers. If it could be helped, no scrap of food was ever wasted.

give to feed the Red Army,[27] as if they were bearing witness to their faith. Or there would be dramatic gimmickry such as farmers celebrating the liberation of Kharkov by speeding up the delivery of grain and hauling it to storage points in a cortege of red carts.[28] Patriotic holidays were used as rallying points to stir patriotic feelings and get more food sent to the front. In honor of the twenty-fifth anniversary of the Red Army, it was announced that about 50 railroad cars filled with gifts were being sent to the front from the Kuibyshev oblast, including 74 tons of smoked foods; 5 tons of dressed poultry, fat, and butter; 42 tons of confectionery goods and homemade fancy bread; 2,500 kilograms of honey; and 12,500 eggs.[29]

Such announcements of contributions were more than proclamations of deeds done; they were also semicompulsory solicitations. In some places rubles and gifts of jewelry were made to the Red Army Fund. Once there was a 1 million ruble gift in 1943,[30] although this mammoth gift had absolutely no impact on the food supply of the army; its function was to sop up some of the excess inflationary pressure in the countryside. Much more modest was the October 1942 collection of 7,000 rubles from a collective farm in Tbilisi with which tobacco, wine, and fruit were bought for the front.[31] It should be noted that the requests for the Red Army Fund always took place in October after obligatory deliveries had been made.

Foreign sources of food

While moving to extract as much food as possible from domestic agriculture, the Soviet government also sought foreign aid. The main foreign source of food was the United States, through the Lend-Lease program. The program did not have the unqualified support of either political party, however, and aid was extended to the Soviet Union in spite of a great deal of opposition by a large part of Congress and the American people.[32] Because of mutual suspicion

---

[27] Kornei Chukovskii, "Fundament Pobedy," April 16, 1943, in *Ot sovetskogo informbiuro . . . 1941–1945*, Vol. 2, Moscow, 1982.

[28] *Pravda*, August 29, 1943, p. 1.

[29] *Pravda*, February 20, 1943.

[30] *The New York Times*, August 9, 1943, p. 8. One of my émigré sources said that this included requests for contributions of gold.

[31] *Pravda*, October 5, 1942.

[32] See, for example, Raymond H. Dawson, *The Decision to Aid Russia*, Chapel Hill: The University of North Carolina Press, 1959. A Gallup poll showed that only 62 percent of Republicans and 74 percent of Democrats even favored the principles of Lend-Lease. *Life*, February 3, 1941, p. 17. Even after the Soviet Union became a military ally, a great

and by mutual Soviet and U.S. agreement, the Lend-Lease food program was designed to feed the Soviet military exclusively. Measured in this way, one can say that the program played an important but not decisive part in feeding the Soviet armed forces.[33]

Lend-Lease assistance to the Soviet Union began with the signing of the First Protocol on October 1, 1941. It was terminated on September 20, 1945, although food deliveries stopped in May 1945. Over the course of three and one-half years, the United States extended $10.9 billion in aid to the USSR, of which food assistance was $1.7 billion, or about 15 percent of the total.[34] Table 6.1 provides a breakdown of the food sent through the Lend-Lease program from October 1, 1941, through May 1945.[35] Food exports were dominated by grain and flour, with meats and fats and oils ranking next in importance.

Although the list is long, the actual quantities of U.S. food sent to the Soviet military were fairly small. Based on the earlier figure of 6,162,000 tons of grain and flour reserves for the armed forces lasting four to six months, the 901,220 tons of grain and flour that the U.S. exported to the Soviet Union would probably have constituted less than one month's supply for the Red Army.

An estimate of the total amount of food per day provided each Soviet soldier by U.S. Lend-Lease during the war is also small. The 4,468,582 tons were sent over a period of 3.67 years (from October 1941 to May 1945), which is an annual average of 1,217,597 tons or 2,435,194,000 pounds of food. Since the average size of the Soviet

deal of hostility remained in the United States and Canada and to this was added an amorphous fear that food from the United States was being squandered on foreigners. The U.S. propaganda machine continually had to argue first that actually very little food was being sent abroad and second that it was in the United States' interest to make sure that Soviet soldiers were well-fed so that they could capably fight the Nazi enemy.

[33] There was Soviet criticism of Western contributions both during and after the war. In 1944, *Pravda* said that food received from the United States amounted to 3.5 percent of total Soviet food stocks during that year. See *Pravda*, March 1, 1944, p. 1. A slightly different version of the same charge in a relatively recent history book maintains that the average yearly wartime imports of U.S. and Canadian grain amounted to less than 3 percent of the average yearly Soviet grain procurements during that period. See *Istoriia Vtoroi Mirovoi Voiny 1939–1945*, Moscow, 1980, Vol. 11, p. 344. Without defending the limited character of U.S. and Canadian food aid during the war, it must be pointed out that neither of these Soviet critiques is helpful in assessing the level of food assistance inasmuch as food aid was by design aimed at assisting the Soviet armed forces. It is the level of aid to the Soviet military that is the proper measure of Western largesse.

[34] DOA, December 7, 1945, memo from Robert M. Cavanaugh to Clinton Anderson.

[35] The program was formally terminated in September, 1945, Soviet food needs notwithstanding.

Table 6.1. *Lend-Lease food exports to the Soviet Union (in short tons)*

Wheat, flour, and other grains and cereals	901,220
Dried peas and beans	270,514
Seeds	37,477
Sugar	703,079
Canned meat and meat products	822,510
Smoked and prepared meats	319,341
Animal fats and oils	446,433
Vegetable oils	520,800
Canned milk	31,021
Dried milk	77,352
Dried eggs	121,144
Cheese	35,021
Soya flour	51,873
Soya grits	19,202
Fruits and vegetable pastes and purees	10,024
Concentrated juices	1,799
Dried fruits	2,340
Dried and dehydrated vegetables	15,687
Dried soups	9,485
Concentrated cereals	9,738
Canned fruits	369
Canned vegetables	1,938
Fresh fruit	183
Fresh vegetables	2,505
Vitamins	1,432
Yeast	1,155
Tea	1,217
Coffee	10,581
Salt	2,181
Spices	655
Flavoring extracts	171
Hazelnuts from Turkey	3,638
Other nuts	58
Other foodstuffs	2,799
Feed	33,631
Other miscellaneous agricultural products	9
Total	4,468,582

Source: Department of State, *Report on War Aid Furnished by the United States to the U.S.S.R.*, 1945, pp. 21–2.

armed forces was roughly 11 million a year during the war,[36] this means that each man received about 221 pounds of food a year or just under 10 ounces of food a day of U.S. Lend-Lease food. On the other hand, the meat and oils were a real addition to the diets of those who received them.

Canada and Great Britain also provided food assistance to the Soviet Union, although in amounts that paled even before the limited U.S. effort. From June 22, 1941, through April 30, 1944, British food deliveries amounted to 138,200 tons, about 3 percent of the U.S. level. Canadian food deliveries went to the Soviet Union under the auspices of Great Britain until July 1, 1943.[37] Canada did not have diplomatic relations with the USSR at the start of the war and this accounted for using the British as a third party.

Centralized food supply and its limits

The supply of food at the disposal of the military was never large compared to the mouths it had to feed even before the war. The slightly more than six million tons of grains and flour that existed on the eve of the war were perhaps as little as half of what it might have been had it not been for the decline of production resulting from collectivization.[38] All of these grain stocks were reserved for the army, according to Stalin himself. In January 1942 he told General D. V. Pavlov, the head of *Glavprodsnab*, that food from state reserves should only be for the troops, although Pavlov was ordered to use these reserves only in exceptional circumstances and when all other possibilities had been exhausted.[39]

In fact, the food supply situation was so strained at the beginning of the war that military efforts had to be directed toward building up food stocks that were considerably smaller than the four to six months of reserves said to exist on the eve of the war. In September 1941 the goal was to have fifteen days worth of rations on all fronts except the northern food deficit areas, where the norm was twenty days for

[36] Sokolov, p. 215. During 1942, 1944, and 1945, the armed forces numbered 10.9, 11.2, and 11.6 million, respectively.

[37] Arnold Rothstein, *Soviet Foreign Policy During the Patriotic War*, Vol. II, London: Hutchinson, n.d., p. 86.

[38] In a recent article, Holland Hunter argues that without collectivization grain reserves would have been 13.7 million tons at the end of 1940 or slightly more than twice the actual level as of that date. See "Soviet Agriculture With and Without Collectivization, 1928–1940," *Slavic Review*, Summer 1988, p. 213.

[39] *Tyl*, p. 197.

the Leningrad front and twenty days for the Karelian front. Once the harvest was in, the norms were amended in October and all fronts were to have at least twenty days of food. By 1943 when the government had a better grip on the food supply, the norm was raised so that all fronts were to have thirty days of food, with the exception of northerly Karelia, for which the goal was a forty-day reserve.[40] A month's reserves is still minimal. Compare this, for example, with the U.S. and Australian goal in early 1943 of trying to build up three-month reserves of nonperishable foods for the 1 million troops in the Southwest Pacific and a year's reserves for 200,000 troops in the South Pacific.[41] It was not until the end of the war that the Soviets were able to achieve the levels of food reserves they sought early in the conflict.

There was also an unrelenting set of distributional difficulties, some the result of organizational problems and some arising from the weakness of the overburdened transportation system. A report by Berlin radio on November 15 purported to cite the diary of a Russian soldier who wrote of a daily diet of crackers and a spoonful of porridge: "Americans will be surprised that a penny should be spent on any army that cannot organize its supplies."[42] The transportation problems were greatest in the first year and a half of the war, but even when the railroads were operating efficiently, as they were said to be in 1943, the pressure on the system to deliver weaponry and troops affected the distribution of food.[43] Eventually the insoluble distribution problem would make it clear that the armed forces, like the civilian population, would have to rely to a much greater degree on local resources.

An example of the unevenness in food distribution can be seen in the wide disparities of specific foods available in the three armies on the southeastern front defending Stalingrad in August 1942 (Table 6.2). The difference in food supplies is dramatic, even when we take into account that the front had been created less than a week earlier to contain Hitler's stepped up drive on Stalingrad. The dietary experience of Soviet soldiers in one army did not necessarily bear any relationship to that of comrades in other armies, even on the same front.

---

[40] Ibid, p. 191.
[41] Paul Hasluck, *Australia in the War of 1939–1945. The Government and the People*, Canberra: Australian War Memorial, 1952, p. 291.
[42] CBS, November 15, 1941.
[43] DOA, "Russian Food Mission and Purchasing Committee" file, October 22, 1943, from Lester B. Pearson to Mordecai Ezekiel.

Table 6.2. *Average number of days of rations per soldier*

	Army		
	64th	57th	51st
Flour, bread, dried bread	2.6	7.6	12
Cereal grains	0.8	6.6	3.7
Sugar	0.5	28.4	0.0
Meat	3.5	9.8	8.1
Fish	0.0	5.8	0.0
Fats	0.0	4.8	59

Source: *Tyl sovetskikh vooruzhennykh sil v Velikoi Otechestvennoi Voine*, Moscow, 1977, p. 199.

Stalingrad

The Battle of Stalingrad lasted from late summer 1942 until the Germans surrendered in February 1943 and reduced to rubble what had once been a living city. It is a heroic metaphor for the determination of the Soviet people to prevail in World War II. The decision to defend Stalingrad was made by Stalin on July 19, 1942, and at that time provisions and livestock were moved to the east bank of the Volga.[44] In the crisis of preparing the defense of the city, however, the matter of assuring adequate food supplies was apparently given a low priority. The battle revealed some of the worst problems faced in trying to feed the Red Army from centralized sources. Therefore, Stalingrad is also a metaphor for hunger in the Red Army.

Not until September 12, 1942, more than a week after the Germans had captured the outer suburbs of Stalingrad and only a month before the German 6th Army drove into the heart of the city, already in a state of annihilation, did the Chief Administration of Food Supplies of the Soviet Army (*Glavprodsnab*) issue a plan for the food supply situation of the troops in the southeast and at the Stalingrad front. *Glavprodsnab* proposed to create a reserve of twenty days of food for the front and a special two-month reserve of meat, and the State Defense Committee approved the plan. The logistical nightmare of getting the food assembled on the left bank and transferred to the right bank on barges and small ships was compounded by constant

[44] John Erickson, *The Road to Stalingrad*, New York: Harper & Row, 1975, p. 363. This brilliant book is an excellent source on the Battle of Stalingrad, especially pp. 362–70, 384–93, and Chapter 10.

German bombing. Then, with the approach of winter when the Volga would freeze, it was decided to set up small supply units with ten days' supply of food on the right bank of the Volga no more than six to eight kilometers from the actual fighting.[45]

The plan to feed Stalingrad did not work at all, something that might have been predicted from the late date at which it was drawn up. Within two weeks the Germans entered the city proper and in a month, despite desperate building by building fighting by the Soviet defenders, they reached the banks of the Volga in the southern half of the city. In the nearly three months of fighting in the rubble that was left of the city, Soviet troops had extremely limited access to food and both they and the civilians faced terrible hunger. Two recent novels convey the full horror. In Vasily Grossman's narrative a group of soldiers have been trapped in a house in Stalingrad and their means of survival is described: "On the way the boy told the officer how they had been in house 6/1 for over two weeks, how they'd lived for some time on a cache of potatoes they'd found in the cellar, how they'd drunk the (foul) water from the central heating system."[46] Valentin Rasputin's antihero, Andrei Guskov, described survival "[i]n Stalingrad, saving himself from starvation with horse meat. . . . Once they had to chop up and boil a dead horse – and they were glad for it, even though they had to drag it away under fire."[47] In the words of one veteran: "Whatever we saw, we ate. There was no regular supply of food. In Stalingrad, I ate horses and dogs."[48] Soldiers and civilians scavenged for any leftover food they could find. Stalingrad was the final proof that central planning and distribution could not be relied upon to feed the Soviet army.

The army turns to local food sources

Even before Stalingrad demonstrated the failure of central policy, a major shift of food procurement policy began to emerge, clearly connected with preparation for the crucial harvest of 1942. In August the army formed procurement groups (*zagotovitelnye gruppy*) responsible for acquiring local food and forage and for processing

---

[45] *Tyl*, pp. 199–200. The plan was to have ten days worth of food on the right bank of the river by October 5 and by October 10 there was to be five to twenty days worth of food reserves in the field warehouses.

[46] Vasily Grossman, *Life and Fate*, New York: Harper & Row, 1986, p. 253.

[47] Valentin Rasputin, *Live and Remember*, New York: Macmillan, 1978, p. 119.

[48] Interview of June 18, 1988.

them in local enterprises. These new organs became the middlemen between the previously existing civilian procurement organs and the army's organs responsible for feeding the soldiers. Furthermore, the army turned directly to local sources for its procurements of food and forage, especially grain, meat, potatoes, vegetables, and hay, using soldiers themselves to collect the food. For the 1942 harvest, each army was assigned an area of up to 30 kilometers behind the front from which it could draw resources to feed itself.[49] Soviet soldiers became expert foragers. As the Red Army began to push out the enemy forces by the end of the year, units were able to take advantage of the fact that farmers had been able to hide a considerable amount of food from the Germans, food that could now be bought or requisitioned for Soviet soldiers. As a result, in the winter of 1942 and 1943, an army moving through a formerly occupied region fulfilled its monthly food needs to the following extent: flour – 54 percent, vegetables – 97 percent, meat – 108 percent, hay – 140 percent, oats – 68 percent.[50] In the second half of 1943, local food sources supplied most of the food of the south and central fronts. This not only relieved the center of responsibility of supplying these areas with food, it also allowed them to concentrate their food on other fronts.[51]

In 1943 and 1944 the turn to local sources of food led to a program to develop a network of subsidiary farms that resembled the practice in the civilian sector. The effort began in 1943 and by the end of the year about 5,000 such farms, with a total sown area of about 298,000 hectares, produced 517,000 tons of potatoes and vegetables, over 2,000 tons of meat, about 6,000 tons of fish, as well as milk, eggs, mushrooms, and greens.[52] In 1944, the role of subsidiary agriculture increased as army farms operated on the Belorussian, Leningrad, Karelian, and Far Eastern fronts, as well as in the South-Ural and Moscow military districts and operated mills in areas formerly occupied by the Germans.[53] Output increased substantially as 867,000 tons of potatoes and vegetables were harvested during the year, livestock herds increased by 71,000 head over 1943, and slightly more than 16.5 million pounds of fish were produced. This output was used to meet regular ration requirements and provide supplementary rations for both officers and soldiers. In some cases the navy also

[49] *Tyl*, pp. 198–9.
[50] Earl F. Ziemke, *Stalingrad to Berlin: The German Defeat in the East*, Washington, D.C.: Office of the Chief of Military History, United States Army, 1968, pp. 147–8.
[51] *Tyl*, p. 206.
[52] Ibid., p. 207.
[53] *Krasnaya zvezda*, February 17, 1945, in NFAS, U.S. Embassy at Moscow, Despatch No. 1540, March 8, 1945.

Table 6.3. *Daily ration norms of the Soviet Army (in grams)*

	Proteins	Fats	Carbohydrates	Calories
Combat units	103	67	587	3,450
Active duty at the rear	84	56	508	2,954
Combat and field units not assigned to the field army	87	48	489	2,822
Guard units and rear installations	80	48	458	2,659
Flying units of the army on active duty	171	125	694	4,712
Hospital patients	91	69	543	3,243

Source: *Tyl sovetskikh vooruzhennykh sil v Velikoi Otechestvennoi Voine,* Moscow, 1977, p. 191.

engaged in subsidiary agriculture, although on a much smaller scale than the army. For instance, in 1942, when Sevastopol was blockaded, the navy used 240 hectares within the city to grow vegetables.[54]

What soldiers ate: the diet of the armed forces

In general, soldiers ate better than civilians, and soldiers at the front ate better than soldiers in the rear. On September 20, 1941, the State Defense Committee established food rations for both the army and the navy, setting the caloric value and ideal daily diet of Soviet soldiers (Table 6.3). By universal standards, the caloric value of the rations were adequate, but not generous, considering the physical demands made on members of the armed services. Actual military rations often fell short of the official rations, however, and there was wide variation in what soldiers ate depending on where they served, their job, their rank, and their own efforts to get food in one way or another.

A doctor who served at the Volkhov front from 1942 to 1943 said that when there was actual combat, the soldiers did not get food regularly and sometimes they would not have food for two days. Food supplies were more regular when there was no fighting and soldiers had rations for three or four days, in most cases dried bread

[54] *Opyt sovetskoi meditsiny v Velikoi Otechestvennoi Voine 1941–1945gg. (Opyt),* Vol. 33, Moscow, 1955, p. 200.

and a piece of sausage. During her two years on the Volkhov front the food situation did not change.[55] In mid–1943, according to U.S. intelligence sources, daily rations in the Red Army were 900 grams of bread plus two hot meals including soup, butter, sugar, and salt. Vodka was a seasonal treat: 400 grams in winter, 200 grams in the spring and nothing in the summer. Soldiers in Moscow division head-quarters received only 600 grams of bread a day, but were also given three daily meals.[56] An officer in training in mid–1943 was fed two meals, a fish soup at 8 A.M. and soup and kasha at 2 P.M., and in the evening he was served tea.[57] Later in the war, a low moisture black bread was baked for soldiers that they could carry around for an extended period of time. Because the bread was so hard, it was the custom to soften it in hot water or tea.

The ration allowances of soldiers improved in the last year and a half of the war. The weight of the daily food ration was increased by 15 percent at the beginning of 1944 and a year later it was increased by another 34 percent.[58] At first, however, the diet of the ordinary soldier remained unvarying. As they moved toward Hungary and Romania, soldiers were given macaroni and noodles to supplement the rather limited choices of finely ground barley, corn, and pearl barley that they had taken from the Ukraine as they marched west.[59] In late 1944, in addition to carrying a kilogram of black bread, the ration of a soldier at the front also consisted of about 400 grams of kasha and about 500 grams of meat.[60] It is worth noting that in September 1944, the rations of Red Army officers were increased to include a category 2 worker ration in addition to their usual ration allowance.[61] The category 2 ration meant another 800 grams of bread a day, as well as a monthly supplement of 1,800 grams of meat or fish, 400 grams of fat, 600 grams of sugar, and 1,200 grams of flour.

Conditions appear to have been better in the navy.[62] The average daily allowance of 3,460 calories for sailors was fundamentally the same as for combat soldiers, with a range from 3,120 for signalmen to 4,000 for certain specialists when at sea, and sailors were supposed

[55] Interview of May 21, 1988. The notion that soldiers in general carried food for three or four days is confirmed by a *Life* magazine report early in the war that said that Russian soldiers carried food for three days. See *Life*, July 28, 1941, p. 17.
[56] NFAS, May 26, 1943.
[57] Interview of January 30, 1988.
[58] *Tyl*, p. 209.
[59] Ibid., pp. 209–10.
[60] NFAS, U.S. Embassy at Moscow, Confidential Report No. 41, October 19, 1944.
[61] *The New York Times*, September 16, 1944, p. 35.
[62] The discussion that follows is drawn from *Opyt*, Vol. 33, Moscow 1955, pp. 194–203.

to receive 100 or more grams of protein a day. Unlike the changes that took place in army diets in 1944 and 1945, naval diets remained virtually the same during the entire war. Food was generally cooked right on board the ship and was heavily salted for the purposes of preservation.

A Soviet medical source said that on some boats people gained from one to three pounds,[63] and this is supported by the experience of an émigré who was drafted into the Soviet Navy in 1938 and served throughout the war on border patrol in the Black Sea. He said they had less food than sailors who were in combat or who served in submarines but, "Before the war started, the food was very good. We had condensed milk, butter, different kinds of meat and fish. The situation got worse when the war started but not much worse. We had no butter." After 1942, his food was mainly U.S. Lend-Lease food:[64] "The worst year was 1943 because when Novorossisk fell it made deliveries of food difficult. So there was no milk, no butter, but enough meat and enough bread. I ate four times a day." He joked that he was so well fed that he thought they were preparing him for slaughter (*kak na uboi*). Even naval rations, however, did not meet the standard for U.S. sailors. In the fall of 1943, when U.S. seamen were temporarily supplied with stores roughly corresponding to the amounts served on comparable Soviet vessels, U.S. officials complained to the Soviet Commissar of Foreign Trade that the quantities provided were "inadequate" and "asked for improvement in supply of fresh vegetables, meats, milk, and sugar."[65]

For large sections of the Red Army there was simply not enough food or enough variety of food. One observer characterized the Soviet soldier as one "who subsisted almost exclusively on what he could carry in the sack he customarily slung over his shoulder or tied to his belt."[66] There was a consistent inability to provide enough food beyond immediate needs. One émigré remembers how he and his army comrades foraged for nettles to make soup and also picked goosefoot (*lebeda*), which they cooked with potatoes to make green cabbage soup. The potatoes were usually frozen, having been abandoned when civilians left an area. They also hunted for garlic and onions, their intuitive belief being that they could get important nutrients from these two foods.[67]

[63] Ibid., p. 197.
[64] Interview of January 30, 1988.
[65] *Foreign Relations of the United States*, Washington, D.C., 1943, Vol. 3, 1943, p. 707.
[66] Ziemke, p. 147.
[67] Interview of November 15, 1988.

Another indication of the inadequacy of a soldier's diet was the need to buy food on the collective farm market. Officers were more able to do this because they had money. However, the ordinary soldier had to resort to illegal activity. Sometimes soldiers would sell part of their uniform to buy food. Soldiers even stole other uniforms to buy food.[68]

Some soldiers pilfered food when possible. One émigré, assigned to kitchen duty in a battalion of soldiers too sick to perform ordinary military duties, was encouraged by two friends to steal some corn oil from the big vat that was the daily supply of corn oil. The agreement was that he would steal a ladleful and the three of them would share the oil: "But I couldn't wait and I drank the whole thing." In the late fall of 1944 the same man was assigned to guard U.S. Lend-Lease food supplies in Archangel. He remembers looking into the big warehouse he was guarding and seeing sugar and *tushonka*:[69]

> I was so hungry and there was so much food. I decided to take a box. It was dark and I hit something and everything fell. The sound was like a shell. It was 35 degrees below zero. I thought this was the end. If they caught me they would shoot me in front of the division. I took a whole case of *tushonka*, sugar, and dried bread. I realized that I shouldn't do this but I opened a can of *tushonka* and ate it. Then I left my post and went to my superior and told him I had the food. He kissed me. We went and ate a couple of cans of *tushonka*. We hid the rest in the fields far away. When we went back to the fields later for the food, someone had stolen all of it.[70]

But to most civilians, army rations seemed like heaven. For those who joined the army after the war was underway, it may have been the first time in a long time that they ate twice a day on a regular basis. And they got more eating military food than they had as civilians. In 1944 and 1945, the per capita consumption of fats and oils in the military was 39.7 pounds, well over twice the 16.3 pounds the civilian population received.[71] The daily bread allowance of 900 grams was more than 100 grams higher than the highest civilian ration. The food was sufficiently inviting that a woman who had survived the siege of Leningrad wanted to join the army to use what she said was

---

[68] Interview of October 28, 1986.
[69] *Tushonka* was a highly popular pork-based product made according to a Soviet recipe in the United States and shipped to the Soviet Union under the auspices of the Lend-Lease Program.
[70] Interview of November 18, 1987.
[71] NFAS, U.S. Embassy at Moscow, No. 8, February 19, 1945. Peasants were not entitled to any ration allowance.

her good German, but also to have better food.[72] A man who entered the army in November 1943 said: "I had no meat, but I got potatoes. You were lucky if you got to peel potatoes. You could keep the skins. To go to the kitchen was like a holiday."[73]

In addition, there were vitamin deficiencies. Emigré physicians regularly reported the absence of vitamin supplements: "Many soldiers suffered from a lack of vitamins. They suffered with scurvy. There were no vitamins manufactured." They boiled pine needles for vitamin C.[74] A doctor I interviewed, whose husband was also a physician who had served at the front, was told by him that although he never saw any hunger in the army, soldiers commonly had gum disease, again reflecting the lack of vitamin C.[75]

More vitamin supplements appear to have been available to the navy, especially later in the war. Specialists who worked in excessively hot areas and some submarine and launch personnel received 2½ mg of vitamin B_1 every day. Sailors also received 25 to 75 mg of vitamin C a day, depending on their job. Naval personnel stationed at the Arctic Circle were also given 500 immunization units of vitamin D every day. The amount of vitamins given to the navy increased every year. By 1945 it was four times what it had been at the beginning of the war.[76] If the amount of vitamins increased so much in relative terms and if we assume that the Soviets did not distribute redundant quantities, then this suggests that early in the war there was a serious shortage of vitamins for naval personnel.

By mid-May 1942 the Soviets were producing vitamin B, glucose tablets with vitamin C, and a drink made from conifer needles that contained vitamin C. These were all specifically designated for the front.[77] There was also vitamin-enriched chocolate produced in the Moscow state vitamin factory Marat late in the war, but it is not known how many of the fourteen-gram pieces were manufactured.[78]

The production of food concentrates

A relatively low level of technology was applied to matters pertaining to the food supply of the army and as a result, the shortages

---

[72] Interview of October 28, 1986.
[73] Interview of November 18, 1987.
[74] Interview of May 21, 1988.
[75] Interview of September 10, 1986.
[76] *Opyt*, Vol. 33, p. 202. Unfortunately the absolute amounts of vitamins produced are not given.
[77] *Pravda*, May 18, 1942, p. 3. My own suspicion, based on conversations with émigrés, is that these vitamins were husbanded for military hospitals.
[78] NFAS, November 19, 1944.

of food were compounded. Consequently, while Soviet production of dry food concentrates as substitutes for fresh food increased during the war, quantitatively it was no match for production in the United States, which jumped from 62,500 tons in 1942 to 1 million tons in 1943.[79] In all, the Soviets produced 506,000 tons of food concentrates during the war. This was not a large quantity and it could provide no more than one-sixth of an ordinary soldier's annual food needs in 1942.[80] Production was coordinated through the Main Administration of the Food Concentrate Industry, created in September 1941 within the Food Commissariat. They made soups, *shchi*, borshcht, and different kashas. The food concentrates had two major defects. First, many took a long time to cook, often longer than soldiers had time to wait for their food. As a result, the concentrates were often used instead as substitutes in communal cooking. Second, the concentrates lacked taste and the only way they became palatable was to add fresh vegetables, potatoes, and greens, items that were not always readily available.[81]

Army food and sanitation

There were several health problems associated with military food. Many food products served to soldiers transmitted typhoid, dysentery, botulism, toxic infections, and other diseases. These diseases were contracted from canned food as well as local unprocessed products.[82] There was also a high incidence of ulcers in the army, attributed by Soviet authorities to the irregularity of the soldiers' diets.[83] Last, a major rodent problem plagued the army and there were army food inspectors who, among other things, were responsible for killing insects and rodents. Although there is no real proof,

---

[79] *The Financial Post* (Toronto), May 13, 1944, p. 13.

[80] The 1942 output of 160,000 tons yielded about 58 pounds a year of dehydrated foods per soldier for an army with a midyear size of roughly 5.5 million men on active duty. If each ration weighed one pound, then dehydrated foods covered about two months worth of rations. A wartime source suggests a much higher level of provisioning with dehydrated rations. The *Moscow News* of February 26, 1944, reported that more than 3 billion concentrated rations had been sent to the front since the beginning of the war. If that were true, it would mean that over a period of 2.7 years an army averaging 6 million men on active duty would have consumed 1.1 billion rations a year for an average of 183 rations per man per year. This figure is so much at odds with the much more recent Soviet assessment, as well as my own sense of what soldiers ate, that I am inclined to view the wartime figure as greatly exaggerated.

[81] *Tyl*, pp. 187, 205–6.

[82] *Opyt*, Vol. 32, Part III, p. 20.

[83] *Opyt*, Vol. 23, p. 110.

Measures taken by the military in their struggle against rodents in the field. The top two pictures show cones placed upside down on tables by the Red Army to prevent rodents from reaching soldiers' food. The bottom picture is a barrel baited with food into which the rodent falls and drowns. *Source: Opyt sovetskoi meditsiny v Velikoi Otechestvennoi Voine 1941–1945gg.* Vol. 32, Part III, Moscow 1955, p. 43. Photo by Gordon White.

it is arguable that rats followed the army, which was better endowed with food than the civilian population. In order to protect the food from rodent infestations, at warehouses, the army built shelves fifty centimeters off the ground and thirty to forty centimeters away from

A trap made by the army from tin cans. *Source: Opyt*, p. 44. Photo by Gordon White.

the walls and placed lids on the water wells and put out rat traps – which often were crudely constructed – of various kinds (see photo).[84] Tables were modified with inverted cones on the legs to prevent rodents from climbing onto tabletops (see photo).[85]

Conclusion

There is every evidence that the armed forces received favored treatment regarding food. In determining how hardship would be distributed, the government always ensured that combat troops were first in line to receive food. Great pressure was placed on farmers to hand over their output at levels above and beyond the call of duty, and soldiers had priority in the receipt of manufactured food and received virtually all food imported from foreign food assistance programs. There is no doubt that the armed forces ate better than civilians. Yet the state was unable to feed the armed forces adequately. When centralized mechanisms were unable to produce and distribute food, the preferred solution was the same as it was in the civilian sector: a wager on localism. Soldiers could not take their food supply for granted; they became foragers. In a figurative and literal sense they were forced to knock on doors and rely on others for their daily bread. It took a combination of state supplies, local supplies, foreign assistance, and individual ingenuity to survive what was often a precarious situation.

[84] *Opyt*, Vol. 32, Part III, pp. 26–27.
[85] Ibid., p. 40.

7 Feeding the cities and towns: civilian rationing

If the armed forces, even with top priority, were not always fed adequately, then it should be no surprise to find that there was not enough food for civilians, especially those in cities and towns. It is understandable why the government in its struggle to win the war gave civilians a lower priority than soldiers, but for many this meant malnutrition or even hunger during most of the war.[1] Food was scarce and the issue that faced the government was how to distribute the short supply among various groups of civilians.

Two systems – a nonmarket mechanism and a market mechanism – operated side by side during the war to allocate food supplies to the civilian population other than the peasantry. The nonmarket mechanism took the form of a complex rationing system that was instituted quite early in the war and eventually spread to cover all urban areas, although not the countryside.

Rationing was the predominant means of allocating food, reflecting the efforts of wartime economic planners to achieve an equitable distribution of severely limited food supplies and thereby make it easier for people to accept deprivation. The market system was found in the collective farm market, an institution that predated the war, but came to play a crucial role in the wartime distribution system. This mechanism was divided into two branches: one in which money was a medium of exchange and a second in which a barter system operated. The food supplies in the free market served not only the interests of buyers and sellers of food, but those of planners as well. Whereas rationing established a minimum standard of subsistence, albeit with

---

[1] The special case of besieged Leningrad and mass starvation is treated separately in Chapter 10.

differential definitions of entitlement by group, the market permitted the pressures rationing inevitably created to vent themselves. This chapter is the first of two that examines the food distribution system. The focus of this chapter is the rationing program that prevailed during the war. The second chapter on the distribution system will focus on the vast network of local producers and markets that sprang up everywhere.

World War II was not the first time since the Bolshevik Revolution that food was rationed. Rationing had been employed during two earlier periods since 1917: first, during the period of the Civil War and its aftermath (from 1918 to 1923) and then during the war against the peasants from 1928 to 1935.[2] In all, during almost half of the quarter of a century that preceded the war the Soviet Union had been under a regime of rationing. With the last rationing episode having ended only six years before, the reintroduction of rationing probably came as no surprise to most, and inasmuch as the population was already accustomed to this system it probably did not have to make a great adjustment in learning how to cope.

Indeed, the rationing system developed during the war fundamentally resembled the system erected in 1929. In both instances rationing was first introduced in Moscow and Leningrad and then spread to the entire urban population. Also, the peasantry was excluded from the system each time. In addition, distinctions in ration allowances were made according to category of worker. One major difference was that the World War II rationing program established maximum consumption norms by food category, whereas the principle behind the 1929 system was that of "a guaranteed minimum at a certain fixed ration-price."[3]

Rationing was officially introduced by a resolution of the USSR *Sovnarkom* on July 18, 1941, only four weeks into the war, although neither the decree nor an announcement about the rationing were published in *Pravda* or *Izvestia*. Actually rationing had begun on July 17 in Moscow, was applied to Leningrad on July 18, and then gradually extended to a number of cities and suburban areas in the Moscow and Leningrad oblasts. The goods covered were bread, bakery goods and flour, groats and macaroni, sugar and confectionery goods, but-

[2] Maurice Dobb, *Soviet Economic Development Since 1917*, New York: International Publishers, 1948. During the period of War Communism daily bread rations in the urban areas fell to an astonishingly low 60 grams. This was the basic cause for the wholesale migration of the city population to the countryside (p. 100); E. H. Carr and R. W. Davies, *Foundations of a Planned Economy 1926–1929*, Vol. 1, Part II, p. 702.
[3] Dobb, p. 368; Carr and Davies, pp. 702–4.

Table 7.1. *The number of people receiving state-supplied bread (in thousands)*

	1942	1943	1944	1945
Urban	40,961	43,188	48,373	53,817
Rural	20,817	24,523	25,626	26,769
Total	61,778	67,711	73,999	80,586

Source: *Istoriia Velikoi Otechestvennoi Voiny Sovetskogo Soiuza, 1941–1945*, Vol. 6, Moscow 1965, p. 76.

ter, vegetable oil, margarine, meat and meat products, and fish and fish products.[4] On August 20, rationing of bread, sugar, and confectionery goods was introduced in 200 cities, worker settlements, and "settlements of the urban type," and in November these same products were rationed in all urban areas. Also in November, meat, fish, fats, coarse grains, and macaroni began to be rationed in forty-three of the largest industrial centers in the Urals, such as Perm, Sverdlovsk, and Cheliabinsk. In a number of cities where ration cards were not issued for these foods, a modified form of control was introduced by having them either sold directly by public catering establishments or through stores with a one-time only coupon. Nonagricultural workers living in the countryside were issued bread rations, but farmers were completely excluded from the state rationing system.[5]

Despite the existence of norms for the five food groups, bread was the only food that was guaranteed to the population. The state supplied bread to about 62 million people in 1942, and the number increased as territory and therefore population was liberated (Table 7.1).

[4] July 18, 1941 resolution, "On the introduction of ration cards for several food and industrial goods in the cities of Moscow, Leningrad and individual goods in the cities and suburban areas of the Moscow and Leningrad oblasts," in *Direktivy KPSS i sovetskogo pravitel'stva po khoziaistvennym voprosam*, Moscow 1957, pp. 705–6. It was a rarity for rationing to be officially acknowledged during the war. For one of those uncommon recognitions, see *Izvestia*, December 21, 1944, p. 1. There was obvious sensitivity to the rationing issue. On November 13, 1942, Moscow radio broadcasted a message in English to North America denying a German radio report out of Belgrade that Soviet bread rations had been cut to 80 grams a day. The Soviet broadcast took the highly exaggerated position that bread rations in the USSR were higher than those in "Berlin, Vichy, and other Axis cities put together." See *Daily Report of Foreign Radio Broadcasts*, November 14, 1942.
[5] *Istoriia Velikoi Otechestvennoi Voiny Sovetskogo Soiuza 1941–1945*, Vol. 2, Moscow, 1961, p. 549. Peasants who produced nonfood crops could obtain food through the stores of the consumer cooperatives at specified levels; U.G. Cherniavskii, *Voina i prodovol'stvie*, Moscow, 1964, p. 71.

By 1945, 80.6 million relied on bread rations. About two-thirds of the recipients in each of the war years were urbanites.

From the very beginning, the system differentiated between groups in the population and, as the war developed, the system of differentiation made more and more distinctions between population groups. Although the norms that were set (that is, the nominal rations) proved to be very different from the actual amount of food that people received, they inform us about the principles of food distribution and may be seen as a declaration of the state's views on the importance of various groups in the population. The differences in allowances were meant to translate into different levels of consumption.

The ration cards had five sets of coupons covering five different food groups: (1) bread, (2) meat or fish, (3) fats, (4) sugar, and (5) flour or meal. The entire population was divided into categories and the ration for each food was determined by the category into which the individual fell. Initially, there were four categories: Category 1 – manual workers (*rabochie*), Category 2 – employees (*sluzhashchie*), Category 3 – dependents, and Category 4 – children. A new first category created on February 1, 1942, included people engaged in critical war industries, scientists, and technicians – in essence those doing heavy work or important work.[6] Shortly before the new category was created a number of occupations were downgraded, effectively decreasing their rations.[7] Individuals who did not fall into one of these categories were not entitled to ration cards. Because virtually every able-bodied person was in the labor force, however, there would have been relatively few people outside of the peasantry who did not receive a ration card.

The bread ration for blue-collar and white-collar workers was divided into two categories. Category 1 workers and employees received the highest daily bread ration. These were workers in the defense, fuel, chemical, metallurgy, machine-building, construction, and transportation industries; coal miners and others performing underground work; and some workers in the ferrous metallurgy and oil industries.[8]

The differentiation between the five population groups for the five

---

[6] USSR: Crop Conditions and Production, 1942–1945. Records of the Foreign Agricultural Service. Record Group 166, National Archives, Washington, D.C. (NFAS). U.S. Embassy at Moscow, Despatch No. 15, March 18, 1942; U.S. Embassy at Moscow, May 26, 1943, telegram.

[7] This was done in December or January. *Foreign Relations of the United States (FRUS),* Washington D.C., 1942, Vol. III, p. 412.

[8] Cherniavskii, p. 74.

Table 7.2. *Monthly ration norms (grams)*

Category	Bread (daily)	Meat or fish	Fats	Sugar	Flour or meal
1	800	2,200	600	600	2,200
2	800	1,800	400	400	1,200
3	500	1,200	300	300	800
4	400	400	300	300	800
5	400	400	200	200	600

Source: DOA, Russian Food Mission and Purchasing Committee File, October 22, 1943.

food groups as defined by the rationing planners can be seen in the ration norms of mid–1943 (Table 7.2).

The importance of bread as the irreducible staff of life is demonstrated by the fact that there were smaller differences in the bread ration than in any other food category. The ratio of the highest ration to the lowest for bread was 2:1, whereas it was no lower than 3:1 for any other food and went as high as 5.5:1 for meat and fish.

On the national level, rations were remarkably stable during the war. The official ration norms introduced at the beginning of the war for meat and fish, cereals and macaroni, and fats never changed during the war years. The sugar and confectionery rations were reduced only once, on April 11, 1942, after the Germans overran most of the territory producing sugar beets. And the bread ration was changed only once, on November 21, 1943.[9]

The infrequency of change in nominal rations can be seen in the case of Vladivostok, where the rationing of bread and sugar began on November 1, 1941. In the next months, the food situation worsened. By the end of February, the U.S. Consulate reported that there was less food available than at any time within the previous year.[10] Yet nominal rations did not change. But there were several ways in which local variations in the norms were introduced, although not with great predictability. First, we can distinguish local and regional variation in the ration norms that can best be explained by the degree to which the local population had access to food outside the rationing system, that is, to the collective farm market. Unlike nations where geographic complexities did not exist, one of the complexities of Soviet

[9] Ibid., p. 82.
[10] NFAS, U.S. Consulate at Vladivostok, Despatch No. 107, February 12, 1942.

rationing involved geographic differentiation in nominal rations. When rationing was first introduced, the national norms were applied everywhere, but we know that by 1944 rations varied by region and it seems likely that they are evidence of the serious regional differences in food availability. An example of such variation can be seen in the norms for Moscow and Murmansk for the months of August and November 1944 (Table 7.3).[11] The port city of Murmansk, north of the Arctic Circle, was much smaller than Moscow, and because its cold climate ruled out local agriculture it was unable to resort to alternative food sources.[12] The ration allowances for workers were uniformly higher in Murmansk than they were in Moscow and an additional category for workers was added. With only one exception, rations for employees, dependents, and children under 12 were the same. The most plausible explanation for the higher rations in Murmansk is the physical demands of the cold climate and the absence of a free market in the area. Murmansk civilians probably were compensated with higher food allowances because, unlike Muscovites, they did not have access to alternative sources of food.

There were other instances of regional variations in ration allowances. In July 1943, the Kuibyshev bread ration for workers was 800 grams, whereas it was only 700 and 600 grams for the two categories of workers in Moscow.[13] In Novosibirsk, in 1942, the food situation was acknowledged to have worsened.[14] An émigré recalls the daily bread ration in the city for both blue-collar workers and employees as 400 grams and for dependents as 300 grams. The meat ration for employees was 1,200 grams. The bread ration for workers and employees was lower than the nominal national norms, although the bread ration for dependents and the meat ration for all these groups was the same as the national norm.[15]

A second form of local variation came when the ration norms were officially lowered in a region, which usually happened in times of extreme scarcity, such as 1943. The bread ration in Moscow for Cat-

[11] The Murmansk data for August were collected by a U.S. official and were not confirmed, for example, by access to actual ration cards. The November ration data were copied from the ration cards of a Category 2 worker and a child under the age of twelve. NFAS, U.S. Embassy at Moscow, Despatch No. 60, November 16, 1944.
[12] Murmansk had a population of 130,000 before the war, which fell to 30,000 before rising to 60,000 in October 1944. Ibid.
[13] NFAS, U.S. Embassy at Kuibyshev, Despatch No. 11, June 28, 1943.
[14] NFAS, U.S. Consulate at Vladivostok, Despatch No. 107, February 12, 1942.
[15] Interview of September 23, 1986. Forty-four years is a long time for someone to remember bread rations. Because this recollection came without prodding and was advanced with such a ring of certainty and because his other figures accurately stated the official national rations, I have chosen to trust his memory.

Table 7.3. *Ration norms in Moscow and Murmansk in August and November 1944 (in grams)*

	Moscow					
	Daily		Monthly			
	Bread	Meat and fish	Fats	Grits	Sugar	Tea
Category 1 workers	650	2,200	800	2,000	500	25
Category 2 workers	550	2,200	800	2,000	500	25
Employees	450	1,200	400	1,500	300	25
Dependents	300	600	200	1,000	200	25
Children under 12	300	600	400	1,200	300	25

	Murmansk						
	August (unconfirmed)						
	Bread	Meat	Fish	Fats	Macaroni or grits	Sugar	Tea
Category 1 workers	1,000	2,500	1,500	1,000	2,500	800	25
Category 2 workers	750	2,200	1,500	800	2,000	500	25
Category 3 workers	500	1,200	1,500	800	2,000	500	25
Employees	450	1,000	*a*	400	1,500	300	25
Dependents	300	600	*a*	200	1,000	200	25
Children under 12	300	600	*a*	400	1,200	200	25
	November (confirmed)						
Category 2 workers	700	4,000*a*		800	2,000	750	*b*
Children under 12	400	2,000*a*		500	1,500	500	*b*

*a*Meat and fish combined.
*b*Not reported.
Source: NFAS, Box 442, U.S. Embassy at Moscow, Despatch No. 60, November 16, 1944.

egory 1 workers, for example, was reduced twice from its July 1941 starting point, first in March 1943 and then in November 1943 (Table 7.4). The rations for the other four categories were cut in November 1943. The reduction of the bread ration was not reported in the Soviet press and foreign correspondents were forbidden from reporting the change so as not to "give aid and comfort to the enemy."[16]

In fact, stated rations were often meaningless. It was a common-

---

[16] *FRUS*, 1943, Vol. 3, p. 789.

Table 7.4. *Official bread ration in Moscow (in grams)*

Category	July 17, 1941	March 1943	November 21, 1943
1	800	700	650
2	600	600	550
3	500	500	450
4	400	400	300
5	400	400	300

Source: DOA, Russian Food Mission and Purchasing Committee file, October 22, 1943.

place for substitutions of inferior foods to be made for the foods listed on the ration cards. As a consequence, the caloric intake of the ration and the nutritional content were likely to be below standards of sufficiency. In effect, the ration card was a set of possibilities, not a set of assurances. With the exception of the bread ration, looking for one's ration entitlement became a perpetual crap shoot for the ordinary Soviet citizen.

Uncertainty was an abiding characteristic of the daily and monthly quest for food. As someone who lived in Rostov during the war said: "So, instead of two kilos of meat per month, you might be given some fish, a few eggs, and also some canned food or honey, without ever being able to understand the mysterious law that governs these substitutions."[17] The fact is that the authorities simply distributed whatever food was available at the time. An émigré who worked at a defense plant in Kuibyshev remembers that during the worst days of the winter of 1941 and 1942 chocolate was a substitute even for bread. "I can't look at chocolate now," she said. "Chocolate was a substitute for everything, for meat, for everything."[18]

The situation in Moscow in the harsh year of 1943 and even afterward serves as an illustration. In July 1943, substitutions took place within all of the major food categories. The bread ration was 70 percent black bread and the better white bread or gray bread was distributed only as available. Sugar was not disbursed at all. Honey, at the weight ratio of one for one, and jam, cookies, or cake, at the ratio of two for one were sold instead. Only 20 percent of the butter allocation was available. The remainder was offered in the form of either corn oil from the United States or inferior vegetable oils, some of which were

[17] K. S. Karol, *Between Two Worlds*, New York: Henry Holt, 1986, p. 251.
[18] Interview of January 30, 1988.

described as having a rancid taste. There was virtually no fresh meat available, a problem that was not new and lasted until nearly the end of the war. Instead fifteen eggs were substituted for one kilogram of meat.[19] A former Soviet citizen remembers that when she and her family returned to Moscow in June or July 1943, they often had to take powdered eggs as a substitute for meat and butter.[20] Occasionally, 800 grams of chicken sausage or 1 kilo of either salted or dried fish replaced 1 kilo of meat.[21] During the latter part of 1943, meat and butter remained unavailable, although bread and cereal were typically obtainable.[22] Only Category 1 and 2 workers received fats in September 1943. In the summer of 1944 sugar remained scarce; in general people received only about one-third to one-half of their quota and in some instances this was received a month late. Eggs and fish were still substituted for meat. Potatoes replaced cereals in April 1944, although in May and June the cereal ration was resumed.[23]

The apprehensions that people must have had about the availability of rations can be understood by looking at what happened during May and June 1943 in a particular store in Kuibyshev. This was a large store to which about 7,000 people were attached – many of them Soviet employees at foreign embassies, teachers, physicians, Intourist employees, and evacuees. Most rations were supplied in May 1943, and there were few deficiencies. There was no fresh meat but at least the substitutions seemed quite reasonable; they included salted fish, smoked fowl, canned crabmeat, fish, cheese, and a few eggs. The fat allowance was met by sunflower oil, cheese, and sour cream. The sugar category was fulfilled by honey, sweet cakes, and candy. But in June, the story was absolutely the opposite. As of June 28, the only foods that had been issued, besides bread, were six eggs in place of the 400-gram meat ration for children under the age of twelve, and 400 grams of sour cream to some workers in place of their 100-gram butter allotment. Even the bread supply was dubious in June. If you weren't on line by 8:30 A.M. you would probably have to settle for flour or zwieback.[24] Much less uncertain was the quality of the substitutes. One Soviet scholar characterized the meat substitutes as inferior to the real thing and said that replacement sweets were made

[19] NFAS, U.S. Embassy at Moscow, Despatch No. 3, August 4, 1943.
[20] Interview of August 19, 1986.
[21] NFAS, U.S. Embassy at Moscow, Despatch No. 3, August 4, 1943.
[22] FRUS, 1942, Vol. 3, p. 479.
[23] NFAS, U.S. Embassy at Moscow, Despatch Number 13, August 15, 1944.
[24] U.S. Embassy at Kuibyshev, Despatch No. 11, June 28, 1943; 600 grams of flour and 500 grams of zwieback equaled one kilogram of bread.

from a low-quality sugar. Instead of fresh fish, canned goods were offered.[25]

The mechanics of the rationing system

The administration of the rationing system was done by a newly created rationing department within the People's Commissariat of Trade (*Narkomtorg*).[26] Ration cards were issued at the beginning of each month and workers were reregistered in the middle of the month.[27] The monthly registration process, although obviously costly from an administrative point of view, showed that the scarcity value of food was much more important than the value of the time it took to check individual eligibility and issue new cards. Able-bodied people who did not work were not issued ration cards. The cards were distributed at the workplace and at educational institutions.[28] People were registered at specific retail food stores and dining rooms (*stolovye*).[29] The ration card would not be honored in any place other than where it was registered.[30] Individuals who came to the city without a residence permit or a job were not entitled to a ration card. But they could obtain coupons for one of the communal dining facilities to eat a single meal a day.[31]

Rationed food was distributed through two channels: closed stores and open stores. The closed stores were associated with state organizations and food was available only to those bearing a permit. The open stores were the ordinary stores under the *Narkomtorg*. Although food was sold at the same prices in both types of stores, supplies were more likely to be available in the closed stores.[32]

Bread was issued only on a daily basis so that the authorities could make sure that several days worth of rations would not be consumed all at once.[33] For all other foods, however, one-third of the monthly allowance was distributed every ten days. In fact, it was only when

---

[25] Cherniavskii, p. 69.
[26] Ibid., p. 96.
[27] NFAS, U.S. Embassy at Moscow, Despatch No. 15, March 18, 1942; Cherniavskii, p. 75.
[28] Cherniavskii, pp. 75, 96.
[29] Ibid., p. 101.
[30] NFAS, U.S. Embassy at Moscow, March 18, 1942.
[31] Vasily Grossman, *Life and Fate*, New York: Harper & Row, 1985.
[32] U.S. Department of Agriculture Archives – World War II files (DOA), "Russian Food Mission and Purchasing Committee" file. October 22, 1943, from Lester B. Pearson to Mordecai Ezekiel; *FRUS*, 1942, Vol. 3, p. 480.
[33] Cherniavskii, p. 72.

the food stores announced the numbers of the coupons that would be redeemed that nonbread goods were offered. Even this did not ensure that the food could be obtained; the supply could be depleted before everyone was satisfied.[34]

A typical ration card was divided into two parts. One part was used to purchase food in stores, while the other part was used to purchase a major meal in the dining room at the enterprise where one worked. Communal dining rooms, such as those found in industrial enterprises, would serve meals twenty-four hours a day in three-shift plants.[35] A Category 2 worker reported that the workplace portion of her card entitled her to 1,800 grams a month of meat or fish (about four pounds), 1,300 grams of groats or macaroni (for which potatoes could be substituted at the rate of two kilograms of potatoes for one kilogram of groats or macaroni), and 300 grams of fat. The meal at the dining room had two courses – the first was a "thin soup made of gritts [groats], or beet leaves, or nettles, or rarely cabbage. The second dish is gritts, or potatoes, (or rarely) meat – little fresh meat, mostly herring or hard coarse sausage made of meat scraps." The meal cost three to four rubles. She had to provide her own bread, which was the standard 600-gram daily ration. Her supplementary rations on the other section of the card were 400 grams of meat, 700 grams of groats or macaroni, 500 grams of fat, 500 grams of sugar or confectionery, 400 grams of salt, and, if it was available, 25 grams of tea.[36]

The adequacy of Soviet rations

A number of serious questions arise with respect to the adequacy of Soviet rations. There are two principal measures of adequacy. One yardstick is the number of calories consumed every day. Were supplies adequate relative to the demands being made under wartime conditions? A second yardstick is the quality of the diet offered by the rations, particularly by the rations actually available, because there was a vast difference between what was offered on the ration card and what was actually available to consumers on a month-to-month basis. General stringencies often translated into the absence

---

[34] NFAS, June 30, 1943; NFAS, U.S. Embassy at Moscow, Despatch No. 15, March 18, 1942.
[35] *Pravda*, April 22, 1942, p. 4.
[36] NFAS, U.S. Embassy at Moscow, June 30, 1943.

Table 7.5. *Relative caloric content of industrial workers' rations (first quarter, 1945)*

Textile industry	100
Light industry	104
Paper industry	124
Heavy industry	124
Construction industry	126
Medium-size machinery industry	127
Ferrous metallurgical industry	139
Oil industry	139
Military supplies industry	146
Tank industry	150
Coal industry	160

Source: U. G. Cherniavskii, *Voina i prodovol'stvie*, Moscow, 1964, p. 78.

of certain foods. Meat and fish were often not available, vegetables seldom, and fruit was a virtual pipedream.

The caloric content of industrial workers' diets varied quite dramatically, reflecting the differences in the importance attached to each industry in the war effort and serving as an incentive system to attract high-quality labor to priority jobs (Table 7.5). The most important workers received rations that were 50 to 60 percent higher than workers in consumer goods industries. But because the rations of workers in the consumer goods industries were low in caloric content, the base is a low one and the diets of even the best-fed workers were deficient.

During 1943, the British Ministry of Food evaluated Moscow's rations. The assessment was based on the assumption that all rations were obtainable and that food could not be obtained through other means. The appraisal of Moscow's ration allowances focused on the daily caloric intake of various groups relative to what was regarded as necessary under wartime circumstances rather than on the mineral and vitamin content of the diet. The total daily caloric intake of Category 1 workers, or those doing the heaviest industrial work, based only on their ration allotments, was estimated as 2,914 calories, whereas the minimum amount of calories considered appropriate for this group was 3,500. Therefore, in the British analysis, Moscow rations for the heaviest work were at least 600 calories less than they should have been. Category 2 workers, those doing manual labor but not the heaviest industrial work, were estimated to need 3,000 calories a day, which is the universal standard for a male performing moderate activity. On the average, this group was estimated to have a ration of 2,394 calories or a 600-calorie deficit from what was considered desirable. A similar gap was found for office workers, for whom the Moscow ration was judged to be 1,867 calories, while 2,500 and 2,100 were considered to be the caloric needs of sedentary male and female workers, respectively. The groups considered to be worst off were adult dependents and children. The composition of the group was such a mixed bag that it was difficult to get even a reasonable approximation. Children aged twelve to sixteen years of age need about 3,000 calories, whereas the aged could get by on 1,600. Only a rough estimate was made of the caloric intake of the fifth category, children under twelve years. The impression of the British evaluation was that the deficit was probably smallest for this group.[37]

The British data are doubly disturbing. Not only do the numbers suggest serious inadequacies in the rations, but they also lead us to conclude that the situation elsewhere in the country was even worse, because Moscow was one of the best-supplied cities in the country and the food was considered to be better.[38] As a former member of *Narkomzem* told a U.S. official in 1943: "The quality of bread in small places is poorer than in Moscow."[39] And for workers in the low-priority consumer goods industries, the situation was even worse.

A responsible Soviet estimate of calorie consumption during the war (Table 7.6) confirms the British appraisal.[40] However, the same Soviet source also makes claims about the diets of children that do not seem plausible. It contends that children up to the age of one year received 1,224 calories a day, including a special milk supplement, children in the day nurseries received 1,440 calories, and those in children's homes got 1,594 calories. And his claim that no children went hungry during the war is simply untrue.[41] These data show that

---

[37] DOA, Feed Our Allies file, October 1, 1943, letter from E. F. Penrose to Averell Harriman.
[38] NFAS, U.S. Embassy at Moscow, June 18, 1943.
[39] NFAS, U.S. Embassy at Moscow, June 30, 1943.
[40] There are two difficulties in comparing these two estimates. One problem is that the definition of the groups within each category is not the same. The second problem is that the date of the Soviet data is not given.
[41] Cherniavskii, p. 79. It seems unreasonable for any scholar to hold the system to such an absolute standard. An émigré of the 1950s who spent much of the war in an orphanage while she was separated from her parents often resorted to edible grasses to survive. Indeed she took a walk in the woods a number of years ago on a return visit and was able to identify the flora that had helped her survive so many years before.

Table 7.6. *The caloric content of Soviet urban rations (per day)*

Dependents	780
Employees receiving a bread ration of	
400 grams	1,074
450 grams	1,176
Workers receiving a bread ration of	
500 grams	1,387
600 grams	1,592
Workers (supplied according to a special list) receiving a bread ration of	
500	1,503
700	1,913
Workers supplied with increased rations (for example, foundry workers, glass workers, oil-well drillers)	3,181
Workers supplied special increased rations (for example, underground workers)	3,460
Coal miners and hewers supplied with increased rations and receiving a cold breakfast	4,114
Coal miners and hewers receiving an additional hot meal	4,418

Source: U. G. Cherniavskii, *Voina i prodovol'stvie*, Moscow, 1964, p. 77. These ration allowances were in force from November 21, 1943, to early 1945.

in every category, except coal mining and underground work, Soviet rations supplied an insufficient number of calories to Soviet civilians. Those worst off according to these figures were dependents, white-collar workers, and the lower categories of manual workers.

Rations as rewards

In principle, any rationing system should modify the effects of the unequal distribution of income where there are unequal money incomes. Rationing should diminish the differences in real incomes. Although Soviet rationing clearly moved in the direction of equalizing differentials, providing a basic level of consumption, it also created inequalities. Food during World War II took on the role of both the carrot and the stick. It was used as an incentive to produce, as a reward for working in difficult conditions, and also could be withheld as a way of punishing those who were viewed as slackers.

The differential bread ration served as a means to channel people into heavier work. In the words of a former factory worker, "The women workers in my factory [in 1944] could have found less physically demanding work in Rostov, but they have chosen to work here because it entitles them to a first- or second-category food ration card, that is to say eight hundred or six hundred grams of bread. I do not underestimate the six hundred grams of bread that comes with my job."[42] Since local authorities had the power to make decisions about ration levels, it was used on occasion as an instrument to coerce more people to enter the labor force. In 1942, able-bodied housewives in Archangel had their rations withdrawn and all able-bodied adults in Moscow who were not in the labor force lost their right to have coupons for meat and fats.[43]

Food was used to reward some of the nation's shining examples of excellence at the workplace. In early 1942 the nine dining rooms of the Moscow auto plant had special tables for Stakhanovites fulfilling the norms by at least 200 percent.[44] In many enterprises, workers who overfulfilled production quotas were allowed a second hot meal at the enterprise.[45] For those working in the hot shops of the meat industries there was also a special ration. They received 1,000 grams of bread a day, or 200 grams more than a typical Category 1 manual worker. But the best workers did not receive the highest rations; those were reserved for high officials. Although these rations were not made public for obvious reasons, U.S. Embassy estimates suggested they were comparable to the ration given in hospitals and sanitoria.[46] Such officials also received their food outside of the regular food distribution network.[47] Special rations were also awarded to invalids and pregnant women.[48]

Those who were hungry could donate their blood in exchange for food. Patriotic appeals to give blood for wounded soldiers were reinforced with additional food rations. In Moscow alone there were 200,000 to 300,000 blood donors, some of whom gave blood occasionally, either a full pint (450 grams) or a half unit (225 grams), and registered donors who gave blood every six weeks. For the occasional donor, the reward for giving a full unit of blood was 250 rubles, a

[42] Karol, p. 215.
[43] FRUS, 1942, Vol. III, p. 480.
[44] Pravda, April 22, 1942, p. 4. Stakhanovism drew its name from the coal miner who in 1935 became a model of socialist rectitude when he developed a technique that allowed his team to haul out an unheard of amount of coal in one day.
[45] Cherniavskii, p. 75. The same benefit was available for workers who worked an extra long day.
[46] NFAS, U.S. Embassy at Moscow, May 26, 1943.
[47] FRUS, 1942, Vol. III, p. 480.
[48] Dmitri V. Pavlov, Leningrad 1941: The Blockade, Chicago: University of Chicago Press, 1965, p. 67.

three-course meal immediately after giving the blood, a worker's ration card for one month, and supplementary ration coupons for 500 grams of butter, sugar, and groats; those donating half a unit received 125 rubles, a three-course meal, a worker's ration card for a month, and supplementary coupons for 300 grams of butter, sugar, and groats. The regular donors received precisely the same payoff, except that the ration card was guaranteed every month whether they actually gave in that particular month or not.[49] The worker ration card was above and beyond whatever ration card was earned on the job. Many people must have given blood out of a sense of patriotism, but the state cemented feelings of patriotism by creating the exchange of two scarce goods – blood for food. For those without any ration card, the sale of blood would have been a key to survival. Given the small number of people who were not employed in the war effort, however, the overwhelming majority of donors were probably giving blood to obtain more food.

Conclusion

The Soviet rationing system was implemented to achieve equity in the distribution of food and hence to distribute fairly the hardship that all experienced. Its failures were not in its conception, but in the impossibility of its execution. The state's efforts were doomed from the start by the inadequate level of food available. For most of the war there was a great deal of uncertainty about the amount of food that would be available as well as the kind of food that would be available. Less nutritious substitutions were as likely as not in this uncertain environment.

Yet nominal rations stayed constant for a very long time in the country as a whole and in any given place, even when the food supply was insufficient and stated coupon allowances could not be met. As a consequence, decreases in stated rations lagged behind the reality of food shortages. These decreases were an expression of shortages. How can the relative stability of nominal rations over time be explained? There must have been a great reluctance on the part of the authorities to lower rations. In view of the constant substitutions that had to be made, and the shortages of so many food items, nominal rations were an illusion. But as long as nominal rations remained at a certain level, for civilians they represented a sense that things could

---

[49] NFAS, U.S. Embassy at Moscow, Despatch No. 3, August 4, 1943.

be better and that the state intended to meet this level of food supply. Any decrease in stated rations represented a concession to a terrifying reality and could only lead to a loss of morale and make it more difficult to maintain the commitment to the war. Therefore, one reason for lowering rations so infrequently was to maintain the nation's spirit of dedication to the task of defeating the Germans.

On a month-to-month basis, the amount of Soviet rationed food was inadequate – even if the promised rations had been fully distributed. Throughout the war, there was a shortage of state-supplied food for civilians. One Western estimate was that for the typical Soviet family, rationed food lasted between two and three weeks, the deficit being determined by the availability of supplies in the state system.[50] As a result, individuals were forced to turn to the free market to make up for the deficiencies in the state retail network. It is to the subject of how these markets worked and the role they played during the war that we now turn.

[50] Lazar Volin, "German Invasion and Russian Agriculture," *Russian Review*, November 1943, p. 85.

8   White and black markets: the safety valve for civilian food supply

What was a highly integrated economic system before the war quickly evolved into a state of partial disintegration. The command economy as represented by the rationing system could not fulfill the food needs of Soviet civilians. The disintegration of the Soviet economic system led to a pivotal role for private markets in the distribution of food.

This chapter explores how private food markets worked during the war. There were in fact two kinds of markets during the war, one in which money served as a medium of exchange, and a barter market in which the ruble played no role except as a reference point for bargaining. The existence of these two markets resulted directly from a new, limited role for the central authorities in the food economy.

The analysis is divided into two parts. The first part examines the functioning of the traditionally organized collective farm food markets that used money. The second part of the chapter examines the *barterization* of Soviet food markets. The rise of barter markets in many parts of the country reflected the primacy of localism even more strikingly than did the collective farm markets where money was used.

In the Soviet Union, free markets – where peasants sold privately grown foodstuffs – had existed since the mid–1930s, although they constituted a large ideological bone that stuck in the collectivist throat of the Marxist regime. In the wake of the violent peasant reaction to collectivization, the institution of the collective farm market served several useful purposes for the regime. It assuaged some of the most bitter feelings of an angry and alienated peasantry, it helped to vent some of the inflationary pressures that had built up as a result of food shortages in the 1930s, and it provided food for the peasantry and their urban counterparts. By the end of the 1930s, however, the government took measures to cut back the collective farm markets.[1]

Once the war began, the peasantry, excluded from the rationing system, had little choice but to turn to their private plots for food and, by its silence, the government implicitly lifted the restrictions on private plot farming. The subsequent growth of output from the private plots also led to a rejuvenated nationwide network of collective farm markets. The food that came onto these markets did not include output from the individual and collective gardens of city dwellers; this food was consumed by the gardeners themselves.[2] Rather, the food came from the private plots of collective farmers. The importance of the collective farm market can be seen in the fact that as a proportion of all food sales, the collective farm market went from 20 percent in 1940 to 51 percent in 1945.[3] That is, the state and cooperative share of retail turnover in food fell from 80 percent to just under half of the total.

The central fact behind the increased importance of the collective farm market was the drastic drop in food production, especially in 1942 and 1943, and the diminished proportion of production that went to civilians. In 1943 overall agricultural production was only 38 percent of the 1940 level. In 1943, however, the Red Army began to recapture agricultural areas of the Ukraine, Belorussia, and the Caucasus and by the next year, 1944, agricultural output had risen to 54 percent of the 1940 level. Not surprisingly, the collapse of the food economy led to astonishing increases in prices. The most rapid *rate* of increase in prices took place in 1942 and began to taper off in mid–1943.[4] The

---

[1] For example, in May 1939 a decree was issued that ordered the confiscation of all private plots in excess of the legal ceiling. Land was to be taken from peasants who had not worked on a continuous basis on a collective farm. Moreover, the land worked in common would no longer be contiguous with the private plots. See Lazar Volin, *A Century of Russian Agriculture*, Cambridge: Harvard University Press, 1970, pp. 268–9.
[2] U. G. Cherniavskii, *Voina i prodovol'stvie*, Moscow, 1964, p. 156.
[3] A. N. Malafeev, *Istoriia tsenoobrazovaniia v SSSR, 1917–1963gg*, Moscow, 1964, p. 234.
[4] If January prices of each year are set equal to 100, then we can see that the rate of price increase was much slower in 1943 than in 1942. The price index is for all food goods, including livestock, bakery goods, potatoes, vegetables, meat, and dairy products.

	1942	1943
January	100	100
February	130	103
March	167	100
April	220	109

(*continued*)

Table 8.1. *Average prices in urban collective farm markets*[a]

Year	January	April	July	October
1941	103	95	88	112
1942	268	636	693	886
1943	1,440	1,602	1,467	1,077
1944	1,317	1,488	1,160	758
1945	754	737	590	417

[a]1940 = 100.
Source: A. N. Malafeev, *Istoriia tsenoobrzovaniia v SSSR (1917–1963gg.)*, Moscow, 1964, p. 235.

highest prices came in 1943, falling slightly at harvest time, but then, in view of the low level of agricultural production, rose again until the second half of 1944 (see Table 8.1).

A year after the war started the overall index of collective farm food prices had risen 8.5 times, and after another year it was almost 19 times the July 1941 level (see Table 8.2). It should be noted that within two years, the prices of potatoes and bakery goods, the two dominant foods in the Soviet diet, had risen by twenty-six times and twenty-three times, respectively; these increases were considerably more than the increases for meat and dairy products. For a period of two years, the overall food price index rose at an average monthly rate of 36.6 percent![5] Such a rate of inflation suggests that those who lived in the cities were bidding for pitifully little on the free market, particularly of the two staples, bread and potatoes.

Footnote 4 (*cont.*)

	1942	1943
May	269	112
June	283	104
July	265	111
August	277	98

Source: Malafeev, p. 231.
[5] The inflation rate is found by finding the value of X that sets $(1 + [X/100])t$ equal to the rise in the price index. In the Soviet case the index went from 100 to 1873 in 24 months. The Soviet inflation rate of 36.6 percent a month during this two-year period was not as high as the rates that prevailed during the seven great European hyperinflations of the twentieth century. See Phillip Cagan, "The Monetary Dynamics of Hyperinflation," in Milton Friedman, editor, *Studies in the Quantity Theory of Money*, Chicago: The University of Chicago Press, 1956, p. 26. However, in terms of duration, the inflation of World War II was roughly the same as the two long periods of inflation experienced in the Soviet Union during the Civil War in 1919 and 1920 and from December 1921 to January 1924.

Table 8.2. *Index of food prices on urban collective farm markets (in 43 cities)*[a]

	July 1941	July 1942	July 1943
All goods (including livestock)	100	854	1,873
Bakery goods	100	921	2,321
Potatoes	100	1,121	2,640
Vegetables	100	711	2,138
Meat	100	769	1,278
Dairy products	100	1,160	1,875

[a] 1941 = 100.
Source: A. N. Malafeev, *Istoriia tsenoobrazovaniia v SSSR (1917–1963gg.)*, Moscow, 1964, p. 230.

The great shortage of food led many urbanites to travel to the suburbs or the countryside to buy food. The character of such collective farm markets is made vivid in the mid–1944 report of a U.S. consular official about the market in Ramenskoe, a town about 30 miles outside of Moscow:

> The market is a few minutes walk from either of the last two stations on the line [from Moscow]. At this time of day, between noon and 1:00 P.M., a large procession was wending its way to the market place, which was also crowded to capacity. Many people were milling around on the inside of the entrance holding their wares in their hands. Along the sides of the market, those vendors with more to sell had their displays on the ground. Such displays, in general, consisted of non-food items such as nails, tools, phonographs, bicycles, shoes, boots, and other items of clothing. Toward the center of the market and beneath open sheds, butter, meat, cheese, and sour milk were sold. On the outside of these sheds, the following commodities were noticed on sale: carrots, potatoes, currants, strawberries, bread, cucumbers, dried fish, sunflower seeds, vodka, et cetera. Towards the far end of the market, cows, calves, young pigs, goats, chickens, and rabbits were for sale. A number of policemen were present to keep order.[6]

Prices on the suburban collective farm markets did not follow economic expectations or logic. This can be shown by a comparison of

[6] USSR: Crop and Production, 1942–1945. Records of the Foreign Agricultural Service. Record Group 166, National Archives, Washington D.C. (NFAS). U.S. Embassy at Moscow, July 1944.

prices in three collective farm markets outside of Moscow, all fre-
quented by Muscovite shoppers: Ramenskoe, about thirty-five miles
southeast of the city; Podolsk, roughly twenty-five miles due south
of Moscow; and Saltikovka, about six miles east of Moscow. The price
data are for summer 1944, gathered on Sundays beginning early in
the season in July and ending in Saltikovka in late August. The five-
week spread over which the data were collected means that some of
the price variations have seasonal explanations. There are fifteen food
items for which we have prices in at least two of the three markets
(Table 8.3).[7] If we think of all three suburbs as being in the orbit of
Moscow shoppers, then we should be able to make predictions about
the nature of the markets. If we take account of seasonal variations,
we might expect that prices in the Podolsk and Ramenskoe markets
would be lower than Saltikovka because people would have to travel
further to these more distant markets. But in a number of cases this
was not true. Probably the constant need to find food and the uncertainty about whether prices would be lower elsewhere led people
to take what they could get when they could get it. Moreover, these
individuals, who worked long hours under trying conditions six days
a week, did not have time to travel to several markets to find out
where to get the best deal. Both the opportunity cost of their time
and the transactions costs were extremely high. In fact, based on the
prevailing prices in these markets, it seems that time and travel costs
had no systematic effect on price differentials. The price of beef was
the same in Ramenskoe as it was in Saltikovka, although it was considerably less expensive in Podolsk. On the other hand, the price of
eggs was precisely the same and for butter and millet virtually so in
markets that were at significantly different distances from Moscow.
The relative prices per kilo of black bread in the three markets makes
no sense in terms of any economic model.

To a limited extent, the fall in livestock numbers brought peasants
to the collective farm market as buyers. Moreover, because the peasants were themselves subject to a price squeeze when prices paid to
collective farmers by the state fell during the war, they brought animals to sell in the market. To a certain extent, farmers were able

---

[7] The number of items for which there are prices in the Ramenskoe research is far
fewer than for the Podolsk market. This is because the observers in Ramenskoe were
stopped by a Soviet policeman: "He remarked that he observed they were interested
in writing things down. He said that he also was interested in writing things down
and proceeded to enter their names in his notebook." That ended their day in the
Ramenskoe market. Similarly, the U.S. Embassy attaché left the Saltikovka market
without pricing all the articles he had observed "due to the watchfulness of a suspicious
militia-man."

Table 8.3. *Prices at three suburban Moscow food markets in the summer of 1944 (in rubles)*

	Saltikovka	Ramenskoe	Podolsk
Beef (kg)	200	130 (first grade) 100 (second grade)	200
Black bread (kg)	95	75	120
Potatoes (kg)	35	30	20
Cucumbers (each)	2–3	12.5	7/7" cuc.
Carrots	5/bunch (each about 3" long)	26/kg.	4/bunch of 5 medium carrots
Apples (each)	—	4 (green)	15 (first grade) 10 (second grade)
Gooseberries	—	10/glass	15/glass
Butter (kg)	450–500	—	450
Eggs	—	12/egg	12/egg
Milk (half liter)	20	9.25–10	—
Sunflower seed	13/glass	—	15/glass
Sunflower oil	—	230/250 gr.	105/250 gr.
Millet (kg)	—	13	12
Flour (kg)	130	—	—
Wheat flour	—	—	125
Rye flour	—	—	90
Sugar (cube)	—	5	3

Sources: Ramenskoe – NFAS, Box 439, U.S. Embassy at Moscow, July 1944; Podolsk – NFAS, Box 444, U.S. Embassy at Moscow, Despatch No. 800, August 9, 1944; Saltikovka – NFAS, Box 441, U.S. Embassy at Moscow, Despatch No. 850, August 24, 1944.

partially to recoup their losses in free market sales. Table 8.4 shows that prices of livestock sold to the state actually fell by 8 to 35 percent (except for above-quota sales of sheep and goats to state purchasing agents and cooperatives), but there were increases of up to 500 percent in prices on sales to other collective farmers and on the collective farm market.

It is quite certain that civilians spent a high proportion of their money income for food in collective farm markets, but in the absence of good statistics we can make only a rough estimate of such expenditures. The average monthly income of such workers in 1943 was

Table 8.4. *Average price per head of livestock in USSR kolkhozy (in rubles)*

	Cattle		Pigs		Sheep and Goats	
	1941	1943	1941	1943	1941	1943
Obligatory deliveries	53.0	41.3	48.9	32.0	11.1	8.6
Above-quota deliveries	355.2	279.4	138.0	127.5	67.6	73.9
Sales to collective farmers	667.7	1203.2	46.8	197.1	98.0	268.7
Sales on the collective farm market	900.8	4346.4	101.2	444.9	193.3	1062.4

Source: Iu. V. Arutiunian, *Sovetskoe krest'ianstvo v gody Velikoi Otechestvennoi Voiny*, Moscow, 1963, p. 204.

about 400 rubles.[8] A U.S. observer estimated that up to 85 percent of family income was spent on food,[9] or roughly 340 rubles of the average wage of 400 rubles. Some would have been spent on food bought under the rationing system. A good estimate of the cost of a month's supply of rationed food can be made based on the July 1943 data from Moscow for a Category 2 worker, if we assume that the maximum ration allowance was purchased. Table 8.5 shows that the maximum amount that could be spent by a worker would have been 86.22 rubles,[10] leaving about 250 rubles of the estimated 340 spent on food to be spent in the free market. Therefore, it seems reasonable to think that if the expenditures on rationed food constituted no more than one-quarter of food expenditures, then the remaining three-quarters would have been spent in the free market. And this estimate may be low because we know that for many, if not most, months it was not possible for individuals to have all of their ration allowances honored.

[8] USSR: Crop Conditions and Production, 1942–1945. Records of the Foreign Agricultural Service. Record Group 166, National Archives, Washington, D.C., Despatch No. 11, U.S. Embassy at Kuibyshev, June 28, 1943. The representative wage for a semiskilled factory worker was defined as 400 rubles, although this was said to be reduced by taxes and other contributions. Janet Chapman estimated that the average annual money wage for all wage earners and salaried employees in 1944, a year later than we are concerned, was 5,270 rubles, or 439 rubles a month. See *Real Wages in Soviet Russia Since 1928*, Cambridge: Harvard University Press, 1963, p. 109.
[9] U.S. State Department Decimal File 1940–1944, Document No. 550.AD 1/1007. In view of the high percentage of Soviet household income spent on food even today, such an estimate seems plausible.
[10] I estimate that exactly the same market basket would have cost 82.37 rubles on January 1, 1940, in Moscow, based on prices found in Lazar Volin, *A Survey of Soviet Russian Agriculture*, Washington, D.C., n.p., 1951, p. 176.

Table 8.5. *Cost of one month's rationed food supply to a Category 2 worker in Moscow (July 1943)*

Bread, 600 grams a day for 31 days (18.6 kg)	
70% at 1.00 rubles per kg	
30% at 2.25 rubles per kg	25.57 rubles
Sugar, 500 grams (5.5 rubles per kg)	2.75 rubles
Butter, 800 grams (26 rubles per kg)	20.80 rubles
Meat, 2200 grams	
virtually no meat given – 15 eggs per kg given instead	
at 6.50 rubles 10 eggs)	21.45 rubles
Grain, 2000 grams (poor-quality rice sold at 6.50 rubles per kg)	13.00 rubles
Tea, 25 grams (1 kg = 90 rubles)	2.25 rubles
Salt, 400 grams (1 kg = 1.00 ruble)	.40 rubles
Total	86.22 rubles

Source: NFAS, U.S. Embassy at Moscow, Despatch No. 3, August 4, 1943.

Table 8.6. *Free market prices in Moscow during July 1943 (in rubles)*

Black bread	150 per kg
Gray bread	250 per kg
White bread	300 per kg
Potatoes	50 per kg
Butter	800 per kg
Eggs	200 for 10
Pork or mutton	600 per kg
Beef	400 per kg
Salt	50 per kg
Sugar (lump)	900 per kg
Milk	50 per liter
Flour, white	280 per liter
Flour, rye	200 per liter
Cabbages	150 per liter
Radishes	8 per bunch
Raspberries	20 per water glass

Source: NFAS, U.S. Embassy at Moscow, Despatch No. 3, August 4, 1943.

The low, fixed prices of rationed food shown in Table 8.5 should be compared to the prices prevailing in the free markets in Moscow in late July 1943 (Table 8.6). Here the approximately 250 rubles a month would buy a kilo of gray bread (an intermediate grade of bread as its name suggests), or a dozen eggs, or not quite a kilo of white flour, or about a pound and a half of beef. In other words, 250 rubles bought very little. Consider the recollection of K. S. Karol, who earned more than the average salary: "With her monthly three hundred rubles Klava could only buy three kilos of bread on the black market, and I could afford on my salary only four and a half kilos."[11] To the extent that rationed foods were not available for any given month, consumers would be even more at the mercy of the high prices of the free market. Unless people engaged in barter, stole, had privileged access to food, grew their own food, or engaged in the second economy, they were in a desperate situation.

Let us consider the whole question of the meaning of free market prices. The Soviet economist Tamarchenko writes that by 1944 average monthly wages of industrial workers had risen by 53 percent in comparison with 1940 and confirms the generally held view that prices on rationed foods remained virtually constant throughout the war.[12] He also says that real wages fell during the war because of the high prices on the kolkhoz market. Malafeev contends more specifically that real wages fell 60 percent, which he also attributes to prices on the kolkhoz market.[13] This would mean that, roughly speaking, people would have been paying 113 percent more in the market for food than they did before the war. But we have indisputable indications that the prices for food on the free market were much higher than slightly double prewar prices. All of this suggests that free market prices were merely expressions of inflationary pressure but had no meaning because, in fact, only the wealthy bought at these prices.

Free-market prices imposed severe hardship on ordinary citizens, as is reflected in the stories of émigrés. One said that her family could not afford to buy meat often, so they would buy a single pound of meat and use it over and over again to make soup: "Most people drank tea or boiled water and few had sugar. If you were lucky enough to have a piece of sugar you had to cut it into small pieces. My mother would tie sugar inside her dress in order to hide it." Tea was scarce and expensive. After multiple uses it was often tannish in color. Her husband remarked sardonically that "people drank yellow black tea."[14] Another émigré said that her family did not have enough money to buy food in the kolkhoz market and that those who had

---

[11] Karol, p. 251.
[12] M. L. Tamarchenko, *Sovetskie finansy v period Velikoi Otechestvennoi voiny*, Moscow, 1967, p. 53.
[13] Malafeev, p. 235.
[14] Interview of September 11, 1986.

enough money to pay free-market prices were "people who were in business," by which she meant those operating in the second economy.[15] Other émigré stories show that the alternative was barter, as in the case of one woman's father who stole items from his plant to exchange for food because "it was impossible for ordinary workers to buy food on the market."[16]

Barter

Barter first came into play during the evacuation. Those refugees who either did not have a lot of money or who did not have the foresight to take a lot of money with them on the trip east were forced to trade clothing and jewelry with peasants at stopping points along the way. Even after the need for this transient market had passed and the circumstances of people's lives had returned to some sort of normalcy, barter continued to be part of the exchange system and became even more important.

The seemingly uncontrollable rise of prices had a profound effect on the operation of food markets. With the real purchasing power of money falling, money ceased to function as the medium of exchange and barter became the primary, if not sole, means by which people purchased food. The acceptance of money implies some further transaction because consumers have to buy a good before they receive satisfaction. But there was little to buy during the war and for most of those sellers engaging in barter, money was not a precondition for the subsistence of the household.[17]

The rise of barter was not just a response to the debauching of the currency. It also reflected the rise of localism, which meant that regional markets were cut off from the central economy; regional autonomy was synonymous with the partial disintegration of the economic union of the country.[18] Barter was positively correlated with local conditions; the more scarce food was locally, the more likely

[15] Interview of March 21, 1988.
[16] Interview of June 18, 1988.
[17] For a good overview of the concept of barter, see John Eatwell, Murray Milgate, and Peter Newman, editors, *The New Palgrave Dictionary of Economics*, Vol. 1, London: Macmillan, 1987, pp. 196–8.
[18] An excellent argument for the emergence of barter under particular socioeconomic circumstances can be found in Caroline Humphrey, "Barter and Economic Disintegration," *Man*, Vol. 20, No. 1, March 1985, pp. 48–72. A narrower analysis of economic adjustments made by politically autonomous societies can be found in Mary W. Helms, "The Purchase Society: Adaptation to Economic Frontiers," *Anthropological Quarterly*. Vol. 42, 1969, pp. 325–42.

were people to use barter; the more geographically remote the region was from the center (and therefore the less engaged it was with central economic control), the more likely was barter to prevail. In these instances, prices expressed in ruble terms at best provided a basis for negotiation; they reflected the degree of scarcity, but not what people actually paid because, in many places, money did not matter. In the broadest view of the Soviet Union during the war, we can see that the barter system never completely took over in the operation of food markets and that a price system and barter operated simultaneously. The system bent, but never broke.

From the individual's point of view, it was frustrating to try to buy food at exorbitant market prices. "Unfortunately, on the black market, money had very little purchasing power. It is almost as if, in switching from one market to another, we were entering another world where everything has increased in value a hundredfold."[19] This meant barter, and each tale about the experience of barter is different.

A Polish woman whose family had owned property in occupied Poland was one of the many thousands deported from eastern Poland after the area was annexed to the USSR in late 1939. Arrested in early 1940, she was sent to a labor camp in Archangel along with her three-year-old daughter. Although entitled to rations, her diet was extremely inadequate. In order to supplement her diet and get milk for the child she would sneak out of the camp and walk nine miles through the forest to a kolkhoz to trade clothing, including a silk blouse and silk underwear, for food. In time, the clothing ran out, although apparently the generosity of the farmers did not. They continued periodically to give her milk for her child.[20] Another woman's story of barter was quite different. Before the war her father had worked as a high-level hospital administrator and, as a consequence, had been able to buy vodka, cigarettes, and even saccharine. He could not possibly have known what foresight he showed when he saved these prizes. When the war came he traded them for food, including U.S. Lend-Lease *tushonka*.[21]

The most significant aspect of barter within Soviet food markets was the emergence of bread as the primary medium of exchange after money. In the Soviet case, bread gained the status of money for varying periods of time in many places. It became the most precious commodity because it satisfied the two most basic definitions of

[19] Karol, p. 251.
[20] Interview of March 14, 1988.
[21] Interview of June 18, 1988.

money. It was accepted by others as a legitimate medium of exchange and it could serve as a store of value.

It was illegal to exchange bread obtained with ration cards for other food products. In fact, there was a flourishing market for ration-card bread among collective farmers. In mid–1943 farmers accepted black bread as payment at the rate of 100 rubles a kilogram and whole wheat bread at 150 rubles (about double the rate of six months earlier).[22] The state prices in 1943 for these two kinds of bread were, respectively, 0.9 rubles and 2.7 rubles a kilogram.[23] There are three explanations for the farmers' willingness to pay these high prices. One is that farmers purchased bread because the state took away their grain, and the best quality grain at that. A second and slightly different explanation is that because no consumer goods were available for purchase during the war, farmers hoarded grain and built up their reserves. Being cash-rich because of the high prices they obtained for food on the open market, farmers could afford to offer a handsome price for rationed bread baked from the better grain that had been extracted by the state.[24] Finally, not all, or even most, peasants grew grain and they were forced onto the free market during the war.

So if a family could afford to part with some of its bread – a situation that could only hold if there were multiple earners – it could improve its diet by trading the bread in the free market, although doing so was illegal. In mid–1943, the following prices prevailed in Kuibyshev, denominated in terms of bread: one kilogram of black bread equalled one-third a kilogram of meat; or one-seventh a kilogram of sausage, suet, or fat side; or one-sixth a kilogram of butter; or six eggs; or two liters of milk; or two kilograms of potatoes; or slightly more than one kilogram of onions.[25]

The role of barter increased as one got farther from the center, a fact related to a larger pattern in interregional price differentials. Typically, prices increased as one went from west to east on the Trans-Siberian railroad. On the average, excluding some local variations, prices in the Primorsk region bordering the Pacific were twice the level found in the European parts of the country. As a corollary to this pattern, the role of barter increased as one moved east.[26] Planners apparently were unable and/or unwilling to distribute as much food

---

[22] NFAS, U.S. Embassy at Kuibyshev, Despatch No. 11, June 28, 1943.
[23] NFAS, L. Michael, "Crop Conditions in the U.S.S.R.," U.S. Embassy at Kuibyshev, June 9, 1943, p. 6.
[24] Ibid., p. 7.
[25] NFAS, U.S. Embassy at Kuibyshev, June 9, 1943.
[26] NFAS, U.S. Embassy at Moscow, Despatch No. 299, October 15, 1943.

to the east. In the summer of 1943, there were "very few areas between Vladivostok and Sverdlovsk [a distance of several thousand miles] where money was the preferred medium of exchange." In the entire region stretching from Khabarovsk to Chita along at least one thousand miles of railroad, peasants were unwilling to exchange their limited produce for anything but bread.[27]

From one end of the country to another, bread had become the coin of the realm. It could be the medium of exchange for services rendered, especially in times of great privation. Vera Inber's diary recording the travails of the winter of 1941 and 1942 in Leningrad has an entry on January 2, 1942, about what happened after people died in the hospital: "Long trenches are dug in the cemetery, in which the bodies are laid. The cemetery guards only dig separate graves if they are bribed with bread."[28] And in Moscow it was a preferred currency for black market services, as can be seen in novels about the war such as Vasily Grossman's *Life and Fate*. Lyudmila used bread to pay a truck driver, a plumber, and the gas man when she moved back to Moscow.[29] And Solzhenitsyn reflected on the strange pact between the mourners and the gravedigger in Leningrad: "This sinister profession was the most badly needed in the besieged city. As a final tribute to the dead, the survivors gave the gravedigger their pauper's morsels of bread."[30]

Clothing was the second most important item of barter in the food markets. It was lightweight and both buyer and seller could transport it, it was useful to the peasantry (unlike, say, a grand piano, although in at least one case a woman from Leningrad succeeded in trading one for bread),[31] and it could be exchanged again by the peasants who had accepted it in the first place. Many émigrés remember exchanging clothing for food at the market. One remembers that in Chernikovsk, which is 200 miles west of Cheliabinsk, her mother began to sell clothing because she and the two children "were always hungry. . . . I remember going to the market with my brother and my mother exchanged a pair of his pants for a piece of bread."[32] Another remembers exchanging a favorite dress for food, and yet another exchanged clothing for butter at the market.[33]

But there was a finite supply of clothing and therefore ultimately

[27] Ibid.
[28] Vera Inber, *Leningrad Diary*, New York: St. Martin's Press, 1971, p. 39.
[29] Vasily Grossman, pp. 445, 448.
[30] Alexander Solzhenitsyn, *The First Circle*, New York: Harper & Row, 1968, p. 261.
[31] Interview of October 28, 1986.
[32] Interview of June 18, 1988.
[33] Interviews of September 23, 1986, and June 27, 1986.

a limitation on the currency of cloth and clothing. Little new clothing was produced during the war and the use of clothing as an item of trade had to end at some point. Therefore, in mid–1943, a U.S. diplomat in Kuibyshev noted that "there is already a considerable degree of [clothing] 'starvation.'"[34] Overall, what transpired was a remarkable redistribution of clothing out of the cities and into the countryside.

In Moscow, vodka and tobacco were also used as mediums of exchange, but they never attained the importance of bread and clothing.[35] In Yaroslavl, after bread, tea, and on rare occasions sugar were accepted as mediums of exchange.[36] I have also seen one mention of grain per se as the medium of exchange on a particular kolkhoz. Peasants paid for such things as nails, cord, brooms, rakes, and house rent with grain.[37]

The collective farm market was a curious combination of a white market and a black market. It was a white market because producers could sell all they wanted as long as they met their obligations to the state, and it was a black market because buyers were trading an illegal currency, ration bread. Yet with some exceptions, the state adopted a very lenient attitude toward the activities in the free market. By and large, the police seemed to have left these markets alone. The accounts of U.S. diplomats suggest that the trading of food for bread went on right under the noses of the militia, who it seems were often present, at least at the biggest markets. One diplomat witnessed a young boy trying to sell about thirty food ration tickets and a watch.[38] Yet some émigrés remember unpleasant incidents involving the police that do not reflect such a hands-off attitude, for instance:

> Once I was with my mother at the market. There was a man with many medals and he started to buy something at the market. The NKVD asked him for his identification papers. Pointing to his medals, the man said, "This is my ID." The police started pushing him and then clubbed him into unconsciousness and dragged him away in their car.[39]

Whatever orders the police may have had, it was certainly not to deal a death blow to free market activity. The presence of the police

[34] NFAS, U.S. Embassy at Kuibyshev, Despatch No. 11, June 28, 1943.
[35] NFAS, U.S. Embassy at Moscow, Despatch No. 15, March 18, 1942.
[36] NFAS, U.S. Embassy at Moscow, Despatch No. 299, October 15, 1943.
[37] Lazar Volin, "German Invasion and Russian Agriculture," *Russian Review*, November 1943, p. 86.
[38] NFAS, U.S. Embassy at Moscow, Despatch No. 850, August 24, 1944.
[39] Interview of August 19, 1986.

at these markets in the main served, I suspect, to minimize the most egregious behavior, for example, the sale of ration cards. The cruelties that may have occurred at these markets were infrequent; in truth, the state looked the other way out of self-interest. The state did not want to undertake the task of feeding the civilian population and therefore left this responsibility to local initiative, whether the activity was legal or not.

But as the tide of war turned, the Soviets were able to recapture once-occupied agricultural areas in the Ukraine, Belorussia, and the Caucasus, and although food remained scarce, the situation began to change. This fact, plus the immediate effect of the 1943 harvest, caused the rate of inflation to slow. By 1944 agricultural output began to increase. Now the government attitude toward the free market clearly changed. However, naked power was not used to destroy the markets. Rather, the terms on which these markets could operate were changed and the institutional environment was altered.

The major change came in 1944, when the government opened commercial stores that directly competed with the private markets. These stores were created as pressure on the food supply was easing. They offered nonrationed food at very high prices that in many cases approached the levels found at the farmers' market. In general, the products sold in the stores were considered to be of higher quality and were handled in a more sanitary fashion than in the collective farm market.[40] It seems likely that the commercial stores began operations for two reasons. First, the government wanted to break the back of the collective farm markets by drawing urbanites away from them. Second, because there was a great deal of money to be made by selling food at high prices, the state also wanted a piece of the action. It was the same response the state had showed when the collective farm markets were successful in the early 1930s. In 1933, at Stalin's behest, the commercial stores that had been created in 1929 to sell nonfood consumer goods at high prices began to sell bread and then other food items. The state's invasion of the market was a huge success, and sales rose from 3.9 billion rubles to 13.0 billion rubles in 1934.[41] This lesson had not been forgotten. The wartime commercial stores allowed the state to sop up some of the inflationary pressure in the food market and to enrich the coffers of the central treasury.

The commercial stores were under the administrative aegis of *Osob-*

---

[40] NFAS, U.S. Embassy at Moscow, Despatch No. 1600, April 3, 1945.
[41] Jasny, p. 387.

torg (Special Trade Organization), and the first ones opened in Moscow on April 15, 1944.[42] As of August 1944, there were twenty commercial stores in the capital.[43] Thereafter, commercial stores were opened in Leningrad, Kiev, Sverdlovsk, Gorky, and a number of other large cities,[44] and several months later they began to function in Central Asia or in the east.[45] The operation of commercial stores did not begin in Vladivostok until November 1, 1944, about six months later than the opening of these stores in the major cities of the European part of the USSR, but once opened they became a major enterprise. These operations included two commercial restaurants, one fish and meat store, and one provisions store whose affairs were managed from Moscow. It was explicitly stated when the enterprise opened that one of its principal goals was to lower prices in Vladivostok's food markets, a goal that was achieved according to a U.S. diplomat's report.[46] Over time the Vladivostok operations lowered their own prices as well. It is virtually impossible, however, to separate out the effect of the rising food supply due to the return of agricultural lands from the effect of the opening of the commercial stores, but between November 1, 1944, and March 1, 1945, the average level of *Osobtorg* prices fell by 9 percent. Military officers received a 20 percent discount in the stores and a 30 percent discount in the restaurants.[47]

The commercial stores also offered a variety of foods often not available on the free market. The following foods are a sampling from the July 1, 1944, offerings available at Gastronom No. 1, one of the largest commercial stores in Moscow: cottage cheese, two grades each of sweet butter and salted butter, buttermilk, canned powdered milk, fresh eggs, smoked salmon, black caviar, red caviar, boiled crabs, several kinds of canned vegetables (squash, tomatoes, peas), green peppers, beef, veal, mutton, pork, cooked ham, liverwurst, bacon, fresh strawberries, dried apricots, and three varieties of raisins.[48] In August, fresh eggplants, cucumbers, and cauliflower, as well as canned apples and peaches, were added to the offerings.[49]

[42] NFAS, Despatch 1255, November 30, 1944.
[43] NFAS, U.S. Embassy at Moscow, Despatch No. 13, August 15, 1944.
[44] NFAS, U.S. Embassy at Moscow, Despatch No. 1362, January 6, 1945.
[45] Ambassador Harriman noted that there were no commercial stores operating in Tashkent or Alma-Ata during a visit he made to these two cities at the end of June 1944. U.S. Department of State, *Foreign Relations of the United States*, 1944, Vol. IV, Washington, D.C., p. 971.
[46] NFAS, U.S. Embassy at Moscow, Despatch No. 1123, April 11, 1945.
[47] Ibid.
[48] NFAS, U.S. Embassy at Moscow, "Food Prices in Gastronom No. 1–A Free or Commercial Store," July 1944.
[49] NFAS, U.S. Embassy at Moscow, Despatch No. 801, August 9, 1944.

Competition from the commercial stores, along with the increased supply of food from the 1944 harvest, began to push down prices on the collective farm market. For instance, in 1944, the amount of food sold in Moscow markets rose substantially over 1943: 40 percent more milk, 70 percent more meat, and 100 percent more potatoes. Moscow prices on the collective farm market simultaneously fell from their 1943 levels. The price of potatoes was one-third of the previous year's level, the price of milk fell 50 percent, and meat prices fell at least 50 percent.[50] The state commercial stores helped push the price decline, along with a series of price cuts. When the commercial stores had opened in mid-April, they charged 450 rubles per kilogram of meat, the same price that had prevailed on the free market during the three prior months of January, February, and March. The commercial stores decreased the price of meat to 360 rubles in May and, partly in response to this, the price of meat was reduced to 200 rubles per kilogram in the free market. Similarly, when the commercial stores reduced the price of meat to 250 rubles per kilogram in October, prices in the free market went down to 150 rubles.[51] And on November 6, 1944, a 30 percent reduction in prices on all items in commercial stores was announced in honor of the twenty-seventh anniversary of the revolution.[52]

Seen in the best light, the commercial stores can be viewed as increasing the quantity and quality and lowering the price of civilian food. It is also arguable that they were used manipulatively to seduce the population away from the free markets by offering lower prices and a wider variety of food. Soviet hostility toward free markets is expressed in the statement by the economic historian Cherniavskii that "one of the great achievements of the Soviet state was breaking the price dynamic of the collective farm market in the middle of 1943."[53] This gives us an insight into Soviet intentions. They wanted the reign of the free market to end, probably for ideological reasons as well as for the purpose of diminishing open inflation.

The state also competed on occasion against the collective farm market in barter trade. In Tashkent, there was a branch of *Torgsin*, the international trade organization, that bought gold jewelry from ordinary individuals and issued paper chits on which the money value of the gold was written. The only place where the chits could be used

---

[50] *Moskovskii bol'shevik*, November 11, 1944, cited in NFAS, Despatch No. 1255, November 30, 1988.
[51] NFAS, U.S. Embassy at Moscow, Despatch No. 1255, November 30, 1944.
[52] *The New York Times*, November 6, 1944, p. 6.
[53] Cherniavskii, p. 91.

was at *Torgsin*, where people could buy not only Soviet-made food, but also U.S. Lend-Lease food, including *tushonka*, cheese, and powdered eggs.[54]

A different sort of blow against the collective farm market was struck toward the end of the war. The RSFSR Sovnarkom issued a decree on December 31, 1944, part of which concerned the question of how to improve the work of the collective farm markets. After naming a large number of major cities in which "collective farm trade is particularly unsatisfactorily organized," the issue of sanitation was raised as being of major concern.[55] The decree ordered that food should not lie on the ground in the markets and that nonfood goods not be sold right next to food stalls, but most important it forbade the sale of meat, fish, dairy, and other products without preliminary examination by the appropriate veterinary and sanitary inspectors of the People's Commissariat for Health. Health is a noble purpose, but why did the state choose the end of 1944 to impose new standards? This was probably a thinly veiled message to farmers that the eyes of the state were upon them once again. From the planners' perspective, with the war about to end, the moment was at hand when the central government would be in full command again, and it was time for latitude and localism to fade away. The system was being recentralized.

Conclusion

During the war, the government jettisoned ideology, in essence turning a blind eye to "exploitative" activities of the peasantry in the collective farm market. It probably had to because the free market served a vital purpose, going well beyond the role it had played before the war. First, it mitigated at least to some degree the brutal shortages that the war imposed. Second, for the party to call attention to the outright profiteering would also have called attention to the fact that central planning could not provide the food that the civilian population required. Finally, if the state had not allowed private markets to flourish, what incentive would kolkhoz farmers have

---

[54] Interview of March 21, 1988. There is no indication of how widespread this practice was in the country.
[55] NFAS, U.S. Embassy at Moscow, Despatch No. 225, May 1945. The places named were the Smolensk, Kursk, Orel, Stalingrad, Rostov, and Voronezh oblasts, the Krasnodar and Stavropol krais, the Penza, Gorky, Ryazan, Novosibirsk, and Moscow oblasts and in the Bashkir and Udmurt autonomous republics.

had to increase their sowings and market surplus agricultural products? Because there was nothing from the socialist sector for farmers to buy with their meager earnings, their only incentive to produce a surplus would have been the need to feed their own families. Only the possibility of earning (and hoarding) cash and clothing persuaded them to work toward supplying wider markets.

The growth of the free market also led to a major redistribution of money and other assets from the cities to the countryside. The regime also must have had ambivalent feelings about this outcome, predictable though it was. On the one hand, the fact that a number of peasants became cash-rich made them an excellent target group for buying the subscription bonds issued during the war. With no goods to buy, the peasants became an important lender to the government. Although urbanites were the dominant purchasers of bonds during the war, hundreds of farmers bought bonds in the range of 30,000 to 100,000 rubles and there were peasants who subscribed for as much as 400,000 rubles.[56] On the other hand, the perverse redistributive effects of wartime economic realities had to disturb the leadership on an ideological level.

So we should not be surprised that as the state became stronger, the wide latitude given the free market in food was restricted and eventually withdrawn. With rising agricultural output in 1944, the pressure on all markets eased. The commercial stores also had some effect in this regard, but it was indirect. The state did not blanket the country with these outlets – for example, there were only twenty such stores in Moscow – and the few that existed could not have been decisive in moderating the inflation of food prices. Nevertheless, because these stores were in competition with the free market, they had a definite if not precisely known impact on prices.

At the beginning of the war, the distribution of food, much like the production of food, was allowed to fall into private hands to a degree unknown before the war. It remained there and the regime kept its hands off until almost mid–1944, when we judge that the regime felt that it had the strength to take charge again. The evidence suggests a conscious policy of allowing free markets to do what the government could not do itself.

[56] NFAS, U.S. Embassy at Kuibyshev, June 28, 1943.

9 Crime and privilege

The government's tolerance of quasi-legal free market activity had limits. Expediency had dictated stretching the definition of what the system would tolerate during the war because the state could not meet the food needs of the civilian population through the rationing system. But for many civilians, the markets that arose to supplement rationing were financially inaccessible and some people chose to operate outside of the system to secure more food, thus engaging in criminal activity. In addition, a second group, the privileged of Soviet society, also operated outside the system. Their greater access to food was legal, even if it violated the spirit of equity implicit in the rationing system.

Food crimes

There were two types of criminal activity: stealing from the state and stealing from other individuals. The most widespread of these, stealing from the state, took several forms. The first was manipulating the ration card system in one way or another to increase one's own food supply or sell food to others. A second form was stealing from the workplace. Those fortunate enough to work in a place involved in the production or distribution of food stole food directly; others stole items that could be exchanged for food. Stealing from individuals came closer to robbery in the usual sense of the word, but also included stealing from individual gardens of peasants and urban victory gardens. Sometimes this merged into stealing from the state. There is, unfortunately, no way to document in any systematic way the amount of crime that took place. We must extrapolate what happened from occasional press reports, observations of diplomats serving in the Soviet Union during the war, and émigré accounts. The limited evidence suggests that there was a great deal of crime and that it increased as the availability of food deteriorated in 1942.

Many ration cards were not acquired through legitimate channels. A market for ration cards developed in a number of places. In 1941 a couple in Rostov developed a business buying and selling ration cards in a market where supply, demand, and price all fluctuated.[1] One could sell one's ration card one day if there was a short-term need for cash and buy a card on some other day, although because of price fluctuations it was never possible to know whether you would benefit from such a transaction. At the extreme, there was outright counterfeiting of ration cards, clearly a criminal act and a natural attraction for the unscrupulous. However, the crime might be altruistic. One Russian Robin Hood would reportedly inundate the market with ration cards, thus lowering the price to all.[2]

Stealing food itself from the state took place on farms and in factories producing food. In 1944 severe shortages of onions and garlic were reported in a number of areas of the country. The shortages were a result of actual theft and the reluctance of farmers to plant these two crops because of the threat of theft. It turns out that thieves found these two crops appealing because they were relatively lightweight, were easy to steal, and sold at very high prices in the free market.[3] One émigré became a brigade leader on a collective farm, which gave him the opportunity to steal food. He usually stole wheat seeds that he pounded into flour and baked. It was heaven when he would get a glass of milk from the kolkhoz chairman to go with his wheat.[4]

The tale of one émigré is particularly revealing. In 1942 the émigré's father worked in a slaughterhouse in Dushanbe. All the meat prepared in the slaughterhouse was supposed to go to the Red Army, but people managed to steal meat by hiding it between their legs and under their arms when they left work. This family had an additional ally, a German shepherd appropriately named *Pirat* (Pirate) who at noon each day would jump the fence of their house, run to the factory where the father worked, and leap the fence there while the security guards looked the other way, knowing full well to whom the dog belonged and why he was there. The father would first give the dog

[1] Karol, pp. 74–5.
[2] Ibid., p. 74.
[3] USSR Crop Conditions and Production, 1942–1945. Records of the Foreign Agricultural Service. Record Group 166, National Archives, Washington, D.C. (NFAS), U.S. Embassy at Moscow, memo of March 22, 1944.
[4] Interview of November 18, 1987.

A woman guarding the fields of the Twelfth Anniversary of October collective farm. *Source:* National Archives.

some food for himself and then tie a small package of meat around the dog's body, which he would carry home. So the family came to depend on the dog and they ate relatively well because of him. One day they could not get the dog to go through his daily routine. He hid in the doghouse and then ran to each corner of the yard as the family members tried to get him to run to the factory. He finally relented and did his duty. But he was shot to death by a new security officer who did not know him. It is clear that the dog had a sixth sense and knew there was danger.[5]

An émigré who worked as a tool and dye maker in a Kuibyshev factory for most of the war said that it was common for workers to steal from the factory and exchange the stolen items for food in the collective farm market: "We didn't steal from each other; we stole to survive."[6] A high level administrator in a defense plant in Uzbekistan was responsible among other things for coal and gasoline supplies. He would siphon off fuel and exchange it for food on the market. As a consequence, his daughter believes her family ate satisfactorily during the war.[7] Nor was food destined for the army regarded as sacred. A Red Army officer spoke of the pilfering of dry bread from trains headed from the interior to the front.[8]

Food was also stolen from individuals in the private sector. In mid–1943 *Pravda* complained about potatoes and other vegetables being stolen from individual gardens in Kuibyshev and Ivanov, implying this practice was common. It blamed local public organizations for not guarding the gardens and allowing so-called hooligans to "act with impunity."[9] An émigré who had been evacuated to Alma-Ata spoke of a great deal of crime: "People robbed other people either to steal food or to steal things they could exchange for food. People were even killed over food. We locked our door at night after 5 P.M. because people would try to break in. Several times we had our windows broken and once our house was broken into."[10]

It is absolutely impossible to determine exactly how much crime occurred. But from several pieces of evidence that suggest a campaign against theft began in late 1942, we may infer that the amount of food crime was on the increase. In December 1942, the campaign was launched by a strongly worded *Pravda* article that urged that those

---

[5] Interview of December 22, 1985.
[6] Interview of March 21, 1988.
[7] Interview of June 18, 1988.
[8] I am grateful to Eric Goldhagen for this information.
[9] *Pravda*, July 4, 1943.
[10] Interview of August 19, 1986.

who stole grain be "severely" punished,[11] an implicit warning. On January 22, 1943, the State Defense Committee, the most powerful administrative organ during the war, adopted a resolution, "On Strengthening the Struggle with Stealing and Selling Food and Industrial Goods," suggesting the seriousness of the problem. The purpose of the resolution was to stop abuses in the distribution of ration cards and the stealing of food.[12] *Narkomtorg*, which already was responsible for food distribution, was made responsible for rectifying the problems. It, in turn, assigned the job to the Chief Department of State Trade Inspection and its affiliates at the union republic and oblast levels. They were supposed to watch out for theft during the delivery of goods to trade establishments and public catering enterprises. The heads of the inspection units were given broad powers in implementing the new decree and an additional 120 inspectors were hired. In view of the vast geographic area to be covered and the large number of state organizations to be monitored, this hardly constituted a major commitment of personnel to the antitheft campaign. However, this was only the beginning.

No more than a week later, on February 1, the presidium of the central trade union organization adopted a resolution to deal with food theft that went beyond the January 22 decree.[13] This time the strategy was to mobilize an army of informers. About 600,000 social controllers (*obshchestvenny kontrolery*) were chosen to watch activities in cafeterias, stores, at the food storage bases, and at the subsidiary farms. In other words, a mass movement of workers was to be given the responsibility of watching their friends and coworkers who were eating as badly or as well as they. Although some progress may have been made in the anticrime campaign, it is unlikely that there was notable success. No doubt there were zealots willing to inform on their coworkers who were stealing from the state, but almost everyone was suffering and it is unlikely that many workers were anxious to engage in anything but a conspiracy of silence. Everyone wanted to survive.

Therefore, the next step by the authorities suggests their continued frustration. A decree issued on July 18, 1943, about preparing for the harvest, otherwise innocuous in its issuance of instructions and exhortations on the harvest and procurement procedures, contained very precise instructions about preventing theft:[14] "In 1943 day and

[11] *Pravda*, December 4, 1942, p. 3.
[12] U. G. Cherniavskii, *Voina i prodovol'stvie*, Moscow, 1964, p. 111–12.
[13] Ibid., pp. 115–16.
[14] NFAS, U.S. Embassy at Moscow, Report No. 196, July 26, 1943.

night watchmen should guard unreaped grain and piled and stacked reaped grain. From 10 to 15 days before the ripening of grain, mounted guards should patrol the fields. Day and night watchmen should guard grain on the threshing premises." Most significantly, the decree stated that those found guilty of stealing grain and other agricultural products from state and collective farms would be subject to the August 7, 1932, law on stealing public property. That law, passed in the midst of the chaos of collectivization and generally regarded as having been written by Stalin himself, provided that anyone stealing from state and collective farms was to be shot, unless there were mitigating circumstances, in which case the penalty would be ten years in prison.[15]

These tough anticrime measures built on concern about the theft of food both before the war and early in the war. In early 1940 a food store manager was executed for hoarding food.[16] Near the end of October 1941, three men were sentenced to death by a military tribunal for stealing and selling 300 pounds of bread.[17] A Moscow radio broadcast in mid-September 1941, shortly after the so-called Stalin harvest had been gathered, counseled workers to protect vigilantly the newly gathered grain.[18] But the 1943 actions show an escalation of concern and punishment, suggesting that crime was increasing as the amount of food available to feed the civilian population decreased.

The 1943 measures came in the wake of the period in which civilians had the most difficulty feeding themselves. It seems likely that a sense of hopelessness led many to commit crimes they would not have otherwise committed. This must have placed some strain on the social order or at least led the authorities to fear that social equilibrium was potentially endangered. For the ordinary citizen, there was a certain degree of acceptance of stealing because survival was something everyone could understand. In the main, people did not steal to profiteer, but to survive. Crime was not ordinarily a way of life for many who engaged in stealing. These were not people whose lives were tied up with crime in the prewar period. Crimes were committed by desperately hungry people. It was tolerated by one's peers, but not by the authorities, who were even willing to execute those who stole because they could not get enough to eat.

[15] Robert Conquest, *The Harvest of Sorrow*, New York: Oxford University Press, 1986, p. 184; J. Stalin, *Works*, Vol. 13, p. 402.
[16] *The New York Times*, January 19, 1940, p. 10.
[17] *The Times* (London), October 25, 1941, p. 3.
[18] *Daily Report of Foreign Radio Broadcasts*, September 16, 1941.

Privilege

There was not the same crackdown on those who obtained extra food through privilege, that is, personal or family connections or party and government status that gave them access to food. Because the authorities themselves were among the privileged, it should not be surprising that they made no attempt to diminish their privileged access to food. Understandably, there was a strong sense of injustice on the part of ordinary citizens toward at least some of the privileged.

In the main, privilege in the Soviet Union was conferred on four major elite groups – the party and government, the upper echelons of the military, intellectuals, and foreigners – during the war. Party and government privilege manifested itself in a variety of ways. Before the war, the father of one émigré was a deputy administrator at a suburban Leningrad hospital that served members of the party and so had a store where one could buy special things not available to the general public, such as vodka, cigarettes, and even saccharine: "Even though my father neither smoked nor drank, he bought these items and saved them." No doubt he stored these valuables against the unknown future: "When the war started, he traded them with the peasants for food. He even traded for *tushonka*."[19]

Party membership conferred special access to food that was not available to nonparty members at what would otherwise be the same level of status in the Soviet hierarchy. As Grossman put it, "Workers – and famous scientists, if they're not Party members – have to beg for their bread."[20] In August 1943, the U.S. ambassador ate dinner in a restaurant in Stalingrad set aside for government officials. He described a meal at which a plate of brown bread was served from which the Soviet diners had the right to eat 200 grams, which was to be deducted from their 800-gram ration the next day. Therefore, the officials were limited to the standard bread ration. The rest of the meal, however, was substantial, nourishing, varied, and inexpensive. He and his Soviet companions ate vegetable soup (1.50 rubles), meat, rice, and cucumber salad (3.2 rubles), and cake (1.30 rubles) for a total bill of 6 rubles or about $.50,[21] a fine meal for the price in mid–1943, especially compared to the shortages that everyone else faced. It suggests that upper echelon officials had privileged access to food.

[19] Interview of June 18, 1988.
[20] Grossman, p. 280.
[21] The ambassador, Admiral Standley, was visiting Stalingrad about six months after the end of the great battle. NFAS, U.S. Embassy at Moscow, report of August 23, 1943.

A former doctor who served at the Volkhov front, not far from Leningrad, said that she, the nurses, and the political workers – about thirty people in all – had their own cook. They also had food that was not available to the wounded soldiers who were their patients, including cooked vegetables, salad dressing, and, sometimes, herring. Occasionally, they also hunted small birds and picked mushrooms. When the hospital was moved to Moldavia, they still had their own cook.[22]

Then, of course, there was dinner with Stalin at the Kremlin, the sanctum sanctorum where there were no food shortages at all. In May 1943, Stalin hosted a four and a half hour state dinner for forty-seven people in honor of U.S. Envoy Joseph E. Davies. Dinner began with "caviar, back of dried sturgeon, herring with dressing, back of sturgeon in sauce, English style roast beef, cold ham, gelatin, olives and spring salads, radishes, cucumbers, and a variety of cheeses." There then followed wild fowl, chicken soup, consommé, Siberian salmon, snipe and fried potatoes, turkey, and cauliflower. Dessert included strawberry tarts and vanilla ice cream, candy, nuts, and liqueurs. All of this was washed down with assorted red and white wines, vodka with hot pepper, and champagne. After dinner entertainment was in the "sumptuous" movie theater of the Kremlin, where each of the guests had a bottle of champagne on a table next to his chair.[23]

The privileged were able to receive discounts at the so-called commercial food stores that opened in the big cities in the spring of 1944. These stores, designed to compete with the free market, offered goods not available on the ration cards at quite high prices, although not as high as the free market prices. They sold such items as butter, meat, eggs, and cheese, which one could buy in the free market, and also prepared foods such as caviar, smoked and canned fish, chocolate bars, and preserved fruits, which were not to be found in the market. It took a great deal of money to shop in the commercial stores, but this was made easier because discounts of from 10 to 40 percent were available to certain privileged groups.[24] A discount of 10 percent was available to workers with a minimum of three years service, white-collar workers with a minimum of six years service, scientific workers, workers in the arts and literature, and engineers. Red Army officers had a 35 percent discount and the top discount of 40 percent went to Heroes of the Soviet Union and Heroes of Socialist Labor.[25]

[22] Interview of May 21, 1988.
[23] *Chicago Daily Tribune*, May 25, 1943, p. 1.
[24] NFAS, U.S. Embassy at Moscow, Despatch No. 13, August 15, 1944.
[25] NFAS, U.S. Embassy at Moscow, July 1944.

Gastronom No. 1 was one of the largest and best supplied of the commercial stores in Moscow. The list of luxury foods one could buy included cheese, black caviar, red caviar, all kinds of canned vegetables, beef and veal, cooked ham, chicken, canned cocoa, cubed and granulated sugar, fresh strawberries, dried apricots, and raisins. There was even fancy crabmeat from Kamchatka with the label printed partly in English. It had the Good Housekeeping label on it, suggesting that it had originally been intended for export to the United States. There was a large section of the store that sold beer, wine, liqueurs, and vodka. One section of the store was reserved for the pro-Soviet Poles living in Moscow during the war. Prices for the Poles were significantly lower than the prices for the Russians and some U.S. products were sold. Many Soviet citizens came into this store more as tourists than as actual shoppers, because the cornucopia of food it offered was simply beyond reach, and people cynically referred to it as *bezbozhni musee*, or the "godless museum," because of the large quantity and varieties of food that were available but were priced so high that only a privileged few could afford to buy them.[26]

In addition, different groups were assigned to "closed stores," where only they could buy food to meet their ration allowances. These stores often, although not always, conferred privileged access to food. A store in Kuibyshev served about 7,000 people, including such groups as Soviet employees of foreign embassies, teachers, physicians, and Intourist employees. Although, according to U.S. reports, most ration allowances were fulfilled in the appropriate month in these stores, there were some food items for which substitutes had to be accepted. In contrast, the railroad workers of Kuibyshev could buy bread and little else from March through May 1943 at the closed store to which they were assigned.[27]

The privilege of the few did not go unnoticed by ordinary civilians. Some complained of favoritism in food distribution, that managers in food stores took care of their friends or people in high places who could offer something in return. Others complained that when a small amount of an item came into the store it was not divided equally, but was sold on a first-come, first-served basis.[28] How much of this is real and how much imagined will never be known. It is enough to say that people perceived injustice at a time when unfairness already seemed to dominate their ruptured lives. As one émigré put it: "Priv-

[26] Ibid.
[27] NFAS, U.S. Embassy at Kuibyshev, Report No. 11, June 28, 1943.
[28] Ibid.

ilege for people in high government and party positions – people resented that."[29]

It should be made clear that there was never any sense of deprivation caused by the fact that soldiers at the front received more food. There was a large gap, however, between the provision of rations that would allow a Red Army soldier to fight with energy and the entitlements that often accompanied officer status. Consider the émigré whose uncle helped his mother get a ration card for a military store in 1944: "Our diet immediately improved. We ate kasha, more and better bread, once a week we had butter and meat, and sometimes we had milk – maybe once a week."[30] Similarly, the wife of a Soviet colonel had special privileges. She had access to the military commissary (*voentorg*) in every city she lived in during the war. Nevertheless, there were times when she had to trade clothing for food on the free market. One of the advantages she had was the right to eat dinner at a special military restaurant every day.[31]

Military officers and officer candidates also were well fed. On the average, cadets at Moscow artillery schools had 3,538 calories and soldiers 3,200 calories in their daily meals.[32] Food and drink were abundant in many headquarters or officer clubs, as we can see from the experiences of foreign correspondent Alexander Werth. He ate an impressive lunch at regimental headquarters on the Vyazma-Smolensk Road where "plain-clothed female attendants served round enormous dishes of roast beef, and half-pound hunks of bread."[33] At the Russian navy club in Archangel he found plenty of vodka and "delicious pale smoked salmon."[34] *Life and Fate*, Vasily Grossman's novel about the war, speaks of "senior lieutenants and lieutenant-colonels who had presented other people's wives with the butter, lard and tinned foods they had brought back from the front."[35]

The highest-ranking members of the Soviet intelligentsia also benefited. Members of the Academy of Science not only had "very liberal rations for clothing and food," but were also able to shop at a special store selling items not typically available.[36] The hierarchy of privilege is described vividly in Grossman's novel. He describes a new canteen in the Institute of Physics of the Academy of Sciences in Moscow that

[29] Interview of September 23, 1986.
[30] Interview of August 19, 1986.
[31] Interview of June 27, 1986.
[32] Alexander Werth, *Moscow War Diary*, New York: Knopf, 1942, p. 192.
[33] Ibid., p. 212.
[34] Ibid., pp. 192, 272.
[35] Grossman, p. 118.
[36] Eric Ashby, *Scientist in America*, New York: Pelican Books, 1947, p. 20.

had six different menus, reflecting the effect of status on access to food. In the canteen there was one menu for doctors of science, one for research directors, another for research assistants, a fourth for senior laboratory assistants, one for technicians, and finally one for service personnel. The first two menus differed only in the dessert offering. If you were titled it was stewed fruit; otherwise you had to settle for a jelly made from powder.[37]

Even in Leningrad in the spring of 1942, just after the nightmarish "hungry winter" but well before anything approaching normalcy would exist, the Writer's House was again serving food that was well above the fare with which ordinary citizens had to be satisfied. Members of the writer's union could get dinner between the hours of 3:00 and 5:00 P.M. without ration cards. There was good barley soup, borscht, kasha, and dessert.[38]

Foreigners, mainly embassy staff personnel, constituted the last group that received special treatment. Even for this elite group, however, there occasionally were serious disruptions in the food supply. Very early in the war, the Soviets explicitly created a dual system, one for foreigners and one for their own citizens. In Moscow, for example, foreigners were entitled to shop at Gastronom No. 1, the famous food store that had catered to the rich before the revolution. Although there were limitations on what foreigners could buy, the limits were considerably higher than for Russians. When sugar was disappearing from the shelves of Moscow stores after the quick German capture of sugar beet acreage in the Ukraine in August and September 1941, foreigners could still buy it.[39]

In the fall of 1941 foreign embassies were evacuated with most of the Soviet government to the city of Kuibyshev, about 500 miles east of Moscow. Those few diplomats who remained in Moscow faced food shortages. In the case of the U.S. Embassy, the State Department was informed that "the Commissary of the Embassy is running low and living essentials are not likely to become purchasable here. Some are not now available." It was requested that the Red Cross immediately ship $5,000 worth of food and other amenities, including canned fruits, vegetables, beans, spaghetti, meats, milk, coffee, tea, and sugar.[40]

---

[37] Grossman, p. 466.
[38] Salisbury, p. 615.
[39] Werth, p. 244.
[40] Records of the Department of State Relating to the Internal Affairs of the Soviet Union 1940–1944. Decimal File 861, Calamities, Disasters, Refugees. Telegram of October 22, 1941, from Ambassador Steinhardt to the State Department.

Kuibyshev was ill-prepared for everybody, including their important foreign guests. But life stabilized for diplomatic personnel and their food situation improved significantly, well before it did for the civilian population of that city. This can be seen from the retail price data for Kuibyshev in January 1942, which shows the differences between the prices paid at the closed stores, the commercial stores, and on the open market (Table 9.1). The closed shops were reserved for foreigners, the Commissariat for Internal Affairs, the Council of People's Commissars, the Commissariat for Foreign Affairs, and selected officials of other organizations, including the armed forces. The commercial stores were open to the general population. Food items could be bought in limited amounts and, as the data show, at prices higher than those prevailing in the closed stores.[41] In the open market prices were determined by the forces of supply and demand, and these prices were several orders of magnitude higher than anywhere else. Table 9.1 shows the prices of twenty-six food commodities that could be bought in both the closed stores and commercial stores or in at least one of these retail outlets and the open market, taken from data gathered by a staff member of the U.S. Embassy. The entire market basket cost 45 percent less in the closed store than it did in the commercial store. In addition, over two-thirds of the food items could rarely be found in the commercial stores, whereas less than one-third were in scarce supply in the closed shops.[42] Privilege provided access as well as low prices.

Conclusion

Crime and privilege are really two edges of the same sword. But there is a certain amount of irony in assessing the role of each. None of this expanded the total amount of food; crime and privilege merely redistributed what was available to those with pluck and those with luck. Both had existed before June 22, 1941, and both existed after the war ended. During the war, desperation was the breeding ground for crime; there were many new entrants into life on the shady side. The privileged had much less to risk and just as much to gain;

---

[41] NFAS, U.S. Embassy at Kuibyshev, Despatch No. 1476, February 3, 1942.
[42] Ibid. Unfortunately, Table 9.1 has very few prices for goods sold on the open market because in winter very few food items were available on the free market and activity was low. The data show that those select few who were given the right to shop in closed stores benefited immensely. The entire list contains forty-six food commodities sold in both the closed and commercial stores.

Table 9.1. *Retail food prices in Kuibyshev in January 1942 (in rubles)*

Commodity	Unit	Closed store	Commercial store	Open market
Bread, white, wheat	1 kg	2.70–4.40	3.40	—
French loaf	1 kg	1.44–2.52	5.00	—
Chocolate candy, best	1 kg	80.40	180.00	—
Cocoa	250 grams	17.75	35.00[a]	—
Coffee, roasted	1 kg	55.00	49.00[a]	—
Sugar, granulated	1 kg	5.50	15.00[a]	—
Sugar, lump	1 kg	6.20	17.20	—
Wheat meal	1 kg	4.30	9.00	—
Macaroni	1 kg	4.80	10.00	—
Flour, 72%	1 kg	2.70	6.00[a]	—
Flour, 30%	1 kg	4.40	10.00	—
Rice	1 kg	6.50	15.00[a]	—
Salt	1 kg	.13	.13	—
Beef steak (fillet of beef) and beef roast	1 kg	12.80	14.0–19.0	70.0–90.0
Pork chops and pork roast	1 kg	16.00	24.0–28.0	120.0–140.0
Mutton chops and mutton	1 kg	12.20–14.00	20.0–23.0	90.0–100.0
Chicken, first quality	1 kg	15.00	37.00[a]	—
Chicken, second quality	1 kg	11.00	28.00[a]	—
Turkey	1 kg	18.00	34.00	—
Herring, salted	1 kg	9.50	13.50	—
Herring, smoked	1 kg	10.50	15.00	—
Sausage, ordinary	1 kg	15.30	20.00	—
Potatoes	1 kg	.65[a]	.65[a]	15.0–18.0
Cucumbers, pickled	1 kg	1.95[a]	1.95[a]	8.0–10.0
Milk, fresh	1 liter	2.10	—	20.00
Butter, first quality	1 liter	24.50	46.00[a]	200.0

[a]Very rarely available.
Source: NFAS, U.S. Embassy at Kuibyshev, Despatch No. 1476, February 3, 1942.

privilege was an indulgence in a world that demanded so many sacrifices, up to and including one's life.

To a certain degree, the thieves and the privileged stretched the social fabric and certainly created a sense of injustice, resentment, and even cynicism, but there is no evidence that either group did any real harm. In the end, crime may have served a valuable purpose. It allowed a certain portion of the society to beat the system, always a feeling of triumph within any social and economic order and a useful outlet for feelings of frustration. The perquisites of rank and status meant that the privileged owed just that much more to the system and the war effort. After all, they had been singled out as a part of an elite to get more and better of what everyone else wanted and needed.

Crime and privilege were clear violations of the fundamental attempt to distribute food in an equitable manner and although the principle of fairness was violated, the small dents it made in the allocation mechanism never threatened the war effort.

10   Death's dominion:
the siege of Leningrad

The story of what happened in Leningrad is a tale of unbelievable horror. Leningrad during the war was different than any other city in the country, because it was neither occupied nor unoccupied. For twenty-eight months, one of the great cities of the world was surrounded by the German armed forces while hundreds of thousands of people died from hunger and cold. Therefore, all the ways that food shortages and food distribution were handled in other parts of the country during this period do not apply to Leningrad. Although there was a rationing system, there was virtually nothing to ration for a very long time. Leningrad was a city in extremis.

This chapter examines the dimensions of Leningrad's starvation – how it succumbed and how it survived. The focus is on what is called the "hungry winter" of 1941 and 1942, when the siege was in full force. The city faced its greatest trials and death claimed victims every minute of the day. We also assess the many ways that the city tried to hold out against the seemingly inexorable confrontation with total destruction, including the construction of a lifeline across the frozen waters of Lake Ladoga and a campaign to plant food in every square foot of open space. Ultimately, this is the story of death and dying and of triumph mixed with elegiac sadness.

Once the Germans decided that they could not capture Leningrad by direct military confrontation, a strategy of blockading the city was adopted.[1] The German ring closed around the city during the summer of 1941. To the south, German troops drove past the city to the Volkhov river by mid-August, and to the north hostile Finnish units

---

[1] The blockade strategy was enunciated in a memorandum prepared by General Walter Warlimont for Hitler himself. It formed the basis for the twenty-eight-month siege of Leningrad. See Harrison E. Salisbury, *The 900 Days: The Siege of Leningrad*, New York: Avon, 1979, p. 405.

reoccupied the territory up to the old 1939 border, barely twenty miles away, and on the east lay the waters of the large inland lake, Lake Ladoga. The city was effectively cut off when Mga, 20 miles southeast, fell on August 29, severing the last rail connection between Leningrad and the rest of the country. The ring closed entirely on September 8, as the city of Schluesselburg on Lake Ladoga was captured by the Germans and the city and the surrounding area on the isthmus were isolated. For the next 872 days, Leningrad would be a city alone.

Leningrad – Peter's jewel that rose out of the swamplands to be the empire's capital, the birthplace of the Revolution, a city of roughly 3 million before the war – was besieged. In July and August, 636,000 people were evacuated on the Leningrad rail line, although probably only 400,000 from the city proper.[2] Responsible officials such as Ivan Andreyenko, at the time deputy chairman of the city soviet, and Dmitri Pavlov, head of food supply for the city and the Leningrad front from September, believe that the number should have been two or three times higher.[3] When the circle closed, 2.5 million people were still left in the city and another 343,000 were living in the outskirts.[4]

The authorities had been careless, to say the least, in making provision to feed the people of Leningrad. Food reserves in the city were very limited. As of the end of October 1940, potato reserves were at 81 percent and vegetables only at 30 percent of the planned levels.[5] The evidence suggests a thoughtless attitude toward food that was available. In the fall of 1940, almost 1 million tons of food sat rotting away in several places outside the city because there were not enough railway cars sent to bring the food into the city, and 15 percent of the fruits and vegetables in the Leningrad processing and distribution system were thrown away because they had become rotten.[6] In the words of Andreyenko: "It has to be said – and it's no news to anyone, that before the war we had not worked out an emergency system of regulating food and consumer goods supplies in case of war."[7]

More important, there were not significant food stocks at the time of the invasion. As of June 21 there were only fifty-two days worth of flour, including an unspecified amount intended for export, coarse

[2] Dmitri V. Pavlov, *Leningrad 1941: The Blockade*, Chicago: The University of Chicago Press, 1965, p. 47.
[3] Pavlov, p. 47; Ales Adamovich and Daniil Granin, *A Book of the Blockade*, Moscow, 1982, p. 122.
[4] Pavlov, p. 48.
[5] *Leningradskaia pravda*, October 27, 1940, p. 1.
[6] *Leningradskaia pravda*, November 1, 1940, p. 3; October 27, 1940, p. 1. Only one of the three potato warehouses built before the war was usable.
[7] Quoted in Adamovich and Granin, p. 122.

grain for eighty-nine days, thirty-eight days of meat, forty-seven days of animal oil, and twenty-nine days of vegetable oil.[8] There was some panic buying on the part of many who lined up to buy food the day after the war started in anticipation of shortages,[9] but there was no sense that the city would be completely cut off two and a half months after the initial attack. Worse yet, the authorities seemed unaware of the danger that Leningrad faced. At the end of his life, Anastas Mikoyan reported that early in the war, as the Germans overran the western parts of the country, he had sent trainloads of grain to Leningrad for storage in the city after their original destinations had been occupied. He did so on his own authority, for in his view, additional reserves in Leningrad would never be "superfluous." But Andrei Zhdanov, head of the Leningrad party organization, said there was insufficient warehouse space in the city. Furthermore, Stalin thought Mikoyan was sending too much food to Leningrad and ordered him not to ship anything above the originally agreed upon amounts.[10]

Even as Leningrad was being cut off, no effort was made to disperse food stocks. This was a costly mistake, both practically and psychologically. The wooden Badaev warehouses, the main food storage depot for the city, were firebombed on September 8 and 3,000 tons of grain and 2,500 tons of sugar were burned.[11] The losses were important, coming as they did on the day the city was fully besieged, although Pavlov's and other Soviet accounts tend to diminish the importance of the event.[12] It seems likely, however, that the fire had a psychological impact on the people of Leningrad and it stands for some historians as an event foreshadowing the doom of Leningrad.[13]

Rationing was instituted in Leningrad on July 18, a day after the system was first applied in Moscow. Not only was it four weeks after the invasion began, but there was no modification of ration allowances in view of Leningrad's vulnerability. The rationing system in Len-

---

[8] A. V. Karasev, *Leningradtsy v gody blokady*, Moscow, 1959, p. 127
[9] Salisbury, p. 241.
[10] A. Mikoyan, "V dni blokady," *Voenno-istoricheskii zhurnal*, No. 2, 1977, pp. 45–6.
[11] A. V. Burov, *Blokada den' za dnem: 22 iiunia 1941–27 ianvaria 1944 goda*, Leningrad, 1979, p. 53.
[12] Pavlov has argued that the losses incurred at Badaev were not decisive in causing hunger in Leningrad. Indeed, he argues that the burnt sugar was made into candy and the actual loss was only 700 tons of sugar (p. 56).
[13] Harrison Salisbury is an advocate of this view. See *The 900 Days*, p. 338. One émigré said that although the local press blamed the Germans for the absence of food in Leningrad, it was the fault of the Soviets for having all this food concentrated in one place (Interview of October 29, 1986). However, after the Badaev loss, Pavlov ordered the dispersal of the stocks of flour that were sitting at the city's two flour combines. Salisbury, p. 343.

ingrad used the standard daily bread allowances for the five categories of recipients: (1) Workers, engineers, and technicians received 800 grams; (2) workers in hot workshops, 1,000 grams; (3) office workers, 600 grams; (4) adult dependents, 400 grams; and (5) children under 12 years of age, 400 grams.[14] All through August as the encircling armies moved closer, the authorities imprudently left ration allowances at the July level. Rations should have been lowered well before the first reduction on September 2. Moreover, commercial dining rooms and restaurants were allowed to operate without ration cards. These establishments accounted for a not inconsequential amount of food: 12 percent of the fats, 10 percent of the meat products, and 8 percent of the sugar and confectionery.[15] In retrospect, the authorities erred in allowing ration allowances to remain as high as they had during July and August.

In the meantime, however, food stocks fell. By the beginning of September, at the rate food was being consumed, there was only fourteen days of flour, twenty-three days of cereal, nineteen days of meat, twenty-one days of fats, and forty-eight days of sugar and candy left in the city for the civilian population.[16] Only at this dangerous point, on September 2, were bread rations lowered. Factory workers were allotted 600 grams a day, office workers 400 grams, and dependents and children, 300 grams.[17]

Only ten days later, after the siege had taken effect, ration allowances for all the major food categories were lowered. The bread ration was really what mattered, however; it was lowered three more times, the last decrease coming on November 20, before it began to rise at the end of December (Table 10.1). At its nadir, daily bread rations were 300 grams for workers, engineers, and technicians, 375 grams for workers in hot workshops, and 125 grams for office workers, adult dependents, and children under the age of 12.[18] Even with such stringent rationing, all food supplies fell throughout 1941. By December fats had virtually disappeared.[19] By the last day of the year there were

[14] The other five food groups – groats, meat, fat, sugar and candy, and fish – were available to four categories of recipients. But as the winter wore on, the ration allowances for each of these groups became largely irrelevant because these foods were virtually nonexistent.
[15] Pavlov, p. 51.
[16] Ibid., p. 49.
[17] Ibid., p. 52.
[18] N. N. Amosov, *Rabochie Leningrada v gody Velikoi Otechestvennoi Voiny*, unpublished dissertation, Leningrad, 1968, cited in R. Bidlack, *Workers at War: Workers and Labor Policy in the Siege of Leningrad*, unpublished doctoral dissertation, Indiana University, 1987, p. 274.
[19] Pavlov, p. 55.

Table 10.1. *Bread rations in Leningrad during 1941 and 1942 (grams per day)*

Type of card	July	Sept. 2	Sept. 12	Oct. 1	Nov. 13	Nov. 20	Dec. 25	Jan. 24	Feb. 11
Workers	800	600	500	400	300	250	350	400	500
Office workers	600	400	300	200	150	125	200	300	400
Dependents	400	300	250	200	150	125	200	250	300
Children under 12	400	300	300	200	150	125	200	250	300

Source: Dmitri Pavlov, *Leningrad 1941: The Blockade*, Chicago: The University of Chicago Press, p. 79.

only 980 tons of flour and only 334 tons of coarse grain left, enough
to last four days, and there was meat enough to last only nine days.[20]

Lake Ladoga – the road of life

What hope existed for the city came from the east, across Lake
Ladoga, which began to play a role in delivering food to Leningrad
once the blockade began. But the amount delivered was extremely
small. For September, only 172 tons a day of food were brought into
Leningrad against an average daily demand by the population for
2,000 tons.[21] For the entire fall only about 45,000 tons of food were
brought across the lake,[22] not nearly enough to make significant in-
roads into the food needs of the city. German bombing and stormy
waters made it extremely difficult to get even this much food across
the lake, and the Soviets lost five tugboats and forty-six barges, leaving them with only seven barges on the lake.[23] As the approach of
winter made the lake no longer navigable, they were forced to bring
food in by air, starting on November 16.[24] The airlift could bring in
only about 40 to 45 tons a day of all supplies, well below the planned
100 to 150 tons.

In the meantime, they waited for the ice on the lake to thicken
sufficiently in order to build a road across the ice to bring food into
the beleaguered city. On November 20, the ice road opened, although
the ice was not yet thick enough to handle the heavy truck traffic that
would have to traverse the lake. During the nine days from November
23 to December 1, only about 800 tons of flour, or less than two days
worth of Leningrad's basic needs, came over the ice, while forty trucks
either sank or became stuck in water holes.[25] Even after the ice had
thickened, the trip was perilous, endangered by a combination of
German bombing, blizzards, and the freezing cold.[26] In all, 1,000

---

[20] Burov, p. 115.

[21] Leon Gouré, *The Siege of Leningrad*, New York: McGraw-Hill, 1962, p. 130.

[22] *Sovetskii rechnoi transport v Velikoi Otechestvennoi Voine*, Moscow, 1981, p. 114. The
food supplies included 27,000 tons of grain, 15,500 tons of flour, 1,300 tons of coarse
grains, 214 tons of meat, 140 tons of butter, and more than 200,000 tons of fish and
meat products.

[23] Ibid., p. 114.

[24] Pavlov, p. 104. However, the food they brought in by plane was nowhere near the
amount that could be brought in by barge. Burov, p. 77.

[25] Pavlov, p. 136.

[26] Burov's January 2, 1942, entry (p. 116) portrayed the danger: "A large caravan of
trucks set off for Leningrad from Borovich but it is not known when they will get to
their destination. It is impossible for the trucks to go straight now and they must make
a big detour so as not to be attacked by enemy planes."

trucks were damaged or destroyed, and many drivers lost their lives.[27] This early period of the ice road was therefore not productive enough to narrow the food shortage significantly.

Although daily deliveries over the lake began to exceed daily food consumption in the latter part of December, it was January before the ice thickened sufficiently to allow fully loaded trucks to cross the lake.[28] On December 22, they were able to bring 705 tons of food over the ice.[29] As a result of the increased shipments, the downward slide of rations could be reversed; the bread ration was increased by 100 grams for workers and engineering-technical workers and by 75 grams for other groups.[30] For the entire winter of 1941 and 1942, only about 262,500 tons of food came over the ice road to Leningrad,[31] so the ice road was clearly not a panacea and hunger continued in the city. This food was not always usable or well-used – for instance, sometimes it could not be stored adequately.[32] On the other hand, the ice road evacuated over 500,000 people during the hungry winter, meaning it did double duty to save Leningraders – food moved one way and people moved the other way.[33] In the spring, of course, the ice melted, but without the ingenuity to build the road and the enormous sacrifice of those who labored to make the system work, during the hungry winter many more would doubtless have died.

The hungry winter of 1941 and 1942

Despite the heroic operations of the road of life across the ice, hunger ruled Leningrad, especially in the first winter of the siege.

[27] Gouré, p. 152.
[28] Ibid., p. 152. Even so, according to Alexander Werth, a great deal of the food taken to Leningrad was wasted because the city did not have an adequate amount of packing material. See his *Russia at War 1941–1945*, New York: Dutton, 1964, p. 332.
[29] Burov, p. 106.
[30] Pavlov, p. 147.
[31] A significant amount of industrial equipment was also moved that first winter before the ice road stopped functioning on April 24, 1942. V. M. Kovalchuk, "Blokirovannyi Leningrad i bol'shaia zemlia," in *Sovetskii tyl v Velikoi Otechestvennoi Voine*, Vol. 2, Moscow, 1974, p. 276.
[32] Alexander Werth, *Russia at War 1941–1945*, New York: Dutton, 1964, p. 332. The country's distribution system was an utter disaster and its inefficiencies cost Leningrad an untold amount of food. The head of the city's vegetable supplies administration during the war years said that the entire crop of potatoes sent to Leningrad in 1942 was infected with the fungus phytophtora, which causes late potato blight. This meant that the potatoes had to be eaten immediately or else the entire crop would have to be thrown out. Adamovich and Granin, pp. 118–19.
[33] Kovalchuk, p. 276.

Table 10.2. *Ration allowances in Leningrad in 1941 and 1942 (grams per month)*

	Workers and engineering technical personnel	Office workers	Dependents	Children under 12
Meat				
July to Sept. 1941	2,200	1,200	600	600
Sept. 1941 to Jan. 1942	1,500	800	400	400
Cereals and macaroni				
July to Sept. 1941	2,000	1,500	1,000	1,200
Sept. 1941 to Jan. 1942	1,500	1,000	600	1,200
Fats				
July to Sept. 1941	800	400	200	400
Sept. to Nov. 1941	950	500	300	500
Nov. to Jan. 1942	600	250	200	500
Sugar and confectionery				
July to Sept. 1941	1,500	1,200	1,000	1,200
Sept. to Nov. 1941	2,000	1,700	1,500	1,700
Nov. to Jan. 1942	1,500	1,000	800	1,200

Source: Dmitri V. Pavlov, *Leningrad 1941: The Blockade*, Chicago: The University of Chicago Press, p. 79.

It was the worst of times. The city was alone, cut off from the rest of the country which itself was in mortal struggle to prevent defeat. The water mains burst in the depths of a bitterly cold winter, trams stopped running, electricity and heat disappeared, and the city sank into cold and darkness. The elegant cultural capital of Leningrad was homogenized into a listless, moribund mockery of a real city. Food was the obsession, survival the only goal.

Rations other than bread were cut in September 1941 and foods such as fats and sugar were cut again in November. Although the amounts on paper were not unbearably low (Table 10.2), often these food groups were not available. People lived on their bread ration and on what they could buy in the market – or worse.

What came to be known as "blockade bread" was bread in name only. The dearth of proper ingredients corrupted the quality of what the city could provide its population. Whereas on September 1, 2,000 tons of flour a day were being consumed, by November 1, this amount was down to 880 tons a day, accomplished not only by cutting rations but by continuing to adulterate the bread.[34] By October 20, the stocks of barley flour that had been used as an admixture with rye were completely gone and Leningrad bread was henceforth baked with flax oilcakes, bran oats, soy, and malt and flour made of moldy grain. Such admixtures amounted to 37 percent of the bread.[35] From November, cottonseed oilcakes, once meant for ship fuel, now became 10 percent of the composition of blockade bread.[36] When bread rations were lowered for the fourth time on November 13, the recipe was also changed and cellulose was added.[37] By the end of the month, the bread recipe was 10 percent edible cellulose, 10 percent cottonseed oilcake, 2 percent chaff, 2 percent flour sweepings and dust from flour sacks, 3 percent corn flour, and 73 percent rye flour.[38] Describing Leningrad's bread, one émigré said, "Maybe it was ten to twenty percent real bread. It tasted like clay." Somebody described it as "black, sticky, like putty, sodden, with an admixture of wood pulp and sawdust."[39]

There was also great attention to using the wild plants and grasses that grew in and around the city. Dandelions disappeared almost as quickly as they appeared; the leaves were used to make soup, and the roots were used to make flat cakes.[40] In the Leningrad area more than 100 types of edible wild plants had potential use as an admixture. Some people marinated wild grasses in a lemon or vinegar mixture for five days, after which they ground and then cooked the preparation.[41] There was even a market for grasses and herbs, with 100 grams of sorrel going for thirty to forty rubles.[42]

The struggle to survive caused people to eat things that would have revolted them but a few months earlier. Almost everything was fair game. Cats and dogs were among the first to go. By November, it was hard to find an animal in Leningrad, and in the market a cat or dog sold for a month's wages.[43] By the beginning of 1942, says Vera Inber, all the cats in Leningrad had been eaten.[44] People also ate oilcakes, which was fodder for cattle: "They boiled leather to use in soup. People killed the pigeons. They were gone – before December.

[34] Burov, p. 82.
[35] Ibid., p. 78.
[36] Pavlov, p. 61.
[37] Burov, p. 89.
[38] Pavlov, p. 63.
[39] Interview of September 11, 1986; Adamovich and Granin, p. 88.
[40] Adamovich and Granin, p. 207.
[41] Karasev, p. 245.
[42] Adamovich and Granin, p. 207.
[43] Gouré, p. 155.
[44] Vera Inber, *Leningrad Diary*, New York: St. Martin's Press, 1971, p. 39.

Rats and mice were trapped. They were considered good food."[45] They used carpenter's glue to make a gelatin, and one old man remembered eating tank grease in the depths of the hungry winter.[46]

Factories were also engaged in eking out more food. For instance, the sausage industry began to make bouillon from bones and by-products, producing 398 tons of such broth in four months. In one confectionery factory, a combination of floor sweepings, sugar dust, and cocoa powder produced forty tons of output and in another confectionery factory they built a special shop to process a synthetic protein out of wood.[47] In the winter of 1941, the amount of natural milk fell rapidly and soybean and cotton oilcakes were used as a substitute. The soya by-products had previously been dumped into the sewer system. People went to any lengths to find food.

There were few risks that people were not willing to take in order to survive and, although Leningrad never came apart as a cohesive politicosocial unit, it had its share of food-related crime, most of which the police were able to do little about. First, there was a thriving black market where everything was for sale. Theft was common in the food distribution system; some of the food was sold in the black market and some was directly eaten.[48] People even stole bulbs from the Botanical Gardens to make soup.[49] *Pravda* made an example of three men who committed food crimes. One stole bread and sugar destined for eighty-three workers; the second, a manager of a bread store and his assistant, stole bread;[50] the third, a store director, was found hiding 175 kilograms of butter, 105 kilograms of flour, and a large amount of coarse grains, cheese, pork, and other products.[51] Concern about theft in the distribution system rose to the point where 3,500 komsomol members were appointed on December 22, 1941, to work in food stores and in dining facilities to ensure that "honest" people worked behind the counters.[52] More broadly, to deal with crime during the war, the civil courts in Leningrad were converted to a military tribunal and the city procurator became a military procurator.[53]

[45] Interview of September 11, 1986. Oilcakes were dangerous when eaten in large quantities and people at times got an intestinal illness.
[46] Adamovich and Granin, pp. 90, 362.
[47] Karasev, p. 196.
[48] Salisbury, p. 352.
[49] Inber, p. 83.
[50] *Pravda,* December 10, 1941, p. 3. The purpose of the article is to give moral instruction. The selfish behavior of the criminals was compared with the altruism of others: "I am ready to work without pay, to live on bread and water alone, if we can soon defeat Germany, to destroy the fascist wretches."
[51] Karasev, p. 193.
[52] Burov, p. 106.
[53] Karasev, p. 193.

A large portion of food crime was associated with the ration card system. Some people simply stole other people's ration cards,[54] and forged and stolen cards were sold on the black market.[55] Others expended great efforts to obtain extra ration cards illegally. Within months the problem had become so bad that in mid-October 1941, everyone was reregistered. Even so, as the food situation worsened, the number of "lost" ration cards grew. In October 1941, 4,800 replacement cards were issued, in November the number rose to 13,000, and in December to 24,000.[56] In an effort to minimize the possibility of forgeries, the printers would not be told the color of the next period's ration cards until six days before the end of the month and they were not allowed to leave the workplace until they handed the new cards over to the authorities, who distributed them to the population.[57] The last gift that the dead could give their loved ones was their ration card – although by law it was a crime. Therefore, it was quite common for a family to hide the bodies of relatives, usually in the house itself, and illegally use their ration card until new cards were issued.[58]

Yet despite all the ways people tried to combat hunger, they could not win. The well-to-do were often as badly off or worse off than the workers. Hunger became a great equalizer. One woman remembers that she sat in her apartment watching life ebb from her body:

> I sold things for food. I sold a grand piano for bread. People sold everything they could. I bought nettles in the market for a hundred rubles a kilo to make into soup, into cutlets, into everything. Sometimes I would drink ten to fifteen glasses of water in the morning and do the same thing at night because I might not have any food during the day. One day a man came to Leningrad who was sent by my mother and sister [who had been evacuated]. He brought four potatoes and two pieces of chocolate. My father and I ate the potatoes slowly rubbing them across our teeth to make them last longer. But my father said we can only eat the chocolate at the last moment of our life. He was put in the hospital when he became very ill. So I was alone. One night I became very sick. I went to the

---

[54] Inber, pp. 42, 56.

[55] Gouré, p. 130. It was difficult to detect the forgeries because dim lighting made it difficult to read the cards.

[56] Pavlov, p. 72. Needless to say, the stories of lost cards posed a dilemma. Many lost cards were either stolen or legitimately lost in air raids, but many who came as supplicants were lying. In any case, the issuance of a new card meant that double rations were being doled out. The solution was to shift responsibility from the raion offices to the main city ration book office. This substantially reduced the number of pleadings.

[57] Adamovich and Granin, p. 106.

[58] Alexander Werth, *Leningrad*, New York: Knopf, 1944, p. 16; Gouré, p. 158.

bathroom maybe forty times. Only it wasn't a real bathroom. It was really a can. I got so weak I couldn't even go to the bathroom so I brought the can to my bedside. I thought I was going to die and I pulled myself to the floor and crawled over to where the chocolate was stored and ate both pieces.

The next morning she was found unconscious by a neighbor with whom she had an agreement, each to keep tabs on the other. She was taken to a hospital where she was told that if she had not eaten the chocolate, she would have died.[59]

Leningraders told a joke about the imminence of death in their lives. It was based on the fact that those who were suffering greatly received a coupon with which they could claim extra food to help them survive, but they had to be in truly desperate straits, on their last legs, to qualify. The coupon was an UDP, for *usilenoe dopolnitel'noe pitanie*, best translated as "intensified supplementary nourishment." But if you received an UDP coupon, the UDP stood for *umersh dnem pozzhe*, meaning "you will be dead the next day."[60]

And people did die, starving to death in their homes and the streets. During the hungry winter Leningrad was death's dominion. Exactly how many died is not known for sure. The official figure of 632,000 first given at the Nuremburg Trials now seems most certainly to have seriously understated the depth of the tragedy. More recent estimates place the number as high as 1 million, probably as much as 40 percent of the city's population.[61] The harvest of death began in the late fall of 1941 when 53,000 died in November and December[62] and reached its zenith in early 1942, when about 200,000 were reported to have died during January and February.[63]

Cannibalism

As death stalked the streets in the winter of 1941 and 1942, hunger forced people over the edge of civilized behavior and into cannibalism, although we will never know to what degree. Understand-

[59] Interview of October 28, 1986.
[60] Interview of October 28, 1986.
[61] Radio Moscow broadcaster Joe Adamov on two different occasions in 1985 said 800,000 and 900,000 had died, respectively. Other estimates are higher. See Bidlack, p. 207. The official Soviet figure for the city's population at the start of 1942 is 2,280,000 (Gouré, p. 285).
[62] Burov, p. 111.
[63] Pavlov, p. 123. It is likely that more died in this period in view of the fact that Pavlov accepts the now rejected figure of 632,000 total deaths from starvation.

ably, Soviet accounts do not discuss the matter[64] and, consequently, we must depend on the limited and self-censored accounts of those who lived through this period. Both Salisbury and Gouré report instances of cannibalism. Gouré says that all of his informants had either heard about cannibalism or had seen evidence of it.[65] According to his account, as well as that of Salisbury, it was rumored that human flesh was passed off as animal flesh in the black market.[66] Berlin radio also talked about cannibalism. The telegraphic-style transcription of a foreign broadcast service quoted a deserting army officer in this way: "I come straight from Leningrad," said Soviet Lieutenant Sokolorski. "Conditions in Leningrad, putrefied corpses used as food. Meat aspic made of glue and human flesh."[67]

Emigré accounts suggest that there was a substantial amount of cannibalism. One émigré remembered her experience: "I went to a bread store that wasn't far from my house. I would walk past people lying dead on the street and then pass these same bodies going home again and parts of their bodies would be missing. It was an hour or so sometimes and body parts would be taken."[68] Another survivor of the war told of her aunt who was a doctor in a Leningrad hospital: "There were so many people dying that it was not possible to bury them all. So they piled the corpses in a backyard near the hospital. Sometimes when I walked by this pile of corpses there were pieces of bodies that were cut off. This I saw with my own eyes."[69] Another said that after the war he and his wife went to live in Leningrad: "We became friends with a woman who said that during the war her six-year-old daughter had died and other people had eaten her."[70] And yet another spoke of people gone mad with hunger: "I saw dead people on the street, frozen, without parts of their bodies. I once saw a man walking on the street with a part of a body sticking out of his pocket. People went crazy. The hunger made people crazy."[71]

Scurvy

Even when the hunger did not kill, people were weakened and became ill. Those who survived the semistarvation were subject

---

[64] For example, a recent book based on a substantial number of eyewitness accounts never mentions the existence of cannibalism. See Adamovich and Granin.
[65] Gouré, p. 216. [66] Salisbury, p. 437.
[67] Columbia Broadcasting System Monitoring Reports, April 21, 1942.
[68] Interview of October 28, 1986.
[69] Interview of June 18, 1988.
[70] Interview of August 19, 1986.
[71] Interview of September 11, 1986.

to diseases.[72] Scurvy was rampant in Leningrad, first appearing in March 1942.[73] The most common disease caused by vitamin deficiencies,[74] scurvy in Leningrad can be traced to the absence of fresh fruit and vegetables; the cure is providing doses of vitamin C as well as food containing the missing vitamin. As early as November 1941 the Vitamin Institute had been instructed by the City Executive Committee to begin work on preparing a vitaminized conifer brew.[75] In mid-April 1942 that committee ordered the shipments of pine needles into Leningrad to make a drink to treat all those ill with scurvy. The drink was to be distributed through all dining facilities.[76] The authorities were only validating what people were already doing on their own. In her diary entry of March 31, 1942, Vera Inber noted that "everyone is carrying pine and fir needles."[77]

During the spring and summer of 1942 a mass campaign to make and use the vitamin drink was launched:

> Thousands of our children and youngsters went out to collect these fresh twigs, and there wasn't a factory canteen, a school, a government office – in fact there was hardly a place in Leningrad where there weren't buckets of this liquid, and everybody was urged to drink of it as much as he could. It didn't taste particularly good, but people drank gallons and gallons of it, as a sort of duty to themselves and to the common cause![78]

More than 16 million doses of the drink were produced in 1942.[79] The use of pine needles as a source of vitamin C continued the following year[80] and at the end of February 1943, when the food situation eased,

---

[72] See also Chapter 12 on the medical effects of food deprivation.
[73] Josef Brozek, Samuel Wells, and Ancel Keys, "Medical Aspects of Semistarvation in Leningrad (Siege 1941–42)," *American Review of Soviet Medicine*, Vol. IV, No. 1, October 1946, p. 71. Scurvy is caused by a lack of vitamin C and the manifestations of the disease are debility, anemia, spongy, ulcerated gums, and skin hemorrhages. See Chapter 12 for more on the presence of scurvy within the general population.
[74] Brozek et al., p. 71.
[75] This use of the drink to treat scurvy was not new to Russia. Archival materials showed that the Russians had exported pine needles as a cure for scurvy and had used it for the same purpose during the war with Sweden. See Adamovich and Granin, p. 40.
[76] Karasev, p. 239.
[77] Inber, p. 74.
[78] This was the description given by a Professor Moshansky, head of the Leningrad Health Department. Werth, *Leningrad*, p. 160.
[79] Salisbury, p. 582.
[80] Burov, pp. 170, 309.

the taste was improved by adding saccharine and berry juice.[81] Employment of the drink ultimately eliminated the disease.[82]

Infants and children

The siege had a great effect on the birthrate and on the health of infants born during this period. Hunger reduced the interest in sex and menstruation stopped. The birthrate fell from 25.1 per 1,000 in 1940 to 18.3 in 1941 to a negligible 6.3 in 1942.[83] According to the records of the Leningrad State Pediatric Institute, in the first six months of 1942, 414 women came to the clinic, whereas in the second half of the year only 79 entered the clinic.[84] Inadequate nutrition increased the number of stillbirths and premature births. In 1942, the number of stillbirths doubled to slightly more than 5 percent of all pregnancies. In the first half of 1942 a shocking 41.2 percent of all infants were born prematurely.[85] The average weight at birth also dropped, by 18 percent for boys and 16 percent for girls.[86] As might be expected, the weakened infants were at higher risk; 21 percent of all children born alive died in 1942 and the morbidity rate of children born in 1942 rose to 32.3 percent.[87]

During the heart of the siege local authorities took special measures to alleviate the conditions faced by children, although these had to be limited. On November 2, 1941, three children's dining rooms were opened, each serving 300 to 400 children a day.[88] A few days after they opened a special treat of 200 grams of sour cream and 100 grams of potato flour was given to the children on the anniversary of the revolution.[89] The dining rooms could not meet children's needs and therefore during the heart of the hungry winter, Leningrad schools

[81] Ibid., p. 319.

[82] Ancel Keys and others, *The Biology of Human Starvation*, Vol. 1, Minneapolis: The University of Minnesota Press, 1950, p. 459.

[83] Salisbury, p. 437.

[84] The following discussion is drawn from A. N. Antonov, "Children Born During the Siege of Leningrad in 1942," *Journal of Pediatrics*, Vol. 30, No. 2, February 1947, pp. 250–7.

[85] Ibid., p. 250. This rate fell to 6.5 percent in the second half of 1942. Clinic records suggest that the women who became pregnant when amenorrhea was widespread were better fed than other women in the city.

[86] The average weight of a baby boy fell from 3.44 kilograms in January to June 1941 to 2.82 kilograms in January to June 1942. Similarly, the average weight of a baby girl went from 3.3. kilograms to 2.76 kilograms during the same period. Antonov, p. 253.

[87] Ibid., p. 255.

[88] Burov, p. 83.

[89] Ibid., p. 86.

fed children twice a day, in the morning and evening. The scanty offerings were foods not ordinarily eaten. First there were pancakes and kasha that were made from the solid residue after the oil has been extracted from the seeds of oil-producing plants, but they simply ran out of oilcakes. Then every day there was a soup with shredded cabbage. One school bought five kilograms of glue and made a gelatin with laurel leaf that was eaten with mustard.[90] In early February 1942, children were sent to the kindergarten twenty-four hours a day when their parents could not take care of them.[91] In the spring of 1942 the schools began to serve children hot food. In Leningrad and the suburbs of Kolpin and Kronstadt, there were 148 schools serving three meals a day to 65,000 children.[92] The weakest children were given an intensified diet.[93] Milk and glucose were provided to children in mid–1943.[94]

One of the saddest aspects of the siege was the children who were orphaned or whose parents could not care for them because of military service or work. In 1943 a network of special kindergartens was opened to cope with the large number of children whose parents were either dead or could not attend to them. The schools became the second home for children, trying to do for them what their parents could not.[95] A doctor who had been sent out of Leningrad to an Omsk oblast village with 2,700 children shortly before the siege began found when she returned with her charges in 1944 that many of them had been orphaned. These children were placed in a special home, given ration cards, and sometimes a bit of sugar.[96] There were special rest homes for working adolescents. They were able to go to these homes for two weeks or a month at a time and were given extra rations, including meat and fish and thirty grams of butter a day.[97]

Unfortunately, the schools could not provide a sense of security for all. Many of the children, especially the younger ones, exhibited obvious signs of depression. One of the teachers in the special kindergartens described how the adversity in the children's lives showed up in their eating habits in school:

> They divided soup into two courses. First they drank off the liquid and then ate the rest. They crumbled bread into tiny bits which they

[90] Burov, pp. 101–2.
[91] Ibid., p. 138.
[92] Karasev, p. 239.
[93] Burov, p. 182.
[94] Inber, p. 152.
[95] *Izvestia*, June 11, 1943, p. 3.
[96] Interview of September 10, 1986.
[97] Werth, *Leningrad*, p. 54.

hid in matchboxes. They saved the bread till last like a delicacy, taking pleasure in eating a little piece for hours, turning it over and examining it as if it were some strange curio. No manner of persuasion had any effect till they became stronger.[98]

Food gardens

By spring 1942 Leningrad was a shrunken city. Its population was now only about 1 million, cut nearly in half by starvation during the hungry winter and by the evacuation of nearly half a million over the ice road.[99] The city was still cut off significantly from the rest of the country, specifically from food supplies. That meant that it had to depend much more on its own resources. The needs of the besieged population gave impetus to party and state support for individual efforts to grow food. On January 11, 1942, the city party committee and the executive political committee discussed the idea of private gardening, speculating unrealistically that gardens could grow enough potatoes and vegetables for 1,500,000 people.[100] Then on February 5, the local party organization issued a resolution creating subsidiary farms in the surrounding countryside to supply Leningrad with potatoes, vegetables, berries, and other products and also began distributing lands for private gardens. Simultaneously it was announced that vegetables and potatoes would be grown in every empty lot, park, garden, and unused area between buildings within the city itself.[101] By late May 1942, Moscow radio announced that about 7,000 hectares of land in the Leningrad area would be turned into vegetable gardens and that more than one-third was for individuals' and workers' own gardens.[102] By late summer these plans had more than succeeded; more than 9,000 hectares were planted in state farms and the suburban farms of enterprises and other organizations,[103] and about 270,000 people were engaged in private vegetable gardening.[104] More than 600 subsidiary farms, planting some 4,600 hectares, were created

---

[98] *The Times* (London), January 5, 1944, p. 5.
[99] In his introduction to Vera Inber's diary, Harrison Salisbury says the population of Leningrad was about 1,100,000 as of April 1, 1942.
[100] Burov, p. 121.
[101] Ibid., pp. 136–7.
[102] *Daily Report of Foreign Radio Broadcasts*, May 21, 1942. Richard Bidlack has pointed out that during the 1930s, when there were food shortages in Leningrad, workers had their own gardens and factories had auxiliary farms on the edge of the city. See "Worker Mobilization During the Siege of Leningrad," paper presented at the 1986 meetings of the American Association for the Advancement of Slavic Studies, pp. 2–3.
[103] *Izvestia*, August 11, 1942.
[104] *Izvestia*, August 11, 1942, p. 2.

on land formerly occupied by state and collective farms.[105] Finally, 176,000 workers and employees joined gardening and consumer amalgamations and planted 1,784 hectares.[106] Alexander Werth was told by P. S. Popkov, chairman of the City Executive Committee in September 1943, that there were 12,500 hectares of vegetable plots in Leningrad and the immediate area.[107]

Open areas in the center of the city were also cultivated assiduously. The space in front of St. Isaac's Cathedral became a vegetable garden. Werth described how all the large spaces between the workers' housing at the Putilov works on the eastern side of the city were used to plant cabbages and potatoes, and vegetables were growing on the unused land along the side of an unfinished road on Krestovsky Island.[108] The plots were very small, which is not surprising in view of the large population and the relatively small amount of land that could potentially be used for growing food.[109] In addition, where one lived in the city affected the ability to grow food. One émigré said that she lived in the middle of the city and like others in this part of town, she did not participate in gardening because there was no access to an area where one could have a garden.[110]

In 1942 the total amount of food grown in the individual gardens was 25,000 tons of vegetables,[111] which would mean about 50 pounds of food per capita for a total population of roughly 1 million.[112] And the output of the state farms and subsidiary farms was 50,000 tons of vegetables in 1942. In 1943 individual gardens yielded 60,000 tons of vegetables, more than doubling the output of the year before, and state and subsidiary farms produced 75,000 tons.[113] The output from the subsidiary farms did not belong solely to the enterprise's workers. The workers were entitled to 300 grams a day of the harvest and then in the name of equity whatever was left over was centralized and made available to the general population.[114]

The results were not encouraging at first. Inber's diary reported in

[105] Bidlack, "Worker Mobilization," p. 28; *Pravda,* May 24, 1943, p. 2.
[106] *Pravda,* May 24, 1943, p. 2.
[107] Werth, *Leningrad,* p. 161.
[108] Ibid., pp. 92, 97.
[109] Interview of September 11, 1986.
[110] Interview of October 28, 1986.
[111] *Pravda,* May 24, 1943, p. 2.
[112] Burov, p. 121. We should think of these and other figures for output during the siege as estimates rather than precise calculations. The press would have had an incentive to exaggerate output, and the civilian population would have had an incentive to understate what they produced.
[113] Karasev, p. 286.
[114] Karasev, p. 245.

early August 1942 that "vegetables aren't growing as they should, the cabbage seedlings weren't thinned out. [The leaves] have such a bitter taste that even our hospital horses refuse to eat them."[115] In 1942 the gardeners also operated under the handicap of inadequate agricultural equipment and supplies, and all cultivation was done by hand and with spades. In addition, no fertilizer was used until 1943; the famine had taken most animals and so there was no manuring of the land in 1942.[116] Moreover, the people were so physically debilitated and sapped of strength that it was painfully hard work to plant food. One Soviet historian described fifty women taking three hours to walk less than two miles to where their subsidiary farm was located.[117] Much more capital equipment was available in 1943 than in the previous year and this helps explain the increase in output. Fifty tractor plows, 75 disk and 500 spring harrows, and 900 zigzag harrows were manufactured. More than 90 tractors were also repaired and made ready for the spring planting.[118]

For a long time Leningrad was totally cut off from any significant food supplies and had no alternative but to depend on its own resources. Although the food that was produced made some dent in the shortfall, it was not a real solution. But gardening also had the virtue of keeping people occupied and by its very nature held out the hope that people could improve their lives.

The abandoned city

Leningrad's martyrdom was made worse by a lack of attention from Moscow that ranged from failure to acknowledge the suffering to a failure to take sufficient measures to alleviate it. This lack of attention must be attributed to the failures of the Soviet system in the dark days of the beginning of the war and to human weakness and error as we weigh the terrible price paid by Leningraders in World War II.

The Soviet press was never known for its candor, but during the most trying period of the war, it appears that the leadership made a conscious decision not to tell the story of Leningrad. It is not unreasonable to think that this was an effort to minimize the likelihood of panicking the general population or of endangering national morale

---

[115] Inber, p. 101.
[116] *Pravda*, May 24, 1943, p. 2.
[117] Burov, p. 185.
[118] *Pravda*, May 24, 1943.

when the Germans were still advancing through Soviet territory. For almost a year there was no official hint at the truth about Leningrad. References in the press either ignored the hunger or carried out a charade, as in the December 21, 1941, *Pravda* story in which the correspondent wrote that, "Leningrad has remained Leningrad – a city of work, of science."[119] The general message of the article was that things were fundamentally normal – at least as far as any city can function normally during a war. And *Pravda*'s article about May Day, 1942, in Leningrad spoke not a word about food, hunger, or the siege, nor did a piece a week later written by the Leningrad City Military Commissar.[120] It was not until July 10, 1942, that the Soviet press acknowledged the hunger in Leningrad, when the city was described as "without water, without transportation, half-starving."[121]

The Soviets were also extremely effective in keeping the real situation hidden from the Allies and the Western press. In his diary, Reuters correspondent Alexander Werth's September 29, 1941, entry suggested that he had no idea of what the real situation in Leningrad was like. He recorded a conversation with the trade union leader, Solomon Lozovsky:

> Last night Lozovsky was very reassuring about Leningrad; he said the Germans were losing tens of thousands of dead; and that, however many more tens of thousands they lost, they wouldn't get Leningrad; that communications with Leningrad were still being maintained and that although there were, of course, ration-cards in Leningrad, there was no food shortage.[122]

Major Associated Press stories about Leningrad in December 1941 failed to mention hunger in the city. On the other hand, the *Chicago Daily Tribune* of October 14, 1941, published a story claiming that 250,000 were starving and freezing to death in the city. That was not true at this juncture and probably reflects the strongly anti-Soviet sentiments of the paper.[123] The January 30, 1942, economic report of the British embassy stated that: "No complaints recorded at Leningrad, although anxiety expressed for food supplies and distribution to workmen evacuated to other areas."[124]

---

[119] *Pravda*, December 21, 1941, p. 3.
[120] *Pravda*, May 2, 1942, p. 3, and May 8, 1942, p. 3.
[121] *Izvestia*, July 10, 1942, p. 3.
[122] Alexander Werth, *Moscow War Diary*, New York: Knopf, 1942, p. 245.
[123] See, for example, *The Evening Citizen* (Ottawa), December 18, 1941, p. 1, and December 27, 1941, p. 1; the *Chicago Daily Tribune*, October 14, 1941, p. 5.
[124] *British Foreign Office: Russia Correspondence 1781–1945*, F.O. 371, 1944, Reel 13, Vol. 32920, p. 38.

For the first year, Soviet citizens learned of Leningrad's suffering only when evacuation brought victims into contact with outsiders. For instance, a man who was evacuated to Novosibirsk in July 1941 said that although people in Siberia knew that Leningrad was under siege, they heard about the mass starvation only when people arrived as part of the renewed evacuation in the spring of 1942. A woman who was in a labor camp in Archangel did not learn of Leningrad's suffering until she was on a train headed for Tashkent in the spring of 1942 and met a woman from the city.[125]

Conclusion

The tragic tale of Leningrad is one of the saddest chapters of the war, but the evidence suggests that some of the tragedy and many of the deaths can be attributed to Moscow's attitude toward the city and its people. It appears that the Soviet leadership could have done a number of things to reduce the number of deaths. First, the city was ill-prepared for the invasion. Second, more people should have been evacuated. Third, it is arguable that if the Soviets had dispersed their food stocks earlier, they would not have experienced the substantial losses suffered when the Badaev warehouses were fire-bombed. Fourth, the failure to accept the food that Mikoyan had shipped to Leningrad because of the alleged lack of warehouse space was a shortsighted decision. Fifth, the food that existed in the city before the siege was used unwisely. Rations should have been lowered well before the first reduction on September 2.

How can one account for all these shortcomings? We will not know anything about the motivation of the Soviet wartime leadership until the archives are opened. Until then we are left with educated speculations. It may be argued that more people were not evacuated because the leadership did not want to appear to be abandoning the city, a symbolism that would not have been lost on the rest of the country. Second, there was simple ineptitude. It was careless not to have a plan on how to deal with wartime conditions and it was careless not to have dispersed the food reserves in the Badaev warehouses. The most damaging possible explanation is that Stalin was indifferent or even hostile to the fate of Leningrad. It is puzzling to compare the way the Soviet press treated the suffering of Kharkov with its handling of the siege of Leningrad. In August 1943 *Pravda* wrote that Kharkov

[125] Interviews of September 23, 1986, and March 14, 1988.

"will always be in our consciousness."[126] At the same time, Leningrad was virtually ignored and its fate was certainly never described in the graphic terms that were granted other cities. Why did the press disregard the nightmare of the siege? Could it have been Stalin's suspected dislike and fear of Leningrad that prevented the press from glorifying the martyred city? And does this therefore provide an insight into why more was not done to help the city. After all, it was Stalin himself who ordered Mikoyan not to send extra grain to Leningrad. To ascribe malevolent motives to Stalin is not outlandish, but it is certainly without the kind of proof of which good history is made. At a minimum, the city was unnecessarily endangered; fewer should have died.

[126] *Pravda*, August 28, 1943. There was another article on Kharkov in *Pravda* on August 30, 1943, p. 2.

11 The newly liberated areas: restoring the food supply

When the last units of the Wehrmacht surrendered at Stalingrad on February 2, 1943, after five months of fierce struggle, it was possible for the first time to believe that Germany could be defeated. By February the grain-growing areas of the north Caucasus were back in Soviet hands and by March the front had stabilized at the Donets River. In the late summer of 1943, after the massive tank battle of Kursk, the eastern Ukraine was liberated and by November Kiev and all of the Ukraine east of the Dneper was under Soviet control.

The military successes achieved by the Red Army in 1943 marked a turnaround in the fortunes of the nation. As the victories began to mount over the ensuing months and more and more territory came under Soviet rule once again, the state began to reassert its role in managing the food supply. Beginning in early 1943, there were a number of policy initiatives introduced directed toward reconstructing the food base in the newly liberated areas. The thrust of these initiatives was to breathe life into centralization; localism as a policy was on its way out.

Devastation in the liberated areas

Whether there was to be centralization or decentralization, there was no quick solution to the food problem. The base from which the state would start in the liberated areas had been bludgeoned by German destruction and before that by the scorched earth policy of the Soviets themselves. For many, in the short term at least, liberation did not put food into their bellies. A Western reporter wrote in the fall of 1943 that "even in the inebriation of success, Russia's little man could not forget the harshness of his daily life. . . . For in Russia today, the sharp pangs of hunger come as regularly as the dawn."[1] And as the Soviet counterattack reclaimed the occupied land, the authorities faced serious difficulties in reconstructing a food base in the liberated areas. Lazar Volin correctly predicted that "the reconquered area, at least until the harvest of 1944, will be a liability rather than an asset at least as far as the Russian food supply is concerned."[2] In fact, in some ways things got worse before they got better.

The reconstruction of agriculture was especially difficult because of the conditions in the liberated areas. It was a topsy-turvy world. People, animals, and machinery had been evacuated and scattered in many directions; where possible they had to be returned. The farms that had been destroyed in the wake of either Soviet or German scorched earth actions had to be rebuilt. In September 1944, when Estonia was liberated, one of the first tasks was to gather in the grain. The situation was so disorganized and the food supply so uncertain that the government offered to give 40 percent of the grain to any peasant who harvested the fields where the original residents were absent.[3] Much of the good agricultural land had been scarred by the fighting in 1942 and 1943. And facilities had been destroyed, almost totally in areas of heavy fighting: "The destruction to Stalingrad is indescribable. The great grain elevator of reinforced concrete was a network of twisted iron rods. For 15–20 miles scarcely a building had a roof and the crumbling walls were pockmarked with rifle bullets and shattered with shell holes. . . . The tractor plant (reinforced concrete) was a jumble of sagging, twisted iron rods."[4] Even as late as the spring of 1945 a London *Times* report said that "agriculture in the western areas and even farther east has slipped back to a condition worse in many ways than it was 10 or 15 years ago."[5]

Although there were serious difficulties with restoring the capital stock and the labor supply, particularly skilled personnel, the most immediate problem was to feed people, particularly those who were returning to their former homes. As of the end of 1943, the population of the reoccupied areas was estimated to be 43.6 million, over one-quarter of the total Soviet population of 161.4 million. Of this 43.6

[1] *Time*, September 6, 1943, pp. 28–9.
[2] Lazar Volin, "German Invasion and Russian Agriculture," *Russian Review*, March 1943, p. 76.
[3] *Foreign Relations of the United States*, 1944, Vol. IV, Washington, D.C., p. 919.
[4] USSR: Crop and Production, 1942–1945. Records of the Foreign Agricultural Service. Record Group 166, National Archives, Washington, D.C. (NFAS). U.S. Embassy at Moscow, August 23, 1943.
[5] *The Times* (London), April 10, 1945, p. 5.

Three women carrying sacks returning to their homes in Tsimlyank-saya. *Source:* National Archives.

Children who had hidden for sixty days returning to their native village of Tuapse. *Source:* National Archives.

million, the state was responsible for providing rations to 17.1 million people. The other 26.5 million were peasants who were not entitled to rations; this proportion of the population not eligible for rations was much higher than in the unoccupied areas.[6] For peasants in the liberated areas, it was crucial that the collective farms be reconstructed quickly because 60 percent of them were on their own and could not rely on the state for food.

[6] NFAS, U.S. Embassy at Moscow, October 2, 1944, p. 16. The reoccupied areas and their population, in parentheses, included parts of the Ukraine (19.2 million), Belorussia (3.9 million), the Crimea (0.8 million), the Northwest and Central regions (9.2 million), and the Southern regions (10.5 million). Of the 120.3 million living in unoccupied areas, only 39.8 million, or one-third, were not entitled to rations.

Peasants bringing grain to Odessa in a long procession of wagons.
Source: National Archives.

Unfortunately, the 1943 grain crop in the unoccupied areas and those regions fully reoccupied by the end of March 1943, when the growing season began, was estimated as about one-third less than the prewar average. This reduced crop not only had to feed all the people living there, but it also had to be stretched to help feed people in the areas liberated in the summer and fall who were absolutely dependent on the returning Soviet authorities.[7]

In some ways, the newly liberated areas had all the earmarks of a famine ridden region. In the wheat-rich Ukraine, peasants were forced to substitute corn and millet for the wheat the Germans had confiscated.[8] Some areas, especially the urban areas, needed emergency relief supplies; for example, food was brought into Kiev right after

[7] U.S. Department of Agriculture Archives – World War II files, "Russian Food Mission and Purchasing Committee" file, October 22, 1943.
[8] *Sotsialisticheskoe sel'skoe khoziaistvo*, March 1945, p. 29.

liberation, including some food from the United States such as 480 tons of meat (mainly fat cuts), 200 tons of butter, and 100 tons of sugar.[9] The food was distributed through stores and "soup kitchens," as one observer described them.[10] Special attention was given to feeding children. Cafeterias were opened for all children and facilities for children with special dietary needs were also opened.[11]

But feeding the people of the liberated areas could not continue on this emergency basis. The food base had to be reestablished. The highest levels of the party, government, and economic apparatus were involved in planning the return of personnel and equipment. The Party Central Committee and the Council of Peoples Commissars jointly issued two major decrees regarding the reconstruction of agriculture in 1943.

The first decree was issued on January 23 as Red Army troops moved forward past the trapped remnants of the German 6th Army at Stalingrad. Entitled, "On Measures for the Reconstruction of the MTS and Collective Farms in the Areas Liberated from the German Fascist Occupiers," the decree assigned priority to reconstructing the machine tractor stations and set an extremely optimistic goal of doing so by the beginning of spring planting. The reconstruction was to take place through the reevacuation of fully repaired tractors, combines, motor vehicles, and other agricultural equipment to the liberated areas. The goal was to send 20,000 tractors, 3,500 combines, and 2,000 motor vehicles and tools to these areas by March 1, 1943. In addition, machine operators, mechanics, agronomists, and other agricultural specialists were to accompany the return of this equipment.[12] The goal of centralized and mechanized reestablishment of the agricultural base was not realized, at least partly because of the fortunes of war, including the German counterattack a month later that pushed the Red Army back to the Donets.

The second decree, dated August 21, concentrated on immediate steps to restore practical agricultural work rather than machinery and equipment. Issued in the aftermath of the Soviet victory at Kursk that

---

[9] Fat cuts include pork bellies, beef flank, and sheep breasts. In this case, it is most likely that salted pork bellies were dominant in U.S. exports. Interview with Jane Porter, U.S. Department of Agriculture historian, May 8, 1989.

[10] NFAS, U.S. Embassy at Moscow, November 13, 1944.

[11] U. G. Cherniavskii, *Voina i prodovol'stvie*, Moscow, 1964, p. 109.

[12] The decree also specified the ruble value of spare parts for tractors that were to be sent to the reoccupied areas. January 23, 1943, resolution of the USSR Sovnarkom and Central Committee, "On Measures for the Reconstruction of the MTS and Collective Farms in the Areas Liberated from the German Fascist Occupiers," in *Direktivy KPSS i pravitel'stva po khoziaistvennym voprosam*, Moscow, 1957, pp. 746–50.

opened the road to the Ukraine and Kiev, the August decree specified the allocation of 120,120 tons of seeds to state and collective farms for winter crops, two-thirds of which were regarded as loans and the other one-third as an exchange for other agricultural goods.[13] It contained highly detailed instructions to return livestock and poultry to certain liberated areas, specifying compensation for farmers when their evacuated animals had been used during the war to meet delivery obligations. The resolution also established a contract system that would create incentives to increase livestock herds in the liberated areas, including a sliding scale of reductions in meat delivery obligations for 1943 if the farmers delivered an agreed upon number of animals to the kolkhoz herd. At the same time, the resolution exempted those farmers defined as victims of the German occupation either partially or fully from having to deliver agricultural products in 1943 and the households of partisans and Red Army veterans where able-bodied labor was in short supply were also exempted.[14] However, there were no exemptions from the obligation to supply military units stationed in the area.[15]

Reviving the farms

There were major problems in reestablishing the machinery and equipment base in agriculture, with consequent ramifications for the food supply. The capital stock had fallen substantially – the number of tractors by 36 percent, the number of working bulls by 58 percent and the number of working horses by 72 percent.[16] In some places, devastation was so extensive that resurrecting the food base would be a herculean task There are conflicting views as to how well the job of moving equipment west to assist in the reconstruction process was done. It was particularly crucial to have equipment available in the liberated areas by early 1944 for the spring planting. One Soviet source says that as of January 1, 1944, 27,600 tractors, 2,100 combines, and 1,720,000 head of livestock had been sent from the

---

[13] *Pravda*, February 5, 1944, pp. 2–3.
[14] August 21, 1943, resolution of the USSR Sovnarkom and Central Committee, "On the Urgent Measures for the Reconstruction of the Economy in Regions Liberated from German Occupation," in *Direktivy*, pp. 765–802.
[15] *The Times* (London), August 31, 1943, p. 3.
[16] M. P. Gubenko, "K ekonomicheskoi kharakteristike raionov RSFSR, osvobozhdennykh ot fashistkoi okkupatsii v 1943 g.," *Istoriia SSSR*, Vol. 6, No. 1, 1962, pp. 116, 118–19. For more detail, see Table 3.2 in this book.

Table 11.1. *Shortfall in equipment returned to liberated areas (April 10, 1944)*

	Number to be shipped	Number that arrived
Tractors	28,772	22,043
Plows	20,250	11,866
Seeding machines	7,370	3,315
Combines	2,830	1,548
Motor vehicles	2,028	618

Source: Iu. V. Arutiunian, *Sovetskoe krestíanstvo v gody Velikoi Otechestvennoi Voiny*, Moscow, 1963, p. 252.

eastern regions to the liberated areas.[17] But another Soviet source suggests that not all equipment actually arrived, creating a serious shortfall (Table 11.1).

The shortfall was much greater for the return of evacuated livestock, a fact that is not surprising considering the logistical nightmare of retrieving animals. The herds that had been moved eastward two years previously began their march west in 1943. From roughly the end of August to the middle of September 1943, emissaries from the liberated areas were sent to the regions to which livestock had been evacuated. As one reporter put it, these census takers

> will, in many cases go far afield in search of their horned cattle, sheep, goats, and horses; from the Smolensk province across the Volga to beyond Kuibyshev, from Voronezh into Asiatic Kazakhstan, from Rostov and Stavropol over the Caucasus range through whose passes the splendid cattle of the Kuban streamed last year.[18]

Then in September and October before the winter set in, the drive of animals back home took place.

The collective farms of the liberated areas received 1,159,000 cattle, 1,418,000 sheep and goats, 86,400 pigs, and 268,400 horses.[19] Not surprisingly, however, the number of animals returned was always less than the number sent out. In Stalingrad, for example, the number of cattle returned was 25 percent less than the number evacuated.[20]

---

[17] I. I. Vinogradov, *Politotdely MTS i sovkhozov v gody Velikoi Otechestvennoi Voiny (1941–1943gg.)*, Leningrad, 1976, p. 122.
[18] *The Times* (London), August 31, 1943, p. 3.
[19] Iu. V. Arutiunian, *Sovetskoe krest'ianstvo v gody Velikoi Otechestvennoi Voiny*, Moscow, 1963, p. 265.
[20] NFAS, U.S. Embassy at Moscow, August 23, 1943.

The machines arrive in the liberated regions: a thresher working on the 20 Years of October farm, Orel region. *Source:* National Archives.

In some places the losses were staggering. Reports from the Ukraine toward the end of 1944 indicated that only 10 to 15 percent of the prewar numbers still existed in the republic.[21] In fact, in all the liberated areas, in 1945 there were only 53 percent of the sheep and goats, and 26 percent of the horses that there were in 1941.[22]

There was also an obligation placed on collective farms and individual farmers in the east to help rebuild livestock herds in the liberated areas, a policy couched in terms of brotherly assistance. The Kalinin oblast was given 18,000 head of livestock and bought another 97,000 head of livestock from farms in the east.[23] In addition, the government bought livestock in the east, which in some cases it gave and in other cases sold to farmers in the liberated areas.[24] Whether the government was to be paid depended on the condition of the collective farm; the worse off the farm was, the less likely was it obliged to pay for the animals. Livestock was to be paid for with other agricultural products, such as grain, oilseed, potatoes, vegetables, and hay at rates established by the state.[25] In order to increase meat production, a contract system was developed that exempted collective

[21] NFAS, U.S. Embassy at Moscow, November 13, 1944.
[22] Arutiunian, p. 304.
[23] *Pravda,* October 25, 1943, p. 1.
[24] *Sotsialisticheskoe sel'skoe khoziaistvo,* March 1945, p. 32.
[25] *Pravda,* September 15, 1943, p. 1.

farmers from their 1943 meat delivery obligation if they gave one calf or two lambs to the state.[26]

There was also a shortage of skilled agricultural workers and managerial personnel in the liberated regions. In this case, the shortage of skilled personnel was made worse by the mistrust of specialists who had functioned under the Germans in occupied territory. From an ideological perspective, they were regarded as suspect.[27] Hence efforts to get skilled agricultural workers to return to the liberated areas were especially vigorous. There had been training programs in the rear regions since the end of 1942 to prepare machine operators to work in the areas that would be liberated and a 2,500-ruble allowance was given to leading management personnel and specialists to go to the liberated areas.[28] Nonetheless, it is clear that the number of refugee specialists returning was inadequate. The shortage of skilled personnel in agriculture forced the use of certain groups who were employed in industry. In 1943, joiners, welders, blacksmiths, and carpenters were assigned to machine tractor stations and state farms to repair combines and harvesters, and former combine operators who were working in industry were sent to the countryside to operate the machines.[29] By the end of 1944, about 4,800 management and technical specialists had returned, about 3,100 of them to the Ukraine,[30] and about 20,000 tractor drivers, 2,800 heads of tractor brigades, and 3,000 combine operators went from the rear to the liberated areas.[31]

The understandable subordination of agriculture to the war effort contributed to the shortage of machinery. For the war as a whole, July 1941 to 1945, agriculture only received 9.7 percent of the total investment budget, whereas for the period of 1938 to June 1941, agriculture's share was 11.4 percent.[32] The major factories had been temporarily converted to the production of tanks and they did not return to tractor production until 1944. The Kharkov Tractor Plant, one of the major tractor-producing factories in the country, was not ready to produce its first tractors until the fourth quarter of 1944.[33] Because the tractor industry could not be rejuvenated early enough,

---

[26] Arutiunian, p. 266.
[27] Ibid., p. 241.
[28] Ibid., p. 242.
[29] NFAS, U.S. Embassy at Moscow, Report No. 196, July 26, 1943.
[30] Arutiunian, p. 242.
[31] Ibid., p. 254.
[32] Harrison, p. 136.
[33] *Pravda*, August 25, 1944, in NFAS, U.S. Embassy at Moscow, Despatch No. 947, September 4, 1944.

the 1944 plan emphasized production of agricultural equipment to be used with draft horses rather than outright mechanization. Along with the targets for mechanization, such as 7,000 tractors (6,500 of which were for agriculture), 8,000 tractor plows, and 3,000 tractor cultivators, the plan also included targets for 70,000 horse-drawn plows, 40,000 horse-drawn zig-zag harrows, and 6,000 horse-drawn cultivators.[34] Unfortunately, these goals were overly ambitious. Only 5,100 tractors were produced.[35] Nor were spare parts produced in significant numbers; it was often up to the kolkhozy to fabricate parts for their machinery.[36] Under the best conditions, the MTS could do no more than 40 percent of the basic field work.[37]

As a consequence of the shortage of machinery, there was wholesale substitution of animals. In the city of Makeeva near Stalino there were only 2,000 tractors in late 1944, compared with the 6,000 that existed before the war. But the number of draft horses and draft oxen were only 20 percent and 25 percent less, respectively, than their prewar levels.[38] In place of machines, it was necessary to use cows belonging to the collective farm that were not highly productive milkers as well as privately owned cows, although their use as draft animals reduced their productivity by an estimated 30 percent.[39] The minicampaign to use peasants' cows produced the slightly cynical invocation: "We will teach all the privately owned cows to walk in harness."[40] In the Kursk oblast, half of all field work in the spring of 1943 was done with cows.[41] A year and a half later in October 1944, a U.S. report stated that most of the plowing between Stalino and Moscow was being done by cows. No tractors and few horses were seen.[42] And it was recognized that the shortage of tractors was not just a temporary problem. As a result, the breeding of oxen was encouraged.[43] Indeed, the goal by the end of 1944 in the Moscow oblast was to have 40,000

---

[34] The resolution also set a production goal of 592,000 tons of mineral fertilizer in 1944. March 14, 1944, resolution, "On the material-technical supplying of agriculture," in *Direktivy*, pp. 827–8.
[35] *Istoriia Velikoi Otechestvennoi Voiny Sovetskogo Soiuza, 1941–1945 (Istoriia)*, Vol. 4, Moscow 1962, p. 598. Similarly, only 181,000 tons of mineral fertilizer were produced, well short of the goal.
[36] For example, see *Pravda*, July 24, 1944, p. 3.
[37] Arutiunian, p. 256.
[38] NFAS, U.S. Embassy at Moscow, Despatch No. 342, April 12, 1944.
[39] NFAS, U.S. Embassy at Moscow, Despatch No. 53, October 25, 1944.
[40] Originally in *Pravda*, May 27, 1944, and cited in Arutiunian, p. 256.
[41] *Istoriia*, p. 185.
[42] NFAS, U.S. Embassy at Moscow, Despatch No. 32, October 18, 1944.
[43] NFAS, U.S. Embassy at Moscow, Despatch No. 342, April 12, 1944. Because horse breeding is a slow process, the number of horses could not be increased quickly.

young oxen working in the fields, about half of which were to be available for spring planting in 1945.[44]

The cumulative effect of all these difficulties was a serious grain shortage in the liberated areas, as well as in the rear regions. Both the amount of land harvested and the gross output of grain was considerably less than in the prewar period. Sown area in 1943 was 63 percent of the prewar figure, not much better than the 58 percent of 1942.[45] Although the sown area in 1944 approached three-quarters of the prewar figure, output was not much better than two-fifths of what it had been before the war.[46] With a population that was about 83 percent of the 1940 total (161.4 million against 194.1 million) and with a gross output of grain at about 45 percent of the prewar crop, per capita grain consumption was about only slightly more than one-half of what it had been before the war. In principle, part of this deficit could have been made up by diverting animal grains to human consumption, but there probably was no feed to spare because animals were being used so intensively due to the tractor shortage.[47] Consequently, liberation provided no solution to the disastrous food problem brought on by invasion and occupation.

There were other problems in the liberated areas. There was a severe shortage of seed, especially in 1943 when territory was liberated only shortly before spring planting time. It was necessary for farmers in uninvaded territory to help farms in the liberated areas, as for example, when about 11,000 tons of seeds were sent to Stalingrad from the Volga region.[48] And then, in addition to all the shortages – machinery, livestock, and seed – there was also the danger of working land that had been mined by the Germans. There were so many mined fields that in each oblast of the formerly occupied areas a school was opened to teach people how to clear the land of mines.[49]

All of the statistics and generalizations do not convey the individual tragedies and human endurance of the war. Many of those who returned to the liberated areas were women; they had to grow the food to feed themselves as well as the cities and the newly liberated areas. A peasant woman returned to her village with her daughter and described the experience in this way:

---

[44] *Moskovskii bolshevik*, March 18, 1944, in NFAS, Despatch No. 342, April 12, 1944.
[45] *Istoriia*, p. 186.
[46] Arutiunian, p. 298.
[47] A slightly different version of this idea can be found in Helen C. Farnsworth and V. P. Timoshenko, *World Grain Review and Outlook, 1945*, Stanford, Food Research Institute, Stanford University, 1945, p. 107.
[48] Columbia Broadcasting System Monitoring Reports, February 16, 1943.
[49] Arutiunian, p. 248.

After a couple of weeks we returned to our village. It had been completely destroyed, and there were bodies all over the place. The air was almost impossible to breathe. We tried to find places to sleep, and used grass as blankets. But we were almost devoured by flies. I remember how I tried to console my little Tonya who was five. I caressed her and caressed her; that was all I could do for her. But we survived. Later, soldiers came and helped us bury the dead. And we began to try to live there; a wall went up here and there. All that was left of our two brick houses were two corners, and we tried to build from there.

When spring came we had to walk to get seed – sixty kilometers back and forth – and we had to carry sixteen kilos each. It was early spring; we had tied rags around our feet and were wet the whole time. We carried the seed home, but all the fields were ruined because they had made trenches there. So the women had to till them up again. Look at my fingers; they're ruined from that work! They don't hurt, but it's not nice to have fingers like that. And then we had to plow, and we had to use spades. I traveled to several other kolkhozy where they had horses; we didn't even have a cow. Everything was gone. Finally we managed to get three horses and plows, and later we got a tractor, too.[50]

The return to the liberated areas was another of the several trials that civilians endured during the war. The damage was so complete that in the short term, it was a mixed blessing to go home. Liberation was only the first stage on the road to the health of the nation. Although it was the most important stage – because it meant victory over the Germans – the joy of emancipation was mitigated by the harsh reality of lives that had to be rebuilt from the bottom up, often without loved ones and almost always without enough to eat.

[50] Carola Hannson and Karen Liden, *Moscow Women,* New York: Pantheon Books, 1983, p. 132.

12 The wages of hunger: direct and indirect consequences of wartime food shortages

The unoccupied portion of the USSR experienced long-term food shortages unlike those of belligerents that escaped wartime occupation. The consequent hunger had many aspects – some starved, most were poorly fed and poorly nourished, and some suffered illness as a consequence of malnutrition. Hunger was chronic and so, therefore, was the accompanying malnutrition. There was nothing selective about the tyranny of food shortages; for most people, life was lived on the margin for most of the war. Those who survived the war did so by dint of a strong will.

The wartime diet of the Soviet people

The fate of agriculture largely determined the diet of the Soviet people during the war. The deficits translated into both a decrease in caloric value of the Soviet diet as well as a change in the structure of the diet. The diet, already biased in the direction of potato and grain consumption, became even more dependent on these items. The startling decline in food industry output from 1940 to 1945 can be seen in Table 12.1; no sector of the food economy was spared from the calamitous results.

However, it is difficult to be sure what the caloric intake was for the average Soviet citizen. During the war itself Soviet sources did not frequently discuss the adequacy of the typical diet and when they did there was at best a lack of candor. More recently, Soviet sources have offered data on daily caloric intake during the war, but they seem unreasonably high. If the data in Table 12.2 are to be believed,

Table 12.1. *Food industry production in 1940 and 1945 (in millions of centners)*

	1940	1945	1945 (as a % of 1940)
Flour	287.9	145.8	51
Bread and bakery products	239.9	109.9	46
Cereals	16.6	10.5	63
Macaroni products	3.2	2.4	75
Granulated sugar	21.5	4.7	22
Confectionery goods	7.9	2.1	27
Vegetable oil	8.0	2.9	37
Butter and other dairy products			
(in milk equivalents)	65.0	29	45
Butter	2.26	1.17	52
Cheese	0.42	0.25	59
Meat	15.0	6.6	44
Sausage and smoked foods	3.9	1.4	36
Fish	13.9	11.1	80
Canned goods (in millions of			
standard tins)	1113	558	50

Source: U. G. Cherniavskii, *Voina i prodovol'stvie*, Moscow, 1964, p. 58.

Table 12.2. *Daily caloric intake of the Soviet urban adult population*

Year	Calories	In % of 1939
1939	3,370	100
1942	2,555	76
1943	2,751	82
1944	2,810	83

Source: U. G. Cherniavskii, *Voina i prodovol'stvie*, Moscow, 1964, p. 179.

then caloric consumption by the urban population was not very different from the 1945 levels found in the U.S. (3,100 calories) and Canada (3,200 calories).[1]

Perhaps one can accept the relative changes suggested by the data,

---

[1] *The New Republic*, April 9, 1945, p. 475, citing "official analysis." The international standards for daily caloric intake say that a man weighing 150 pounds and doing moderate physical activity requires 3,000 calories and 70 grams of protein. A male doing hard physical work needs 4,500 calories and 70 grams of protein. Ancel Keys and others, *The Biology of Human Starvation*, Vol. 1, Minneapolis: The University of

but the absolute calorie figures seem exaggerated. Certainly they do not square with all the other evidence we have about Soviet diets. It was estimated that in 1943 per capita caloric consumption by Soviet civilians was about half of the U.S. level and about two-thirds of the British level, and that the nutritional level was about one-third below the level necessary to maintain health.[2]

Recent Soviet émigrés remember terrible food shortages. Workers in a defense plant in the small town of Kubandik near Cheliabinsk ate potato skins and 600 grams of bread a day, working 12 to 16 hours per day. The food situation in this area remained disastrous through 1943.[3] A woman employed at a defense plant in Kuibyshev worked 12 to 15 hours a day, living mostly on soup with an occasional glass of powdered milk.[4] A British study cited earlier showed caloric deficiencies of 600 calories a day or more in the diets of Soviet citizens, and Edward R. Stettinius, Jr., Director of the Lend-Lease Administration, estimated that in 1942, Soviet defense workers were at best consuming two-thirds of what an American would regard as necessary for sound health and that other groups were even worse off.[5] It

Minnesota Press, 1950, p. 344. According to prewar data, Soviet laborers doing hard work were receiving 132 grams of protein a day in contrast to Sweden – 189, Italy – 114, France – 135, and England – 151. U.S. lumbermen and college athletes received 160 to 270 grams. Ibid., p. 346. At any given body weight, women require somewhat fewer calories. Whereas a 140-pound moderately active man requires 2,850 calories, a moderately active woman of the same weight requires 2,600 calories. Their protein needs are the same. James S. McLester and William J. Darby, *Nutrition and Diet in Health and Disease*, 6th edition, Philadelphia: Saunders, 1952, p. 606. These data are from the Canadian dietary standards.

[2] Bela Gold, *Wartime Planning in Agriculture*, New York: Columbia University Press, 1949, pp. 38, 307.

[3] Interview of January 30, 1988.

[4] Interview of January 30, 1988.

[5] See Chapter 7, p. 19; Edward R. Stettinius, Jr., *Lend Lease: Weapon for Victory*, New York: Macmillan, 1944, p. 226. Eric Johnston, president of the U.S. Chamber of Commerce, after returning from a trip to the Soviet Union, stated that the average Soviet citizen was getting 1,600 calories a day. (*Chicago Daily Tribune*, September 17, 1944, pp. 1, 8) *The New Republic* (April 9, 1945, p. 475) cited an "official" figure of an average of 2,000 calories a day for Soviet consumers, barely above the basal metabolic rate for a 150-pound man. The basal metabolic rate can be thought of as the level of energy over which the body has no control or as the least amount of heat produced in the state of wakefulness. The body uses about 80 calories per hour lying down or sleeping and 100 calories an hour just sitting. Thus, roughly speaking, the human organism needs about 1,920 calories a day to keep body weight constant, even in a lethargic state. See Eva May Nunnelley Hamilton, Eleanor Noss Whitney, and Frances Sienkowicz Sizer, *Nutrition: Concepts and Controversies*, 3rd edition, St. Paul: West, 1985, p. 175. George F. Cahill says that a 70-kilogram man has a basal expenditure of 1,800 calories a day. See "Starvation in Man," *The New England Journal of Medicine*, March 19, 1970, p. 668. There is a decrease in the basal metabolic rate in starving individuals, because during starvation the human organism goes through a series of adaptations to secure

Table 12.3. *Changes in the diet of workers during the war (per capita consumption as a percent of September 1940)*

	1941	1942	1943	1944
Bread and flour	96.9	98.0	98.0	83.5
Groats, legumes, macaroni	95.4	73.5	91.0	114.0
Potatoes	128.2	131.6	198.7	234.1
Vegetables and melons	66.1	41.4	44.7	40.9
Milk and milk products	90.4	58.3	67.3	69.5
Meat and meat products	111.3	42.1	55.8	59.5
Animal and vegetable oils	56.4	65.4	79.9	106.5
Fish and herring	87.3	78.4	105.6	111.6
Sugar and confectionery goods	50.6	33.8	25.3	22.4

Source: *Istoriia Velikoi Otechestvennoi Voiny Sovetskogo Soiuza, 1941–1945*, Vol. 6, Moscow, 1965, p. 77.

is thus no surprise to hear that in 1942, the average Muscovite was reported to have lost 15 pounds.[6] The bleakness of the food situation was soberly expressed by a U.S. diplomat's report in late 1942:

> The urban population in general is suffering from undernourishment to such an extent as to hamper its normal capacity for work. The absence of a balanced diet is having ill effects even though for many years bread, which is the most plentiful food available, has been the staple diet of Russia. In our opinion unless considerable quantities of foodstuffs, particularly fats and sugar, can be obtained from abroad the suffering in many districts will be severe and during the later part of the winter and the spring great numbers of persons will die as a result of undernourishment and the health of many more will be seriously impaired.[7]

The data in Table 12.3 suggest the disintegration of the Soviet food supply from 1941 through 1943 or 1944 depending on the food product in question. Meat and dairy products fell by 1943 to roughly one-half to two-thirds of the prewar level. The 1941 meat figure showing a temporary increase in consumption was likely the result of the slaughter of animals associated with the evacuation. The implications of

energy and conserve protein. The main point is unchanged; Soviet caloric intake for a great part of the war must have been at the margin.
[6] Columbia Broadcasting System Monitoring Reports, June 3, 1943, citing a story in *The Evening Standard* (London) without giving the date.
[7] *Foreign Relations of the United States*, Washington, D.C., 1942, Vol. III, pp. 480–1.

extraordinary slaughter early in the war was the absence of meat in subsequent years. The official meat figures for the war cohere with the postwar assessment of Naum Jasny, who estimated that the 1947 per capita consumption of the major meats was about half of what it had been in the late 1930s and only about 40 percent of the 1928 figure of 24 kilograms a year.[8]

Only in the case of grains and potatoes was the prewar level of consumption either maintained or increased. The data show that per capita bread and flour consumption were about the same during the first three years of the war as they were in 1940, but the maintenance of the supply of bread and flour is something of an illusion. There was a shift to the planting of low-quality millet and a sharp decline in high-quality wheat production. In 1940, just under 6,000,000 hectares of millet were planted, but in 1944 8,400,000 hectares were planted, an increase of 40 percent. Meanwhile, the acreage going to winter and spring wheat fell in the same period from 40 million to 22.6 million hectares, a decline of about 44 percent.[9] In the most difficult times, the Russian peasant always shifted to the inferior millet, which requires less seed and can be sown late in the spring, enabling farmers to have more time to prepare the land. As a proportion of total grain sowing, millet went from 5.4 percent in 1940 to 10.2 percent in 1944. Wheat, on the other hand, fell from 36 percent to 27 percent in 1944.[10]

One of the most dramatic changes in the food supply was the substantial increase in potato consumption, which had doubled by 1943 and then increased even more in 1944. The drive to get people to grow potatoes bordered on the deification of the tuber. In the words of one author, "Potatoes were the second bread."[11] President Kalinin said in March 1942, "It is unnecessary to prove the importance of the potato in the national diet. This year the significance of the potato will be even greater."[12] A month later he said, "If you wish to take part in the victory over the German fascist invaders, then you must plant as many potatoes as possible."[13] Potatoes were called upon to substitute for virtually every other category of food.

---

[8] Naum Jasny, *The Socialized Agriculture of the USSR*, Stanford: Stanford University Press, 1949, p. 85.
[9] Iu. V. Arutiunian, *Sovetskoe krest'ianstvo v gody Velikoi Otechestvennoi Voiny*, Moscow, 1963, p. 409.
[10] Jasny, p. 267.
[11] Ia. E. Chadaev, *Ekonomika SSSR v period Velikoi Otechestvennoi Voiny*, Moscow, 1965, p. 358.
[12] *Pravda*, March 1, 1942, p. 2.
[13] *Pravda*, April 2, 1942, p. 3.

As the data show, sugar practically disappeared from the Soviet diet, falling to about one-fourth of the prewar level of consumption. The great Russian passion for sugar with their tea produced a poignant expression during the war: *"Pit' chai v prigliatku,"* which literally meant to drink tea with your imagination, that is, the Russians would drink tea imagining there was sugar in it.[14]

The structural changes in the Soviet diet can be seen in the recipes published in the popular women's magazine, *Rabotnitsa* (*The Woman Worker*). A sampling of recipes from the prewar period, during the war, and after the war, shows the shifting availability of different kinds of food. If we look at recipes from 1937, when there is a dominance of recipes that use vegetables, the recipes also call for dairy products and some meat. For instance, one 1937 issue included several recipes for five persons. The first, *botvinnia*, a cold fish and vegetable soup called for beets, cucumbers, kvass, green peas, and about a pound of sturgeon or pike. A cold olive salad called not only for vegetables and potatoes, but also for "leftover ham, game, veal, beef," and used sugar in the dressing. And the recipe for strawberry jam used sugar.[15]

These quite typical recipes of the prewar period call for ingredients such as fruits, vegetables, meat, and dairy products that are not used in recipes published in the same magazine during the war. The recipes published in the November 1943 issue of *Rabotnitsa* exemplify the hardships of the war. None of the six recipes – a pureed vegetable soup, vegetable cutlets, vegetable ragout, potato loaf, stuffed cabbage, and vegetable stuffed cabbage roll – mentions meat, dairy products, poultry, or greens. The pureed vegetable soup is dominated by potatoes and cabbage, calling for 250 grams cabbage, 500 grams potatoes, 100 grams carrots, 50 grams celery, 50 grams onions, one tablespoon of flour, and 50 grams of oil. The cabbage is stuffed with 500 grams of chopped carrot plus rice or some other coarse grain. If we use these recipes as an indication of the food available to Soviet households, then the dominance of potatoes and cabbages is manifest and as we would expect, *Rabotnitsa's* wartime recipes were variations on the perpetual theme of 100 ways to eat potatoes and cabbage. In the August–September 1944 issue it was "cabbage provencale," using cranberries or red bilberries for sweetening.[16] Cabbage provencale showed up again in the August 1945 issue, but this time, the recipe

---

[14] Interview of November 18, 1987.
[15] *Rabotnitsa*, No. 20, 1937.
[16] Ibid., No. 11, November 1943; Nos. 8–9, August–September 1944.

called for one-half glass of granulated sugar, suggesting this had become more readily available.[17]

Not until 1946 did *Rabotnitsa* again publish recipes calling for meat, although hardly at a luxurious level. Three recipes in the March 1946 issue contained meat. The first ingredient listed in the recipe for a soup with a meat bouillon was 500 grams of meat, and the other two recipes were a cabbage dish with meat, and potato balls with meat sauce.[18]

Lurking behind the decline in caloric intake and the substitution of bread and potatoes for meat and fats is the question of whether the deprivation of food led beyond hunger and malnutrition to starvation. We know that about 1 million people starved to death in Leningrad, but we know little about how many starved elsewhere. A recent Soviet source refers to civilian wartime deaths from starvation in "the central regions, in the Volga, in the Urals, [and] in Siberia," but offers no estimate of the number of deaths due to food shortages.[19] Indeed, there is virtually nothing in the literature published in the Soviet Union about starvation, nor was starvation discussed or even admitted during the war. Even if the Soviet wartime archives are eventually opened to public scrutiny, we may never know how many starved because of political or human unwillingness to admit the fact. Based on the available evidence, however, it seems most reasonable to conclude that there was some starvation in many parts of the country outside of besieged Leningrad, but that the abiding state of the overwhelming number of Soviet citizens was malnutrition, perhaps even chronic malnutrition, rather than starvation. Many lived with great hunger, perhaps even on the edge of starvation. Yet the food that was available, meager as it was, somehow saw people through.

During the war (and afterward), however, every effort was made to hide the facts about the degree of deprivation, even from the Soviet people themselves. Newspaper accounts simply did not discuss hunger or starvation. An extreme example of this avoidance was the "Letter from the Leningrad Front" published in the December 21, 1941, issue of *Pravda* during the so-called hungry winter, in which there was not a single word about hunger, much less starvation.[20]

---

[17] Ibid., No. 8, August 1945.
[18] Ibid., No. 3, March 1946.
[19] V. Ia. Gorov and A. M. Samsonov, "1941–1945. Na podstupakh k istine," in *Istoriki sporiat*, Moscow, 1980, pp. 313–14.
[20] *Pravda*, December 21, 1941, p. 3.

Stalin's speeches also ignored both hunger and starvation, substituting instead empty cheerleading statements, such as the one he made
on the anniversary of the November Revolution in 1942: "Our collective farms and state farms are . . . conscientiously and punctually
supplying the population and the Red Army with foodstuffs, and our
industry with raw materials."[21]

Despite efforts to banish hunger officially through the press and
speeches, the ubiquitous food shortages were difficult to hide and
word of mouth spread the truth.[22] The cynicism of the time about
such lying by silence or evasion is captured in a sarcastic passage
from Vasily Grossman's novel about the war, describing what it would
be like if newspapers really printed the truth: "You learn why there's
no buckwheat in Moscow instead of being told that the first strawberries have just been flown in from Tashkent. You find out the
quantity of a kolkhoz worker's daily ration of bread from the newspapers, not from the cleaning-lady whose niece has just come to
Moscow to buy some bread."[23]

Given the silence of traditional historical sources, the chronicler
must turn to the accounts of survivors to hear testimony to starvation.
A number of the émigrés I interviewed attested to seeing or learning
of starvation during 1942 and 1943. Some of them literally saw people
die on the job, such as the defense plant worker in Kuibyshev whose
story was told in Chapter 2. Others heard about workers dying of
hunger, such as the workers in the Chernikovsk defense plant who
died in the Urals during 1942 and 1943.[24] Even in Kuibyshev, a privileged city that became the temporary capital and housed the diplomatic corps, there was general deprivation: "People starved to death
in Kuibyshev, especially those who didn't work at the defense plant.
People starved en masse who worked in small enterprises and in the
kolkhozy. Kuibyshev was not a city prepared for all the [evacuees]
who came."[25] And in Chernikovsk there was a special dining room
for children with extraordinary health problems where for a minimal
charge a child was fed a decent meal, usually soup and sometimes a
small amount of meat and either millet or barley kasha for the cereal.
Always lurking on the periphery of the dining room were the so-

---

[21] See Joseph Stalin, *The Great Patriotic War of the Soviet Union*, New York: Greenwood
Press, 1969.
[22] See, for example, the testimony of émigrés in Chapter 10.
[23] Grossman, p. 276.
[24] Interview of June 18, 1988.
[25] Interview of January 30, 1988.

called *dokhodiagi*, people who were on the verge of death from starvation. They would hang around the dining room and when the
children had finished eating they would lick the plates.[26]

Starvation took its toll among the evacuees, who also saw starvation
as they moved through the country. The story of a Polish woman
incarcerated in a Siberian labor camp along with 30 other Polish families sheds light on several kinds of starvation. In February 1942, these
Poles were told they were free to leave the camps and could go
anywhere in the country, although without ration cards because they
were not registered in any town. Ten families pooled their money,
booked passage on a freight train, and hired someone with a horse
to take them all to the railroad station 350 miles away. On February
12, 1942, en route to the railroad the woman's youngest daughter,
who was one year old, "died of starvation in my arms. . . . You can't
blame anyone; it was the war situation, everyone suffered." Her other
child had pneumonia. They were waiting for the train at the station
and somebody went for a doctor. The doctor said: "Don't cry, don't
cry. Let her die. She will be better off. I have no medicine and your
baby is suffering." Pointing to others, the doctor said: "That family
lost five children, that family lost three children." They finally got on
a train traveling to Tashkent:

> On the way I saw [dead] people piled up at the railroad stations.
> Some of them were from Leningrad. At one station a woman came
> banging on the door of our car, yelling, "Poliaki, Poliaki, let me in."
> This woman was traveling from Leningrad. Her twelve-year-old son
> had died and she was carrying him dead in her arms wanting to get
> to Tashkent where her mother lived and bury the child there. But
> other people wouldn't let her keep her dead child [for fear of disease]
> and threw the child on a pile at the railroad station.[27]

The stories from Central Asia are mixed. From one émigré we hear
of starvation in the Central Asian capital of Ashkhabad. There, this
woman said, her mother's cousin, his son, and his parents all starved
to death in the winter of 1942 to 1943.[28] When the Polish woman
arrived in Tashkent in March 1942, she "didn't see dead people on
the stations anymore."[29] Nevertheless, it appears that hunger may
have affected the children of Tashkent later in the war. A U.S. dip-

[26] Interview of June 18, 1988.
[27] Interview of March 14, 1988.
[28] Interview of November 18, 1987.
[29] Interview of March 14, 1988.

lomat traveling to the city in mid–1944 observed even this late in the war that "a good many Uzbek children in the old city of Tashkent have puffed up bellies," although he remarked that "in general the populace looked well fed."[30]

Even the peasants, the growers of food, suffered from food deprivation. In the villages the diet was deficient in fats and vitamins, limited to bread, potatoes, vegetables, and milk. The amount of bread available was often half of what it had been before the war and meat consumption, already at a low level in 1940, fell by half during the war. Sugar, candy, canned goods, and sausage completely disappeared from village tables. In some places, peasants were forced to resort to eating edible weeds.[31] Or in an otherwise bankrupt community, one successful crop might dominate the diet of villagers.[32] A U.S. diplomat traveling on the Trans-Siberian railroad in the summer of 1943 said that the poorest areas appeared to be that from Sverdlovsk to Omsk and the Jewish Autonomous Region.[33] People evacuated from cities dreaded being sent to villages. An émigré sent to Sverdlovsk at the end of 1942 remembers that his work unit was divided into two groups: those that would work for the Urals Machine Building Factory (*Uralmash*) and those who were sent to villages to build a rail line. Each man knew that those who went to Uralmash would be the better fed, whereas those who went to the village would be badly off.[34] One woman told me that people who were evacuated from Kiev to villages starved to death.[35]

There were rumors of cannibalism. In Kaminsk-Uralsky an émigré and her family were warned not to buy the *piroshki* (small meat pies) because they were said to be made of human flesh.[36] And even if there were no instances of cannibalism, the fact that people thought there were reflects a situation of extreme deprivation.

---

[30] USSR Crop Conditions and Production, 1942–1945. Records of the Foreign Agricultural Service. Record Group 166, National Archives, Washington, D.C. (NFAS), U.S. Embassy Report 752, July 31, 1944.
[31] Arutiunian, pp. 356–7.
[32] See Valentin Rasputin's satirical description of such a situation in a Siberian community: "The bread was yellow, made with peas – a pea kingdom reigned in the village now, with pea music for accompaniment: the kolkhoz suddenly had gotten generous and had turned over almost a ton of peas to the workers, so now they shoveled pea porridge with pea bread, and had a side dish of boiled peas with it." *Live and Remember*, New York: Macmillan, 1978, p. 77.
[33] NFAS, U.S. Embassy at Moscow, Despatch No. 299, October 15, 1943.
[34] Interview of January 30, 1988.
[35] Interview of January 30, 1988.
[36] Interview of November 18, 1987.

The health implications of food deprivation

In addition to the immediate effects of hunger – and, at the worst, starvation – the deprivation of food during the war had significant effects on the health of the Soviet population. First, there were serious problems with germ-ridden food during the war. Many canned products and local uncanned products that were served to soldiers carried typhoid, dysentery, toxic infections, botulism, and other diseases. There were food inspectors who were responsible, among other things, for killing insects and rodents. In an effort to defend against rats, they built shelves at the food warehouses fifty centimeters off the ground and thirty to forty centimeters away from the walls and did such things as put lids on water wells.[37]

The absence of proper nutrition led to a variety of medical problems. For instance, the number of cases of and the rate of death from tuberculosis increased. Although the absence of food is not the sole cause of tuberculosis it is an important contributor, and so wartime malnutrition increased the incidence of the disease, with the effects manifesting themselves after the worst hunger. During the first year of the war there were deaths from tuberculosis, but only 4.6 percent of them occurred during the first half of this period, July 1 through December, whereas the other 95.4 percent came in the second half of this period, January 1 to June 30, 1942. Most cases in Leningrad occurred after the time of the worst nutritional deficiencies.[38]

There was also a high incidence of gastritis.[39] People in the occupied areas were especially victimized by gastritis because they ate a great deal of cold food, spoiled food, and food that had not been cooked completely. The generally poor quality of bread also may have contributed to gastritis. Often people suffered from gastritis after eating frozen bread. Probably the main cause was that hungry people stuffed themselves with too much food that was "often cold, hard to digest, coarse, or not cooked completely."[40] Gastritis was also noted among soldiers who had been under siege and people who lived under oc-

---

[37] *Opyt sovetskoi meditsiny v Velikoi Otechestvennoi Voine 1941–1945gg. (Opyt)*, Vol. 32, Part III, Moscow, 1955, pp. 20, 26. See pp. 132–4 for more detail.
[38] Ibid., Vol. 25, pp. 206, 210.
[39] Gastritis, which is an inflammation of the stomach, particularly the mucous membrane, is a pathology that occurs because of nutritional irregularities such as the poor quality of food and meal irregularity, as well as a limited quantity of food, the use of dehydrated food products, and eating food that is hard to digest.
[40] *Opyt*, Vol. 23, pp. 34–5. This is plausible because the wartime diet possessed low satiety values (i.e., people did not eat food that left them feeling satisfied). Bread and potatoes have very low satiety values. The foods with high satiety values, such as meat and whole milk, seldom graced the tables of the populace.

cupation. Many suffered from gastritis because they ate the meat of dead animals, raw mushrooms, rotten vegetables, grass, shredded tree bark, and other edible weeds.[41]

Ulcers were evident in both the military and among the civilian population as a consequence of food conditions. One cause of peptic ulcers during the war was the deficiency of vitamins C and K.[42] It was also argued that ulcers were caused to a large extent because of the changes in diet. During the Leningrad siege, when eating was highly irregular and vitamin deficiency was extreme, there were few ulcers. But after the blockade was lifted most ulcers became apparent, suggesting that the extreme hunger had caused "symptomless ulcers."[43] And there was a great deal of diarrhea and dysentery associated with food problems. A doctor who brought 2,700 Leningrad children to an Omsk oblast village remembers the way illness struck her charges: "The children got diarrhea because the water was impure and the food wasn't clean; the cooking wasn't sanitary. A couple of children died of dysentery. There was not enough medicine. I needed rice, but there wasn't rice."[44] Dysentery was prevalent throughout the country and hospitals provided special diets for people with the disease.[45]

Deprivation of vitamins, which in the Soviet Union were almost entirely obtained through food intake rather than as supplements, had several significant effects. The absence of vitamin C led to rampant scurvy in the military as well as in the civilian population. Indeed, during World War II, the only European country to report scurvy was the Soviet Union.[46] As a consequence of the prevalence of scurvy, there was a great deal of gum disease.[47] One émigré told me that her family bought garlic at 150 rubles a head to deal with scurvy.[48] This use of garlic may explain why so much of it was stolen from fields.[49] The Soviet population gave every indication of lacking vitamin A. The USSR, like the United States and Great Britain, had

[41] Ibid., p. 38.
[42] V. M. Kogan-Yasny, "Some Aspects of Peptic Ulcer During Wartime," *American Review of Soviet Medicine*, Vol. 2, No. 3, February 1945, p. 235.
[43] *Opyt*, Vol. 23, pp. 109–10.
[44] Interview of September 10, 1986.
[45] *Opyt*, Vol. 33, p. 212. The special diet was farina kasha with milk and butter, farina kasha with vegetable bouillon, farina kasha with fruit and powdered eggs, rice pudding, meat souffle, rice kasha with extra calcium, buttermilk made from powdered milk, and buttermilk made with condensed milk.
[46] Keys et al., *The Biology of Human Starvation*, Vol. 1, 459.
[47] Interview of September 10, 1986.
[48] Interview of November 18, 1987.
[49] See Chapter 9.

relied on imports of Norwegian cod liver oil and were cut off from this source during the war.[50] A Polish émigré incarcerated in an Archangel labor camp received no eggs, milk, butter, fruit, or meat in her diet and as a consequence, along with others, she developed worsening eyesight. Her condition improved when she was taken to a *feldsher* (medical assistant) who gave her cod liver oil.[51]

Children were especially subject to the effects of malnutrition, particularly the deprivation of vitamins at crucial points in their development. In mid–1943, even after the food supply had improved in Kuibyshev, a U.S. diplomat observed "considerable evidence of malnutrition, particularly among the babies, many of whom seem undersized and pale."[52] After the war, Soviet doctors attributed a number of neuropsychiatric disorders in children to conditions arising from the German occupation, including a lack of food and near starvation.[53] Moreover, the postwar implications of wartime food deprivation on children were great. For instance, Mark Field has suggested that increases in infant mortality of the 1970s may have been at least partially attributable to the fact that their mothers had been born during World War II and were nutritionally deprived for several years as children.[54]

What stands out in this review of the effects of food shortages in the Soviet Union is the relative lack of government attempts to ameliorate the situation. This is true across the board, from public education about nutrition, to manufacturing vitamin supplements as replacements for natural vitamin sources, to developing new foods or new food technologies. Without making a full-fledged comparison, the contrast becomes clear when looking at some of the key advances made in the United States where, for example, dehydration technology developed rapidly during the war[55] and vitamin A was developed in powdered form for the first time.[56]

---

[50] DOA, "Feed Our Allies" file, February 12, 1944. It was not until the end of 1943 that the United States developed vitamin A in a powdered form.
[51] Interview of March 14, 1988.
[52] NFAS, U.S. Embassy at Kuibyshev, Report No. 11, June 28, 1943.
[53] G. E. Sukhareva, "Psychologic Disturbances in Children During War," *American Review of Soviet Medicine*, Vol. 5, No. 1, December 1947–January 1948, p. 33.
[54] Field raised this issue at the Kennan Institute for Advanced Russian Studies in a talk on November 9, 1987. There is no evidence emanating from the Soviet Union supporting this view and neither Field nor I know of any public discussion of this view.
[55] See, for example, *Food Field Reporter*, January 24, 1944, p. 37.
[56] Ibid., p. 35. It was the first vitamin A concentrate in nonoil form in the United States. See *Food Field Reporter*, January 24, 1944, p. 35.

There were few vitamin substitutes in the USSR to compensate for the shortage of natural vitamins supplied by food. The evidence is that as late as February 1945 vitamin supplements played an extremely limited role in the life of the ordinary Soviet citizen. Even where they existed, a Moscow newspaper complained, people generally viewed vitamins as having a curative function and did not understand their preventive purpose.[57] In part this may have resulted from their prevalent use in hospitals, where virtually all patients were given vitamins because of the many cases of vitamin deficiency. Patients showing a deficiency were daily given 100 to 300 milligrams of vitamin C and as the deficiency diminished their dosage was cut to 50 to 100 milligrams. They also received 2.5 milligrams of vitamin B. Sometimes niacin, yeast, castor oil, vitamin A, and liver extract were given. The use of vitamins in hospital diets increased during the war.[58]

There appears to have been only one factory in the country manufacturing vitamins, the Marat factory in Moscow, which operated under the aegis of the Commissariat of the RSFSR Food Industry. It produced six different vitamin preparations, including vitamins A, B_1, C, a combination of C and B_1, D, and niacin.[59] It is not known how much of its output was slated for the military and how much for the civilian population. In the kindergarten in Chernikovsk, a teaspoon of vitamin C in the form of a syrup was given only to the weakest children, suggesting a general shortage.[60]

Furthermore, public education on nutrition was virtually nonexistent. It was not until late in the war that Rabotnitsa carried an article on how to ensure that there was an adequate supply of vitamins in the family diet. The article, which focused on vitamins A and C, indicated that people should have 50 milligrams of vitamin C every day and informed the readership about the foods that supply vitamin C. It spelled out how much of the vitamin content is lost under various cooking conditions and urged women to preserve the vitamins of the food they cooked.[61]

[57] Vechernaia Moskva, January 18, 1945, cited in NFAS, U.S. Embassy at Moscow, Despatch No. 1463, February 10, 1945. Vitamins were sold in the pharmacies. There were plans at this time to open a special department for the sale of vitamins at the Dietetic Shop No. 2 on Gorky Street in Moscow. I have no way of knowing whether that occurred.
[58] Opyt, Vol. 23, p. 61.
[59] NFAS, U.S. Embassy at Moscow, October 19, 1944.
[60] Interview of June 18, 1988. The interviewee said: "The nurse loved me and after she had given all the children their vitamin C she would put my tea in the cup which had contained the syrup."
[61] Rabotnitsa, July 1945, No. 7. The lack of education on vitamins and nutrition is in vivid contrast to the United States, where enormous efforts to educate the public on

It was state policy to shift grains destined for animal fodder into human consumption. As early as October 1941, an article in *Pravda* discussed reducing the grain content of pig fodder by 15 to 20 percent and giving the extra grain to the state.[62]

There was an effort to produce edible yeasts (*pishevye drozhzhi*) as a protein source to compensate for the loss of meat, milk, fish, and eggs. There was some production of albuminous yeast during the Leningrad blockade, but it appears that there was more talk about the virtues of yeast than real efforts to produce it. The Soviets were capable of producing about 12,000 tons of dry edible yeast a year (the nutritional equivalent of 30,000 tons of meat) and apparently they opened yeast shops in hydrolysis plants as a by-product of alcohol production. Yet after mid–1943, the effort disappeared from public discussion.[63]

There was not a total absence of research on new foods, but instead it was a case of too little, too late. It was not until late 1944 that unripe walnuts were found to have a high concentration of vitamin C and a method was developed for producing their juice.[64] By 1946 wartime research had identified other sources of vitamin C, including the fruits of wild oranges (cherry laurel).[65] Indeed, it was admitted at the end of 1943 in a leading journal that little research was being carried out in some crucial areas, such as finding new strains of grain and developing insecticides.[66] The resources were simply not there to invest in alternative foods for the civilian population.

Conclusion

There can be no disputing the fact that for much of the war, most Soviet citizens lived at the margin of existence. The decline of

these matters became routine. A survey in 1941 showed that 19 percent of Americans had a "considerable interest" in vitamins and 45 percent had a "moderate interest." In 1942, those figures jumped substantially to 30 percent and 46 percent, respectively. See *Food Field Reporter*, October 12, 1940, p. 40.

[62] *Pravda*, October 9, 1941, p. 3. Helen C. Farnsworth and V. P. Timoshenko conjecture that "considerable portions of such feed grains as barley and corn have been diverted to human consumption," although neither they or any other source knows how frequently such diversions took place. See their *World Grain Review and Outlook, 1945*, p. 102.

[63] See *Pravda*, October 26, 1942, p. 3, and May 26, 1943, p. 3.

[64] *The Food Industry*, No. 10, 1944, in NFAS, U.S. Embassy at Moscow, Report No. 469, November 1944.

[65] G. K. Sergeev, "Pomerantsevye plody kak istochnik vitamina c," *Voenno-meditsinskii zhurnal*, Nos. 7–8, July–August, 1946, pp. 50–51.

[66] *Sotsialisticheskoe sel'skoe khoziaistvo*, December 1943, pp. 48–51.

the quantity and quality of the diet took its toll in terms of weight loss and physical and mental illness during and after the war. Its long-term negative implications remain a matter of speculation, although concern seems legitimate.

Few could have been protected from the ravages of food deprivation. Even for a worker in a high-priority defense plant, the food situation was disastrous and was compounded by a work regimen of twelve-hour days and seven-day work weeks. At the very time when the most demands were made on the human spirit and body, there was little to feed the spirit, and even less to feed the body.

Conclusion

In 1941 the USSR was invaded by a power that had run roughshod over a large part of Europe and seemed capable of conquering the USSR with the same dispatch it had shown in the first two years of the war. But the war was long and for the Soviet Union it ended on May 9, 1945, only after a series of paroxysmal crises involving invasion, evacuation, occupation, and liberation. During the four years of war, at least twenty million, and perhaps as many as thirty million, had died.[1] There were also massive economic losses, possibly as much as seven years of earnings for the prewar population.[2] The nation's spirit was bent, but never broken, its resources strained, but never depleted. The country survived. The triumph not only preserved the USSR, but also made it an imperial power; control over Eastern Europe was a spoil of victory.

Although the Soviet Union proved itself to be a nation great enough to defeat a mighty military power, it was not a nation rich enough to fight a great war, that is to feed, clothe, and supply its army and also to feed its civilian population. Of the Allies, the United States was rich enough to fight the war and feed its people well during wartime. Great Britain fought and ate respectably, although not plentifully, because Canada shared its wealth with its British cousin. But the Soviet Union was neither endowed with a bountiful food supply nor was there a friendly nation to share freely from its agricultural cornucopia. Alone among the Allies, the Soviet Union had to fight two wars at once: one against Germany and one against hunger.

The Soviet victory over Germany is clearer than its victory over

---

[1] Recently Soviet Foreign Minister Eduard Shevardnadze stated that 26 million people died during World War II (*The New York Times*, February 3, 1990, p. 1).
[2] James R. Millar and Susan J. Linz, "The Cost of World War II to the Soviet People: A Research Note," *Journal of Economic History*, Vol. XXXVIII, no. 4, December 1978, pp. 959–62.

food shortages. In the field of food policy, the Soviet central authorities retreated almost immediately and handed over part of the responsibility for fighting the daily struggle to feed the civilian population to local areas, probably the most logical policy they could have pursued in view of the existing confusion and the limited alternatives that were available. The defenses against hunger were to be erected in every town, village, enterprise, and school in the country through private plots, private urban gardens, factory farms, and local markets. Having been given increased responsibility during the war to feed themselves, civilians adapted quickly and efficiently, developing local production and distribution systems that had been much less developed on the eve of the war.

Could the central regime have done more to feed the population? On the one hand, it may be argued that there was probably not much more that it could have done, especially in view of the severe shortage of resources. The primary limitation was, of course, the loss of key food-producing areas to the Germans. Nothing could have been done about this until the occupied areas were recaptured. But real constraints on the ability to feed the civilian population during the war had also been inherited from the 1930s. The damage done by collectivization and the inadequate level of investment in railroads were two principal explanations for the food shortages in the unoccupied areas. Moreover, there seems to have been virtually no planning for civilian needs if the Germans attacked, an event that was more likely than not, the Nazi-Soviet pact notwithstanding. There were no food reserves for the civilian population, there was no plan for relocation, and therefore chaos and hunger existed in many places in the rear. For a nation that was paranoid about the outside world's intentions, there was surprisingly little preparation for invasion, much less a long war.

Yet in the face of ongoing food shortages, what is striking about the civilian population is how it accepted the need to endure the enormity of the sacrifices it was being asked to make. Even taking account of the atmosphere of fear under which they lived, it is clear that people not only accepted the secondary priority they had after the army, but were also willing to accept a diet that kept them at the margin of hunger for so much of the war. In spite of the fact that hunger hovered over their lives like an angel of death, civilians were willing to bear this burden in the name of patriotism.

The rationing system, the state's primary means of distributing food, was in many ways a farce simply because there was so little to offer through the state distribution network. Yet there existed an acceptance here as well. Although some turned to criminal activity, especially as food shortages worsened, there was an overwhelming sense that the hardship was being fairly distributed. Some gained through privilege, but not enough to damage the sense of common effort to win the war. And even if we eliminated all the unfairness that existed, there still would not have been a significant improvement in the civilian food supply.

If the Soviet Union won the war in part because of the system of centralized, hierarchical planning that had been installed at the end of the 1920s and the authoritarianism that had existed even longer, the same cannot be said about how the civilian population survived. Civilians were fed not because of the system, but in spite of it. The regime used its limited resources to win the war and feed the army; as a consequence civilians were thrown back on their own resources to a much larger degree than before the war. For as long as it was deemed efficacious, central authority focused its limited resources on more imminent goals. But as soon as it became clear that the tide of the war had turned in favor of the Soviet Union, the regime began to retrieve the power it had temporarily and expediently ceded to the population.

There was a predictable redistribution of wealth during the war from the cities to the countryside. Food shortages made peasant private plot production even more important than it had been before the war. Did the peasants exploit their urban brethren? The answer partly depends on how one weighs the efficiency of a market in distributing output against the immorality of raising food prices in a time of acute shortages. Many peasants grew relatively rich feeding the people of the cities. But those tempted to charge the peasantry with wartime rapacity should remember that the authorities excluded them from the rationing system and left the farm population to feed itself. Moreover, in retreating from responsibility for feeding the civilian population, the authorities were implicitly expecting the peasantry to help feed urban dwellers. Yet after the war, the regime punished the peasantry for its wartime activity. A currency reform in December 1947 required the entire population to exchange their rubles at the rate of 1:10; the enormous cash holdings that so many peasants had accumulated during the war were essentially wiped out. This action was coupled with the conversion of state bonds to one-third of their face value and the reduction of the interest rate.[3] Not

---

[3] Alec Nove, *An Economic History of the U.S.S.R.*, London: Penquin, 1969, p. 308.

for the first time in Soviet history did the peasantry bear an unjust burden.

The bread of affliction was a spare and bitter offering. It was half a loaf shared by millions who were condemned to years of deprivation. To have made the bread last until the end was the deed of a heroic people.

Bibliography

Adamovich, Ales, Yanka Bryl, and Vladimir Kolesnik, *Out of the Fire*, Moscow, 1980.

and Daniil Granin, *A Book of the Blockade*, Moscow, 1983.

Aniskov, V. T., "Kolkhoznaia derevnia v 1941–1945gg.," in *Sovetskii tyl v Velikoi Otechestvennoi Voine*, Vol. 2, Moscow, 1974, p. 192–200.

Antonov, A. N., "Children Born During the Siege of Leningrad in 1942," *Journal of Pediatrics*, Vol. 30, No. 2, February 1947, pp. 250–9.

Armstrong, John A., *Ukrainian Nationalism, 1939–1945*, New York: Columbia University Press, 1955.

Arutiunian, Iu. V., *Sel'skogo khoziaistvo SSSR v 1929–1957gg.*, Moscow, 1960.

Sovetskoe krest'ianstvo v gody Velikoi Otechestvennoi Voiny, Moscow, 1963.

Ashby, Eric, *Scientist in Russia*, New York: Pelican Books, 1947.

Bidlack, Richard, "Workers at War: Factory Workers and Labor Policy in the Siege of Leningrad," unpublished doctoral dissertation, Indiana University, 1987.

Brandt, Karl and associates, *Management of Agriculture and Food in the German-Occupied and Other Areas of Fortress Europe*, Stanford: Stanford University Press, 1953.

Brozek, Josef, Samuel Wells, and Ancel Keys, "Medical Aspects of Semi-starvation in Leningrad (Siege 1941–42)," *American Review of Soviet Medicine*, Vol. IV, No. 1, October 1946, pp. 70–86.

Burov, A. V. *Blokada den' za denem: 22 iiunia 1941–27 ianvaria 1944 goda*, Leningrad, 1979.

Bykov, Vasil, *Sotnikov*, Moscow, 1975.

Cagan, Phillip, "The Monetary Dynamics of Hyperinflation," in Milton Friedman, editor, *Studies in the Quantity Theory of Money*, Chicago: The University of Chicago Press, 1956.

Cahill, George F., Jr., "Starvation in Man," *The New England Journal of Medicine*, Vol. 282, March 19, 1970.

Calvocoressi, Peter and Guy Wint, *Total War: Causes and Courses of the Second World War*, New York: Pantheon, 1972.

240

Carr, E. H. and R. W. Davies, *Foundations of a Planned Economy 1926–1929*, Vol. 1, Part II, New York: Macmillan, 1969.

Chadaev, Ia. E., *Ekonomika SSSR v period Velikoi Otechestvennoi Voiny*, Moscow, 1965.

Chapman, Janet, *Real Wages in Soviet Russia Since 1928*, Cambridge: Harvard University Press, 1963.

Cherniavskii, U. G., *Voina i prodovol'stvie*, Moscow, 1964.

Chernik, S. A., *Sovetskaia shkola v gody Velikoi Otechestvennoi Voiny*, Moscow, 1975.

A Citizen of Kharkiw, "Lest We Forget: Hunger in Kharkiv in the Winter 1941–1942," *The Ukrainian Quarterly*, Vol. IV, No. 1, Winter, 1948, pp. 72–9.

Conquest, Robert, *The Harvest of Sorrow*, New York: Oxford University Press, 1986.

Dallin, Alexander, *German Rule in Russia 1941–1945*, New York: St. Martin's Press, 1957.

Dawson, Raymond H., *The Decision to Aid Russia*, Chapel Hill: The University of North Carolina Press, 1959.

Deborin, G., *Secrets of the Second World War*, Moscow, 1971.

Direktivy kpss i sovetskogo pravitel'stva po khoziaistvennym voprosam, Moscow, 1957.

Dobb, Maurice, *Soviet Economic Development Since 1917*, New York: International Publishers, 1948.

Dyadkin, Iosif G., *Unnatural Deaths in the USSR, 1928–1954*, New Brunswick: Transaction Books, 1983.

Ehrenburg, Ilya, *The War: 1941–1945*, Cleveland: World, 1964.

and Vasily Grossman, *The Black Book*, New York: Holocaust Publications, 1981.

Erickson, John, *The Road to Stalingrad*, New York: Harper & Row, 1975.

Eto bylo na Kalinskom fronte, Moscow, 1985.

Farnsworth, Helen C. and V. P. Timoshenko, *World Grain Review and Outlook, 1945*, Stanford: Food Research Institute, Stanford University, 1945.

Fisher, H. H., *The Famine in Soviet Russia, 1919–1923*, New York: Macmillan, 1927.

"Food Rations in Axis and Occupied Countries," *Monthly Labor Review*, Vol. 57, No. 1, July 1943, pp. 37–9.

Furman, L., "Ob ispol'zovanii korov na sel'skokhoziaistvennykh rabotakh," *Sotsialisticheskoe sel'skoe khoziaistvo*, Nos. 3–4, March–April 1943, pp. 24–7.

Fyodorov, A., *The Underground Committee Carries On*, Moscow, 1952.

German, Alexei, director, "Proverka na Dorogakh," USSR, 1972.

Gold, Bela, *Wartime Economic Planning in Agriculture*, New York: Columbia University Press, 1949.

Gorodetsky, Gabriel, *Stafford Cripps' Mission to Moscow, 1940–1942*, Cambridge: Cambridge University Press, 1984.

Gouré, Leon, *The Siege of Leningrad*, New York: McGraw-Hill, 1962.

Great Patriotic War of the Soviet Union, Moscow, 1974.

Gridnev, V. M., "Nemetsko-fashistskii okkupatsionnyi rezhim v sel'skoi mestnosti zapadnykh i severo-zapadnykh raionakh RSFSR (1941–1944gg.)," *Istoriia SSSR*, No. 1, 1972, pp. 110–18.

Grossman, Vasily, *Life and Fate*, New York: Harper & Row, 1986.

Gubenko, M. P., "K ekonomicheskoi kharakteristike raionov RSFSR, osvobozhdennykh ot fashistskoi okkupatsii v 1943 g.," *Istoriia SSSR*, Vol. 6, No. 1, 1962, pp. 114–21.

Guderian, Heinz, *Panzer Leader*, Washington, D.C.: Zenger, 1952. Reprinted 1979 by Dutton.

Hamilton, Eva May Nunnelley, Eleanor Noss Whitney, and Frances Sienkiewicz Sizer, *Nutrition: Concepts and Controversies*, 3rd edition, St. Paul: West, 1985.

Hannson, Carola and Karin Linden, *Moscow Women*, New York: Pantheon Books, 1983.

Harrison, Mark, *Soviet Planning in Peace and War 1938–1945*, Cambridge: Cambridge University Press. 1985.

Hasluck, Paul, *Australia in the War of 1939–1945. The Government and the People, 1942–1945*, Canberra: Australian War Memorial, 1952.

Helms, Mary W., "The Purchase Society: Adaptation to Economic Frontiers," *Anthropological Quarterly*. Vol. 42, 1969, pp. 325–42.

Howell, Edgar M., *The Soviet Partisan Movement 1941–1944*, Washington, D.C.: Department of the Army, 1956.

Humphrey, Caroline, "Barter and Economic Disintegration," *Man*, Vol. 20, No. 1, March 1985, pp. 48–72.

Hunter, Holland, "Soviet Agriculture with and without Collectivization, 1928–1940," *Slavic Review*, Vol. 47, Summer 1988, pp. 203–16.

Soviet Transportation Policy, Cambridge: Harvard University Press, 1957.

Inber, Vera, *Leningrad Diary*, New York: St. Martin's Press, 1971.

Inkeles, Alex, and Raymond Bauer, *The Soviet Citizen*, New York: Atheneum, 1968.

Istoriia Velikoi Otechestvennoi Voiny Sovetskogo Soiuza, 1941–1945, 6 volumes, Moscow 1960–1965.

Istoriia Vtoroi Mirovoi Voiny 1939–1945, 12 volumes, Moscow, 1973–1982.

Jasny, Naum, *The Socialized Agriculture of the USSR*, Stanford: Stanford University Press, 1949.

Joravsky, David, *The Lysenko Affair*, Cambridge: Harvard University Press, 1970.

Karasev, A. V., *Leningradtsy v gody blokady*, Moscow, 1959.

Karol, K. S., *Between Two Worlds*, New York: Henry Holt, 1986.

Keys, Ancel and others, *The Biology of Human Starvation*, Vol. 1, Minneapolis: The University of Minnesota Press, 1950.

Experimental Starvation in Man, Vol. 2, Minneapolis: The University of Minnesota Press, 1945.

Kievshchina v gody Velikoi Otechestvennoi Voiny 1941–1944, Kiev, 1963.

Kogan-Yasny, V. M., "Some Aspects of Peptic Ulcer During Wartime," *American Review of Soviet Medicine*, Vol. 2, No. 3, February 1945, pp. 233–7.

Kovalchuk, V. M., "Blokirovannyi Leningrad i bol'shaia zemlia," in *Sovetskii tyl v Velikoi Otechestvennoi Voine*, Vol. 2, Moscow, 1974, p. 271–8.

Kovalev, I. V., *Transport v Velikoi Otechestvennoi Voine (1941–1943gg.)*, Moscow, 1981.

Krawchenko, Bohdan, "Soviet Ukraine under Nazi Occupation, 1941–4," in Yuri Boshyk, editor, *Ukraine during World War II*, Edmonton: University of Alberta Press, 1986.

Kulischer, Eugene M., *The Displacement of the Population in Europe*, Montreal: International Labour Office, 1943.

Kumanev, G. A., *Na sluzhbe fronta i tyla*, Moscow, 1976.

Sovetskie zheleznodorozhniki v gody Velikoi Otechestvennoi Voiny, Moscow, 1963.

Kuznetsov, A. Anatoli, *Babi Yar*, New York: Bantam Books, 1971.

League of Nations, *Wartime Rationing and Consumption*, Geneva, 1942.

Liberman, Sanford R., "Crisis Management: The Wartime System of Control and Administration," in Susan J. Linz, editor, *The Impact of World War II on the Soviet Union*, Totowa, N.J.: Towman & Allenheld, 1985.

"The Evacuation of Industry in the Soviet Union During World War II," *Soviet Studies*, Vol. XXXV, No. 1, January 1983, pp. 90–102.

Likhomanov, M. I., *Khoziaistvenno-organizatorskaia rabota partii v derevne v pervyi period Velikoi Otechestvennoi Voiny (1941–1943gg.)*, Leningrad, 1975.

"Razmeshchenie i ispol'zovanie evakuirovannogo naseleniia v vostochnykh raionakh," in *Sovetskii tyl v Velikoi Otechestvennoi Voine*, Vol. 2, pp. 181–91.

Lorimer, Frank, *The Population of the Soviet Union: History and Prospects*, Geneva: League of Nations, 1946.

Malafeev, A. N., *Istoriia tsenoobrazovaniia v SSSR (1917–1963gg.)*, Moscow, 1964.

and V. Milovanov, "Perestroit' zhivotnovodstvo na voennyi lad," *Sotsialisticheskoe sel'skoe khoziaistvo*, September 1941, No. 9, pp. 29–38.

McLester, James S. and William J. Darby, *Nutrition and Diet in Health and Disease*, 6th edition, Philadelphia: Saunders, 1952.

Medvedev, Zhores A., *The Rise and Fall of T. D. Lysenko*, New York: Columbia University Press, 1969.

Soviet Agriculture, New York: Norton, 1987.

Merinov, I., "Trudovye resursy kolkhozov i ikh ispol'zovanie," *Sotsialisticheskoe sel'skoe khoziaistvo*, No. 3, March 1941, pp. 16–24.

Mikoyan, A., "V dni blokady," *Voenno-istoricheskii zhurnal*, No. 2, 1977, pp. 45–54.

Miriasov, Z., "O rasshirennom primenii fosforitnoi muki," *Sotsialisticheskoe sel'skoe khoziaistvo*, Nos. 7–8, July–August 1941, pp.63–8.

Narodnoe khoziaistvo SSSR za 70 let, Moscow, 1987.

Nove, Alec, *An Economic History of the U.S.S.R.*, London: Penguin, 1969.

Opyt sovetskoi meditsiny v Velikoi Otechestvennoi Voine 1941–1945gg., Vols. 23 (1950), 25 (1951), 32, Part III (1955), 33 (1955), Moscow.

Osvobozhdenie gorodov, Moscow, 1985.

Ot sovetskogo informbiuro . . . 1941–1945, Vol. 2, Moscow, 1982.

Pavlov, Dmitri V., *Leningrad 1941: The Blockade*, translated by John Clinton Adams, Chicago: The University of Chicago Press, 1965.

Paxton, Robert O., *Vichy France: Old Guard and New Order, 1940–1944*, New York: Knopf, 1972.

Petrov, Vladimir, *June 22, 1941*, Columbia: University of South Carolina Press, 1968.

Porter, Jack Nissan, editor, *Jewish Partisans*, 2 volumes, Washington, D.C.: University Press of America, 1982.

Rasputin, Valentin, *Live and Remember*, New York: Macmillan, 1978.

Riasanovsky, Nicholas V., *A History of Russia*, 2nd edition, New York: Oxford University Press, 1969.

Robbins, Richard D., Jr., *Famine in Russia 1891–1892*, New York: Columbia University Press, 1975.

Russia Fights Famine: A Russian War Relief Report, New York, n.p., n.d. [probably 1943].

Salisbury, Harrison E., *The 900 Days: The Siege of Leningrad*, New York: Avon, 1979.

Schapsmeier, Edward L. and Schapsmeier Frederick H., *Encyclopedia of American Agricultural History*, Westport, Conn.: Greenwood Press, 1975.

Scott, James Brown, editor, *The Hague Conventions and Declarations of 1899 and 1907*, New York: Oxford University Press, 1918.

Sergeev, G. K., "Pomerantsevye plody kak istochnik vitamina c," *Voenno-meditsinskii zhurnal*, Nos. 7–8, July–August, 1946, pp. 50–1.

Shabalin, N., "O povyshenii proizvoditel'nosti traktorov v mts," *Sotsialisticheskoe sel'skoe khoziaistvo*, Nos. 3–4, March–April 1943, pp. 21–3.

Shilagin, T. I., *Narodnoe khoziaistvo sssr v period Velikoi Otechestvennoi Voiny*, Moscow, 1960.

Shvankov, I., "V verkhov'iakh volgi," *Eto bylo na Kalinskom fronte*, Moscow, 1985, pp. 59–61.

Sokolov, P. V., *Voenno-ekonomicheskie voprosy v kurse politekonomii*, Moscow, 1968.

Solzhenitsyn, Alexander, *The First Circle*, New York: Harper & Row, 1968.

Sontag, Raymond James and James Stuart Beddie, editors, *Nazi-Soviet Relations, 1939–1941*, New York: Didier, 1948.

Sovetskaia ukraina v gody Velikoi Otechestvennoi Voiny 1941–45, Vol. 1, Kiev, 1980.

Sovetskii rechnoi transport v Velikoi Otechestvennoi Voine, Moscow, 1981.

Stalin, Joseph, *The Great Patriotic War of the Soviet Union*, New York: Greenwood Press, 1969.

Stalin's War Speeches, London: Hutchinson, n.d.

The Statesman's Yearbook 1945, New York: Macmillan, 1945.

Sukhareva, G. E., "Psychologic Disturbances in Children During War," *Amer-*

ican Review of Soviet Medicine, Vol. 5, No. 1, December 1947–January 1948, p. 32–7.

Tamarchenko, M. L., *Sovetskie finansy v period Velikoi Otechestvennoi Voiny,* Moscow, 1967.

Tel'pukhovskii, V. S., *Velikaia Otechestvennaia Voina Sovetskogo Soiuza, 1941– 1945,* Moscow, 1959.

Trial of the Major War Criminals Before the International Military Tribunal, Vols. II, III, IV, VII, VIII, IX, Nuremburg, 1947.

Tsynkov, M., and M. Sysoev, "Ispol'zovat' vse rezervy kolkhoznogo zhivotnovodstva," *Sotsialisticheskoe sel'skoe khoziaistvo,* Nos. 7–8, July–August 1941, pp. 37–42.

Tyl sovetskikh vooruzhennykh sil v Velikoi Otechestvennoi Voine, Moscow, 1977.

Ukrainskaia SSR v Velikoi Otechestvennoi Voine Sovetskogo Soiuza 1941–1945gg., Vol. 1, Kiev, 1975.

U.S. Department of State, *Documents on German Foreign Policy 1918–1945,* Vol. XIII, *The War Years,* Washington, D.C., 1954.

Foreign Relations of the United States 1941–1945, Washington, D.C., 1958.

Report on War Aid Furnished by the United States to the U.S.S.R., Washington, D.C., 1945.

Soviet Supply Protocols, Washington, D.C., 1948.

Vainer, M., "Maksimal'no sokratit' raskhod zhidkogo topliva," *Sotsialisticheskoe sel'skogo khoziaistvo,* Nos. 7–8, July–August 1941, pp. 28–33.

Vinogradov, I. I., *Politotdely mts i sovkhozov v gody Velikoi Otechestvennoi Voiny (1941–1943gg.),* Leningrad, 1976.

Vishnevskaia, Galina, *Galina,* New York: Harcourt Brace Jovanovich, 1984.

Vlasiuk, P., "Ispol'zovanie otkhodov margantsevorudnoi promyshlennosti na udobrenie," *Sotsialisticheskoe sel'skoe khoziaistvo,* Nos. 1–2, January– February 1943, pp. 75–6.

Voinovich, Vladimir, *Pretender to the Throne,* New York: Farrar Straus Giroux, 1979.

Volin, Lazar, *A Century of Russian Agriculture,* Cambridge: Harvard University Press, 1970.

"German Invasion and Russian Agriculture," *Russian Review,* Vol. 3–4, November 1943, pp. 75–88.

"The 'New Agrarian Order' in Nazi-Invaded Russia," *Foreign Agriculture,* Vol. 7, No. 4, April 1943, pp. 75–84.

"The Russian Food Situation," *Annals of the Academy of Political and Social Science,* January 1943, pp. 89–91.

"The Russo-German War and Soviet Agriculture," *Foreign Agriculture,* Vol. 5, October 1941, pp. 390–406.

A Survey of Soviet Russian Agriculture, Washington, D.C., n.p., 1951.

Voznesensky, N. A., *The Economy of the USSR During World War II,* Washington, D.C.: Public Affairs Press, 1948.

Vse dlia fronta!, Sverdlovsk, 1985.

Vyltsan, M. A., *Zavershaiushchii etap sozdaniia kolkhoznogo stroia,* Moscow, 1978.

Waletzky, Josh, director, *Partisans of Vilna,* European Classica, 1986 film.

Wallace, Henry A., *Soviet Asia Mission*, New York: Reynal & Hitchcock, 1946.
Werth, Alexander, *Leningrad*, New York: Knopf, 1944.
  Moscow War Diary, New York: Knopf, 1942.
  Russia at War, 1941–1945, New York: Dutton, 1964.
Wilcox, Walter W., *The Farmer in the Second World War*, Ames: Iowa State College Press, 1947.
Williams, Ernest W., Jr., *Freight Transportation in the Soviet Union*, Princeton: Princeton University Press, 1962.
Young, Vernon and Neven S. Scrimshaw, "The Physiology of Starvation," *Scientific American*, October 1971, pp. 14–21.
Zaleski, Eugene, *Stalinist Planning for Economic Growth, 1933–1952*, Chapel Hill: The University of North Carolina Press, 1980.
Zelenin, N. E., "Sovkhozy SSSR v gody voine," in *Sovetskii tyl v Velikoi Otechestvennoi Voine*, Vol. 2, pp. 201–11.
Ziemke, Earl, "Composition and Morale of the Partisan Movement," in John A. Armstrong, editor, *Soviet Partisans in World War II*, Madison: University of Wisconsin Press, 1964.
  Stalingrad to Berlin: The German Defeat of the East, Washington, D.C.: Office of the Chief of Military History United States Army, 1968.

Periodicals

Chicago Daily Tribune
The Evening Citizen (Ottawa)
The Financial Post (Toronto)
Food Field Reporter
Izvestia
Leningradskaia Pravda
Life
The New Republic
The New York Times
Pravda
La Prensa (Buenos Aires)
Rabotnitsa
Sotsialisticheskoe sel'skoe khoziaistvo
The Times (London)
Voenno-meditsinskii zhurnal

Archives

British Foreign Office: Russia Correspondence 1781–1945, London.
Daily Report of Foreign Radio Broadcasts.

Foreign Broadcasts as monitored by the Columbia Broadcasting System, August 1939–March 1945.

Records of the Department of State Relating to Internal Affairs of the Soviet Union, 1940–1944. Decimal File 861, Calamities, Disasters, Refugees, Washington, D.C.

Records of the Reich Ministry in the Occupied Territories, National Archives, Washington, D.C.

State Department Decimal File, National Archives, Washington, D.C.

U.S. Department of Agriculture Archives–World War II files, Washington, D.C.

USSR: Crop Conditions and Production, 1942–1945. Records of the Foreign Agricultural Service. Record Group 166, National Archives, Washington, D.C.

Index

Soviet and East European Studies